Cyprus: Ethnic Conflict and International Politics

From Independence to the Threshold of the European Union

Joseph S. Joseph
Assistant Professor of International Relations
University of Cyprus

Published in Great Britain by
MACMILLAN PRESS LTD
Houndmills, Basingstoke, Hampshire RG21 6XS and London
Companies and representatives throughout the world

A catalogue record for this book is available from the British Library.

ISBN 0–333–67836–2 hardcover
ISBN 0–333–79036–7 paperback

Published in the United States of America by
ST. MARTIN'S PRESS, INC.,
Scholarly and Reference Division,
175 Fifth Avenue, New York, N.Y. 10010

ISBN 0–312–17623–6 clothbound
ISBN 0–312–22720–5 paperback

The Library of Congress has cataloged the hardcover edition as follows:
Joseph, Joseph S., 1952–
Cyprus : ethnic conflict and international politics : from
independence to the threshold of the European Union / Joseph S.
Joseph.
p.   cm.
Includes bibliographical references (p.   ) and index.
ISBN 0–312–17623–6 (cloth)
1. Cyprus—Politics and government—1960–   2. Cyprus—Ethnic
relations.   3. Cyprus—Foreign relations.   I. Title.
DS54.9.J68 1997
956.9304—dc21   97–13513
                                                            CIP

First edition (*Cyprus: Ethnic Conflict and International Concern*, Peter Lang) 1985
Second edition 1997
Reprinted 1999

This book is printed on paper suitable for recycling and made from fully managed and sustained forest sources.

10   9   8   7   6   5   4   3   2   1
08   07   06   05   04   03   02   01   00   99

Printed and bound in Great Britain by Antony Rowe Ltd, Chippenham, Wiltshire

For Eleni and our daughters Savina and Lina

Contents

Preface

This book is about the domestic aspects and international implications of the ethnic conflict between the Greeks and the Turks on Cyprus. Since the 1950s, the island has been a place of tension, friction, and violence caused by the clashing interests and claims of the two local ethnic groups, and three NATO allies – Greece, Turkey, and Britain. The far-reaching consequences of the conflict, seen in connection with the strategic location of the island, have also presented dangers and opportunities to the United States and the Soviet Union, and caused superpower intervention. The Cypriot dispute has also presented a threat to international peace and security, and caused UN and EU involvement in various ways and settings.

This study attempts to shed some light on these aspects and implications of the problem, and provide some insight into the dynamics and complexities of ethnopolitics and international politics. In the first chapter, some conceptual and analytical considerations define the theoretical framework of the study. The second chapter provides an essential background of the domestic ethnic conflict. The third chapter focuses on Greek and Turkish involvement, especially the role played by cross-boundary ethnic ties in generating and internationalizing the conflict, and the spill-over effect the conflict has had on Greek–Turkish relations. The fourth chapter examines the causes, process, and consequences of American and Soviet involvement. In the fifth chapter, the focus is on the impact that the conflict has had on NATO, and the reactions of the Western alliance to the conflict. In the sixth chapter, the role of the UN in Cyprus is examined. In the seventh chapter, Cyprus–EU relations are examined. Chapter 8 summarizes the major observations and conclusions. Finally, the Epilogue contains some thoughts about the necessity for a settlement of the conflict.

An earlier edition of this book was published in 1985. Since then, the world has gone through many changes. The Cold War is over and the USSR has been dismantled. Germany has been united and the Berlin Wall is gone. The EC of ten member states has now become the European Union of fifteen. The Non-Aligned Movement has weakened considerably while Japan is becoming an important centre of economic and political power. The gap between the North (rich countries) and the South (poor countries) is as wide as ever, while ecological problems and concerns are increasingly becoming major issues on the international agenda.

While drastic changes have been taking place in the world, the situation on Cyprus has remained the same. Although many efforts have been made to reach a settlement, no progress has been achieved. The island is still a *de facto* divided country in a state of no peace no war. Hopes for a settlement are reviving again as the prospects for Cyprus' accession to the EU are creating new opportunities and challenges. The people of Cyprus and the other parties involved are presented with a unique opportunity to overcome their differences and reach a long-overdue settlement.

This second, updated, expanded, and revised edition of the 1985 edition of *Cyprus: Ethnic Conflict and International Concern*, is published with the hope that it can make a contribution in understanding and solving the problem. Although it is based on the first edition, its many new elements prompted a modification in the title to reflect the new content. The entire text has been rewritten. In many cases the revision was substantial and substantive. Chapter 7 is a brand new addition and so is the Epilogue. Several new pages have also been added to the old chapters, some of which have been restructured. About 225 new notes have been added along with a chronology and new appendixes. Emphasis was also placed on updating and expanding the bibliography and the index.

My thanks and appreciation go to the many individuals and institutions who helped me in the writing of this book by educating, inspiring, and supporting me. Collectively, I thank my colleagues and friends in the Departments of Political Science at Miami University, Gustavus Adolphus College, University of Alabama, and the University of Cyprus. Exchanging views and ideas with them was always helpful. The encouragement and support I had at the Center of Middle Eastern Studies at Harvard helped me enormously in preparing this book. I am especially grateful to my editor, Tim Farmiloe, whose enthusiasm for the book was a constant source of strength to me. I also appreciate the help of Sunder Katwala and Jo North. My particularly warm thanks go to Professor William A. Hazleton of Miami University who reviewed the manuscript and offered advice. His suggestions made a difference. I am especially indebted and grateful to my parents whose support and devotion provided guiding inspiration. Both passed away before this project was completed, but they are very much part of it. My wife Eleni and my daughters Lina and Savina were also a constant source of support and inspiration. I express to them my deepest gratitude.

While many people contributed in the preparation of this book, the views, judgements, and interpretations contained in it are mine, and so are any errors of omission or commission.

JOSEPH S. JOSEPH
University of Cyprus

Acronyms and Abbreviations

AKEL	*Anorthotikon Komma Ergazomenou Laou* (Progressive Party of the Working People)
CENTO	Central Treaty Organization
CIA	Central Intelligence Agency
CPSU	Communist Party of the Soviet Union
EC	European Communities
ECSC	European Coal and Steel Community
ECU	European Currency Unit
EEC	European Economic Community
EMU	Economic and Monetary Union
EOKA	*Ethnike Organosis Kyprion Agoniston* (National Organization of Cypriot Fighters)
EU	European Union
EURATOM	European Atomic Energy Committee
GDP	Gross Domestic Product
IGO	Intergovernmental Organization
NATO	North Atlantic Treaty Organization
TASS	*Telegrafnoe Agentstvo Sovetskovo Soyuza* (Telegraphic Agency of the Soviet Union)
TMT	*Turk Mukavemet Teskilati* (Turkish Defence Organization)
UN	United Nations
UNFICYP	United Nations Force in Cyprus
US	United States
USSR	Union of Soviet Socialist Republics

Chronology on Cyprus

Second millennium BC	Immigration from Greece
Eighth–fifth century BC	Archaic period
450–323 BC	Classical period
323–30 BC	Hellenistic period
30 BC–330 AD	Roman period
330–1191	Byzantine period
488	Church of Cyprus declared autonomous by Emperor Zeno of Byzantium
1192–1489	Frankish period
1489–1571	Venetian period
1571–1878	Ottoman period
1878–1960	British period
1950	Greek Cypriot *enosis* plebiscite
1955–59	EOKA guerrilla war against British colonial administration
1959	London and Zürich Agreements signed
1960	Cyprus becomes independent
1963	Thirteen-point proposal for amendment of the constitution submitted by Makarios
December 1963	Outbreak of intercommunal violence
1964	Turkish Cypriot officials withdraw from government
March 1964	UN Force in Cyprus created
June 1964	President Johnson sends letter to Prime Minister Inonu
1965	Galo Plaza submits his report
November 1967	Kophinou crisis
19 December 1972	Cyprus–EEC Association Agreement signed
15 July 1974	Coup against President Makarios
20 July 1974	Turkey invades Cyprus
February 1975	'Turkish Federated State of Cyprus' self-proclaimed and condemned by UN Security Council
January 1977	High level agreement between Makarios and Denktash

August 1977	Makarios dies
1979	High level agreement between Kyprianou and Denktash
15 November 1983	Unilateral declaration of independence by the 'Turkish Republic of Northern Cyprus'
18 November 1983	UN Security Council adopts resolution 541 condemning the unilateral declaration of the 'TRNC'
19 October 1987	Additional Protocol to the Cyprus–EEC Association Agreement signed
4 July 1990	Cyprus applies for membership to the EC
30 June 1993	Opinion on Cyprus' application for membership to the EC issued by the Commission
7 February 1994	EU appoints Serge Abou as observer to the Cyprus peace process
June 1994	European Council meeting at Corfu confirms that Cyprus will be included in the next enlargement of the EU
December 1994	European Council at Essen confirms the Corfu decision
6 March 1995	EU Council of Ministers decides that accession negotiations will start six months after the end of the Intergovernmental Conference
29 January 1996	The Council of the EU appoints Federico Di Roberto the Presidency's representative for Cyprus
June 1996	The European Council at Florence confirms that accession negotiations will start six months after the completion of the Intergovernmental Conference
15 July 1996	The Council of the EU appoints Kester Heaslip as the Presidency's representative replacing Federico Di Roberto

1 Conceptual Considerations and Analytical Contexts

> Nothing has such power to broaden the mind as the ability to investigate systematically and truly all that comes under your observation in life.
>
> Marcus Aurelius Antoninus

SCOPE

This chapter presents and discusses some of the basic concepts and relationships of domestic ethnic conflict and its international implications. Its purpose is to identify, define, and refine certain notions the use of which is essential for the study of ethnic conflict at both the domestic and the international level. Far from being an attempt at developing a coherent conceptual scheme, the discussion merely explores some of the fundamental concepts and relationships of ethnicity and world politics.

A fundamental premise of the theory and practice of contemporary international affairs is that there is a two-way relationship between domestic and external politics. Domestic politics is greatly affected by external factors while international politics mainly revolves around competing national policies and internationalized domestic issues. This is largely the result of interaction and interdependence that characterize the world of nations in the forms of conflict and co-operation. Relationships of 'reciprocal effects among countries or among actors in different countries',[1] as Keohane and Nye call relationships of interdependence, have created a global village, a 'world without borders'[2] characterized by interconnectedness. The study and understanding of contemporary 'global politics',[3] 'the global agenda',[4] and 'the global condition in the late twentieth century'[5] require global perspectives and approaches.[6]

Economic growth and technological advancement 'have shrunk global distances and resulted in increased international and transnational contacts'.[7] As Rosenau points out, 'modern science and technology have collapsed space and time in the physical world and thereby heightened interdependence in the political world'.[8] Hoffman confirms that, 'technology and the universal quest for economic growth have created, if not a world society, at least an unprecedented interdependent milieu'.[9] Advancement in the fields of communication, transportation, and weaponry has been a major cause of interdependence and the globalization of politics. Modern means of communication have established global links of awareness on a global scale. Advancement in transportation has globalized the economy by destroying barriers to the mobility of people, goods, capital, and services. The development of weapons of massive destruction has led to the creation of a unifying global sense of insecurity and uncertainty. In response to these changes, many students of international relations began shifting their focus from the territorial state to the global system and its patterns of interdependence.[10]

POLITICIZATION OF ETHNICITY

Technological progress and modernization have also contributed in the politicization of ethnicity. The expansion and sophistication of communication have heightened ethnic awareness within and across states and intensified political differentiation along ethnic lines. Socioeconomic development, the expanding role of the state in determining needs and allocating resources, and the growing sense of ethnic singularity have been transforming ethnic groups 'into political conflict groups of the modern political arena'.[11] Ethnicity, ethnic groups, and their politics are, therefore, increasingly becoming more relevant to the study of both domestic and international politics and receive their fair share of attention.[12] As Said and Simmons put it in the mid-1970s, '[w]e have entered the age of ethnicity in international politics'.[13] Other scholars write about 'the early phase of a new era in world history, one that does not yet have a name...[an] era of ethnic challenges to world order and security'.[14] Writing in a similar vein about the new phase of world politics, Huntington argues that '[t]he great divisions among humankind and the dominating source of conflict will be cultural. Nation states will remain the most powerful actors in world affairs, but the principal conflicts of global politics will occur between nations and groups of different civilizations. The clash of civilizations will dominate global politics. The fault lines between civilizations will be the battle lines of the future.'[15]

These changes are taking place as we are witnessing a proliferation of states and international organizations in a shrinking and interdependent world of intense complexities. The 'ethnicization' of world politics became more evident after the dismantling of the Soviet Union and the collapse of the Cold War bipolar system. According to Gurr and Harff, '[s]ince the 1960s increasing numbers of ethnic groups have begun to demand more rights and recognition, demands that are now recognized as the major source of domestic and international conflict in the post-Cold War world'.[16]

Ethnicism transcends legal, geographic, and political boundaries. Its international political consequences are largely determined by the very fact that it has not, and cannot, be contained by such boundaries. Ethnopolitics, especially open ethnic conflicts, undermine the unity of the state as an international actor and as an analytical unit, thus making ethnic groups significant actors in world politics. Gurr and Harff go a step further to argue that '[e]thnic groups have become recognized independent actors in international politics'.[17] Referring to the ethnic challenge facing the world system, Shiels writes that governments, nation-states, and the 'global political arena accustomed to corporate states, ideological crusades, anticolonialism, and the broad creep of internationalism among capitalist, communist, and Third World states alike are now faced with the paradox of an array of new tribalisms'.[18] Ethnic considerations are becoming important determinants of the domestic and foreign agendas of governments, especially when defining their positions and policies on ethnic-related issues within and outside their boundaries. This has been clearly manifested in some former Soviet republics and other countries of Central and Eastern Europe where, following the collapse of communism and the creation of an ideological vacuum, ethnicity became a key factor in shaping attitudes, claims, and policies. With the collapse of the political system and the eclipse of ideology which bound ethnically different peoples and countries, 'old rivalries have re-emerged, and neighbors have again become antagonists fighting for power, status, and control for adjacent territories'.[19]

Traditionally, ethnic groups and their politics were 'accommodated' analytically within the framework of the state and, therefore, they were not treated as factors directly interacting with the international environment. But as the world is changing, ethnic politics, especially ethnic conflict, no longer fits neatly into analytical frameworks based on the legal–geographic concept of the state. The study of foreign policy and international relations can no longer be pursued without paying attention to the role played by ethnicity in world politics, in that ethnic considerations have become important factors influencing the behaviour of states.

DEFINITIONS

Conflict, as a social phenomenon, appears when two interacting parties are pursuing incompatible goals. The mere existence of conflicting values does not dictate a conflict situation in the sociopolitical sense. Value differences, however, present a potential for conflict. A conflict manifests itself when incompatible objectives are formulated by different parties and steps are taken towards their achievement. As Wright put it in his classic definition, the meaning of conflict in the sociological sense should be limited 'to situations where there is an actual or potential process for solving the inconsistency'.[20] Coser, in another classic definition, defines conflict as a 'struggle over values, and claims to scarce resources in which the aims of the opponents are to neutralize, injure or eliminate their rivals'.[21] In broad conceptual terms, we can define conflict as the pursuit of mutually exclusive or incompatible goals by different parties.

A conflict is resolved when one or more of its constituent elements are eliminated. Thus, the decrease of parties to one, ending of interaction, or termination of the pursuit of incompatible goals bring a conflict to an end. The means used for the resolution of a conflict are a manifestation of the conflict itself and can be violent or non-violent. An exchange of words is a form of non-violent conflict and conflict resolution, while an exchange of bullets is a violent form of conflict and conflict resolution.

For analytical purposes, a distinction between domestic and international conflict can be drawn. International conflict refers to confrontation between parties across borders. The parties to an international conflict can be states, groups of states, or subgroups from different states. Domestic conflict refers to confrontation between parties within a single state. Such parties usually are groups identifiable with reference to certain characteristics, such as geographic region, socioeconomic status, ideology, race, language, religion, or ethnicity.

Ethnicity has been defined as 'a set of attitudes related to a sense of ancestral identification with a segment of the world's population'.[22] An ethnic nation is one whose people share the same 'sense of ancestral identification'. Members of many ethnic nations are scattered across boundaries and form ethnic groups within two or more states. Schermerhorn defines an ethnic group as 'a collectivity within a larger society having real or putative common ancestry, memories of shared political past, and a cultural focus on one or more symbolic elements defined as the epitome of their peoplehood'.[23] The most common of these 'symbolic elements' of peoplehood which contribute to the creation and maintenance of the shared sense of ancestral identification are language, kinship, religion, culture, and physical type. These elements perform three basic functions within an ethnic group. First, they provide links of continuity from generation to generation. Secondly, they help maintain a certain cohesion within the group. And thirdly, they distinguish the group from other ethnic groups.

An ethnic group or an ethnic nation is different from the population of a state. The population of a state can be composed of several ethnic groups or include only part of an ethnic nation. Gurr and Harff classify politically active ethnic groups into four categories: ethnonationalists, indigenous peoples, communal contenders, and ethnoclasses.[24] Ethnonationalists seek to establish (or re-establish) their own states. Indigenous peoples want to protect primarily their land and culture, preferably through autonomy. Communal contenders compete for, and seek, maximization of their political power while ethnoclasses demand equal rights and opportunities within existing states.

A state is an institutionalized arrangement combining territory, population, government, and authority into a sovereign political unit that is recognized as such by other states. Geographic state boundaries do not necessarily coincide with ethnic boundaries and, in fact, most of the world's states are multiethnic. Groups of people sharing the same ethnicity are scattered across state boundaries and form parts of different states. Murdock in his *Ethnographic Atlas* identified as many as 862 ethnic societies, but he suggests that a completely exhaustive research would raise that number to over a thousand.[25] The fact that the number of states (approximately 200 today) is about one-fifth of the number of ethnic nations indicates how salient the potential for ethnic diversity and conflict can be within and among states. Connor has summarized this diversity in his ground-breaking article 'Nation-Building or Nation-Destroying', where he found that the vast majority of states are ethnically fragmented mosaics and only a small number of countries could be considered ethnically homogeneous.[26]

Based on the above discussion, domestic ethnic conflict can be defined as the situation where two or more segments of a population, constituent elements of the same state, but with different ethnic identifications, are pursuing incompatible or mutually exclusive political goals.

A serious form of ethnic conflict is the one resulting from ethnic politicization and the pursuit by different ethnic groups of incompatible goals such as control of the state, legitimization or delegitimization of the government, or secession. Ethnic politics tend to be more intense, violent, and dangerous than class divisions and interest group politics because a politicized ethnic group provides a channel through which a broad range of needs and interests, both material and psychological, can be articulated, promoted, and satisfied. Conflicting ethnopolitical goals can lead to a zero-sum game where not only economic and political interests are at stake, but also ethnic and cultural values that fulfil fundamental human needs of self-identification and group-belonging. In a setting of politicized ethnicity, confrontation, uncertainty and high emotional intensity, if not ethnic fanaticism, it is not easy to resolve differences through bargaining in a give-and-take manner. On the contrary, this mixture of conflicting material interests, ethnic values, and blinding fanaticism makes ethnic conflict prone to violence with little hope for peaceful political therapy. A conflict situation can be further complicated by the dynamics of majority–minority relations, where the majority may be tempted to seek control and the minority may seek protection through autonomy, secession, or external intervention.

ETHNICITY AND STATE-BUILDING

Ethnicity has been a factor in state-building since the emergence of the modern secular territorial state in seventeenth-century Europe. The political differentiation of peoples along ethnic lines, however, became more intense with the culmination of the movement of self-determination in the twentieth century. Especially after the Second World War, nationalism provided the heart for movements advocating independence from colonial rule, but in the aftermath of independence new multiethnic states were facing the challenge of ethnonationalism.

The politicization of ethnicity under the umbrella of ethnonationalism grew rapidly during the last five decades, raising issues of legitimacy in old and new states alike. The growing assertiveness of ethnic groups of the former Soviet Union and Yugoslavia are recent illustrative cases. Following the disintegration of the Soviet Union and its sphere of influence in Eastern Europe, the 'increased sense of isolation is being circumvented by a heightened ethnic awareness and a steady growth in intolerance toward members of other groups'.[27] Ethnic groups are becoming conscious of their singularity and distinctiveness which they relate to the political process by defining and pursuing ethnopolitical goals. Real or perceived inequalities in power, status, and wealth stimulate assertiveness and bring ethnicity into the political arena, thus transforming ethnic groups into political groups or competing power blocs. In multiethnic states – old and new alike – political identification and loyalty are increasingly shifting from the political nation and the territorial state to the ethnic group. With this shift in loyalties, ethnicity becomes a major source of legitimization or delegitimization of governments and political systems, and an effective instrument for channelling ethnic-based interests, needs, and objectives.

The effectiveness of ethnicity as a political instrument emanates from the emotional attachment of the individual to a group which he sees as a primary framework of reference for his life and a good channel through which to promote political, economic, social, and cultural interests. With the politicization of ethnicity, the primordial sentiments of ethnic identification and group belonging turn into a drive for self-fulfilment through political assertiveness and vindication. The example of the former Soviet republics suggests that 'ethnic awareness may be the first step toward a new national identity'.[28]

ETHNIC CONFLICT AND WORLD POLITICS

A domestic ethnic conflict takes place mainly within a state, but its causes and consequences may extend far beyond geographical boundaries. Ethnic groups, especially the ones on the weak side, may be inclined to look for affinity and support beyond state boundaries. Governments may also link their foreign policy to domestic and external ethnic issues in other countries and continents. As the world is becoming more ethnic and less geographic, it is safe to say that ethnicity will be a major force in domestic and international politics for many decades to come. It is, therefore, essential to pay attention to the role played by ethnicity at both the domestic and the international level.

For the purposes of this study, international environment can be defined as the total of interacting elements common to the world system and all aspects and consequences of their action and interaction. The interacting elements are actors which are capable of acting and being acted upon as parts of the world system. Such actors are primarily states and international organizations. The aspects and consequences of their interaction include the various manifestations of their relations, the principles governing them, and the instrumentalities through which they are carried out.

Although domestic ethnic conflict can be seen as a primarily domestic phenomenon, it affects and is affected by the conditions of the world within which states live, act, and interact. An understanding of the causes, options, and effects of the interaction between ethnic politics and the international environment is essential for a fruitful study of ethnic conflict. The external ramifications of the flare-up in Bosnia-Herzegovina after the dismantling of the former Yugoslavia, including involvement of outside powers and international organizations, show how far-reaching the consequences of a domestic ethnic conflict can be at the international level.

State behaviour and actions in the international arena are determined by a plethora of factors. Rosenau puts the sources of national behaviour (or foreign policy) into five broad categories: external, societal, governmental, role, and individual.[29]

The external sources refer to the international environment within which states live and interact. The organizational structure of the world, the international legal system, the behaviour of other states and organizations, ideological challenges, geographic realities, and socioeconomic conditions are some of the features of the international environment.

The societal sources refer to an amalgam of elements of the domestic society. Such elements are culture, history, traditions, norms, social institutions, degree of national unity, level of education, economic system, mass media, and interest groups.

The governmental sources refer to the organizational structure of the state, especially those institutions which formulate and implement foreign policy. These institutions influence state behaviour by influencing the process of foreign policy-making and implementation.

The role sources refer to government offices (roles) seen in the context of public expectations set upon the individuals occupying them. These expectations influence the behaviour and decisions of the role occupants and, therefore, the policies of states.

The individual sources refer to the personal characteristics of decision-makers. Such characteristics are the idiosyncrasies, psychological predispositions, values, skills, perceptions, experiences, and knowledge of the individuals who are responsible for the formulation and implementation of national policies.

The above five source categories include congruent and conflicting factors which place constraints on foreign policy formulation and implementation. In the setting of an ethnic conflict these factors are coloured by ethnicity. In a country experiencing ethnic conflict, foreign policy, like domestic politics, is a major area of confrontation. It becomes an ethnicized issue, part and parcel of the means and ends for which the rival ethnic groups are contesting. The foreign policies of other countries towards that country and the rival groups may also be influenced by ethnic factors. The presence of cross-boundary ethnic ties and domestic ethnic lobbies can be particularly influential sources of foreign policy. Consequently, in the context of an ethnic conflict, the behaviour and relations of states can be heavily influenced by ethnic considerations. Ethnic lobbying, which is widely practised, especially in the United States, is an example of how ethnicity can influence domestic and external politics.

A manifestation of inter-state relations is the international governmental organization (IGO) which is a mechanism designed to secure a better functioning of the state-centric system. It has been defined as 'an institutionalized arrangement among members of the international system to solve tasks which have evolved from systemic conditions'.[30] States create IGOs to cope with problems which cannot be effectively or adequately resolved by individual states. Problems of war and peace, and social and economic development have provided the impetus for the establishment of hundreds of regional and global IGOs. As reflections of inter-state relations, IGOs are more than the sum of their parts; they represent patterns of interaction and have qualities and functions different from those of the constituent states. They are processes of state interaction in a world of interdependence, conflict, and co-operation.

International organizations can become involved in ethnic conflicts in various ways and settings. They can provide a forum for the practice of diplomacy or they can get actively involved in peacekeeping and peacemaking operations. United Nations involvement in the Congo, Cyprus, Lebanon, and Bosnia-Herzegovina illustrates this point. It is interesting to note that, in recent years, about half of the UN peacekeeping operations were aimed at keeping apart ethnic antagonists.[31] Depending on their nature and goals, international organizations may also side with one of the contesting parties and provide political, diplomatic, economic, or military support. Political and military organizations are more likely to feel the repercussions of ethnic conflicts. Since they represent articulation of interests and clashes of power in the world arena, they are concerned with the impact that ethnic conflicts may have on the domestic, regional, and international balance of power. If members of an organization are directly involved in the conflict, the whole issue is likely to become a direct source of trouble for that organization.

POWER AND DIPLOMACY

States and IGOs interact within a world system lacking a central authority with effective legislative, judicial, or executive functions. The process of world politics takes place within a basically anarchic environment where power plays a dominant role. As Morgenthau points out in his classic definition, 'international politics, like all politics, is a struggle for power'.[32]

Institutions, norms, and legal rules provide a framework and instrumentalities for the operation of international politics, but the real driving force behind the process of conflict and co-operation among states is 'the concept of interest defined in terms of power'.[33] Power is a relational concept. It can be defined as the ability of actor A to influence the behaviour of actor B. It is a means used for the achievement of ends, but it is also an end in itself. States seek to maximize their power as a first step towards the achievement of other goals. As Burton writes, 'there is probably no greater common factor in all thinking on international relations than the assumption that states depend for their existence upon power, thus making the management of power the main problem to be solved'.[34]

The quest for power also dominates ethnic politics. Rival ethnic groups seek to maintain, increase, or demonstrate power as a step towards the achievement of their ethnopolitical goals. With the internationalization of the conflict, external power politics are linked to the domestic power struggle. External parties look at the conflict as an opportunity for demonstration of power and the promotion of favourable changes in the domestic and external distribution of power. The impact of external power politics on ethnic conflict can be decisive; it can greatly influence the process and outcome of the conflict. Therefore, an understanding of the nature and implications of power in domestic ethnopolitics and international politics is essential for a better understanding of the dynamics of interaction between ethnic conflict and the international environment.

A major instrument in the conduct of international politics is diplomacy.[35] It provides channels and principles facilitating interaction among states, IGOs, and other actors on the world scene. Diplomacy can be defined as the conduct of international politics by pacific means. Barston writes that '[d]iplomacy is often thought of as being concerned with peaceful activity, although it may occur for example within war or armed conflict'.[36] Its most common manifestation is negotiation, that is, the settlement of differences through bargaining in a give-and-take manner. Negotiations can be bilateral and can take place within the setting of a regional or global organization, or an *ad hoc* conference. Diplomacy is a major device for peaceful change and order maintenance in the world system. As a manifestation of the international political process, it is greatly affected by the distribution of power among states. A symmetrical power relationship is favourable for the practice of diplomacy, the maintenance of world order, and peaceful change.

Ethnic conflicts tend to become items of international diplomacy when the rival ethnic groups fail to reach a settlement within a domestic setting. External intervention by diplomacy can be as influential and effective as the use of force. It provides an opportunity for demonstration of power at the bargaining table. Interaction between domestic and external factors takes place largely within diplomatic channels and circles. Therefore, for a better understanding of this interaction one has to study the process of communication between the various parties involved in a conflict.

Sometimes, we think of domestic and international politics as two separate fields of study. The distinction is an analytical and arbitrary one. A clear-cut distinction between the two fields cannot be drawn. The two domains overlap and interact with one another. This is especially true in the modern world system which is characterized by interdependence.

The establishment of patterns of interdependence in the fields of war and peace, economic and social development, and political organization have enhanced mutual sensitivity and vulnerability among states. These patterns of interdependence are especially conducive to the internationalization of ethnic conflict. Therefore, the origin, process, and consequences of ethnic conflict should be examined in this context of an interdependent world comprising mostly multiethnic states.

The above presentation of concepts, issues, and relationships aims at providing a guiding bottom line for the study of domestic ethnic conflict in an international context. In sum, this book suggests that domestic ethnic conflict should be seen as an issue that affects and is affected by the international environment. Therefore, its study will be more fruitful if carried out within an international context and against the background of interdependence, power politics, conflict, and co-operation which characterize the world of nations.

FRAMEWORK OF ANALYSIS

A framework of analysis guides thinking, research, and writing on the subject under study. It organizes ideas and facts, and defines the boundaries of a project. A definition of boundaries is a selective process. It selects the variables to be employed, the events to be analysed, and the relationships to be examined. The outline of the framework reflects the direction and focus of the enquiry.

The analytical framework of this study selects and highlights certain aspects of the Cypriot ethnic conflict and its interaction with the international environment. Six analytical contexts (contextual settings) are defined to guide our enquiry on the subject. They are the following:

1 The domestic setting of the ethnic conflict in Cyprus.
2 Greek–Turkish relations.
3 American–Soviet relations.
4 The North Atlantic Treaty Organization (NATO).
5 The United Nations (UN).
6 The European Union (EU).

The first analytical context refers to the domestic setting within which the ethnic conflict between the Greek Cypriots and the Turkish Cypriots took place, especially in the 1960s, right after the declaration of independence. It aims at providing an essential background of the problem and examining the relationship between political division and ethnic conflict. Emphasis is placed on the geographical, historical, social, cultural, and institutional factors which contributed to the political separation of the two communities and the generation of the ethnic conflict.

The second analytical context places emphasis on the role played by ethnic factors in generating and internationalizing the domestic ethnic conflict. The relations of Cyprus, Greece, and Turkey as well as their internal politics have been affected by the conflict. Greece and Turkey have ethnic ties with the island and consider themselves the motherlands of the two Cypriot communities. Both countries consider the Cyprus issue as their 'national issue'. Greek–Turkish rivalry over Cyprus has repeatedly brought the two countries to the brink of war. Geographic proximity, strategic considerations, and the long history of Greek–Turkish antagonism are additional factors affecting the triangle of Greek–Cypriot–Turkish relations.

The third analytical context focuses on superpower involvement in Cyprus before the collapse of the Soviet Union. Both the USA and the Soviet Union had reasons for concern and involvement in the Cypriot conflict. Their superpower status, their opposed interests in the region, and their positive or negative affiliation with the parties involved in the conflict were the main reasons for their concern and involvement in Cyprus. The impact of the Cypriot conflict on US–Soviet relations is assessed with reference to the attitudes and actions the two superpowers took towards each other and the other parties involved in the conflict.

The fourth analytical context examines the role of NATO in Cyprus. The Western alliance is concerned with the island for two major reasons. First, Greece and Turkey, two NATO allies, are confronting each other over Cyprus. Their confrontation has repeatedly threatened with paralysis the south-eastern flank of the Western alliance. And secondly, NATO is concerned with the security of Cyprus itself. It always had an interest in keeping Cyprus, a non-aligned country, out of the Soviet sphere of influence, and, if possible, bringing it under Western control.

The fifth analytical context directs attention to the causes and consequences of UN involvement in Cyprus. The world organization has been involved in the Cypriot conflict in various ways and settings. Peacekeeping and peacemaking operations have been the main forms of UN involvement in the issue. The UN intervened in Cyprus despite the provision of article 2, paragraph 7, of the Charter stating that '[n]othing contained in the present Charter shall authorize the United Nations to intervene in matters which are essentially within the domestic jurisdiction of any state or shall require the members to submit such matters to settlement under the present Charter'. UN involvement in Cyprus is examined in the light of this provision.

Emphasis is placed on the causes to supersede the principle of non-intervention, and the political implications of UN involvement.

The sixth analytical context examines Cyprus–EU relations, especially after Cyprus' submission of application for accession in 1990. Although the Cyprus problem is the theme still dominating Cypriot politics, the island's prospect of joining the EU is also getting considerable attention and creating a new momentum and hopes for a long overdue settlement. In this context of revived hopes and expectations, the position and involvement of the EU in the efforts to resolve the Cyprus problem are examined.

THREE PHASES OF THE CYPRUS PROBLEM

In recent decades, the Cyprus problem has gone through three main phases. Until 1960, it was a colonial issue which was settled with the granting of independence and the establishment of the Republic of Cyprus. From 1960 to 1974, the problem was basically an internal dispute between the Greek Cypriots and the Turkish Cypriots in which external powers were involved. These powers were primarily Greece, Turkey, and Britain – the guarantor powers of the independence of Cyprus under the 1960 settlement. The United States and the Soviet Union also became involved, at the political level, during the second phase by virtue of their superpower status. The third phase covers the period from 1974 to the present. Following the Turkish invasion of Cyprus in 1974, the dominant element of the problem has been the *de facto* division of the island and the continuing military occupation of its northern part by Turkey.

With the exception of the chapter on Cyprus–EU relations, this book deals primarily with the period from 1960 to 1974. Some background information for the period prior to 1960 is provided in order to have a historical context for the issues discussed. Some of the major developments which followed the 1974 crisis are also presented in rounding up the discussion on the consequences of the ethnic problems that plagued Cyprus at the early stage of its independence.

2 Background of the Domestic Ethnic Conflict

Good is the earth, it suits us. Like the global grape it hangs, dear God, in the blue air and sways in the gale, nibbled by all the birds and spirits of the four winds.

Nikos Kazantzakis

OBJECTIVES

The purpose of this chapter is to provide an essential background of the domestic setting of the ethnic conflict in Cyprus. In doing so, emphasis is placed on the geographical, historical, social, cultural, institutional, and political roots of the conflict. The presentation and analysis of these aspects of the problem serve a twofold objective. First, they define the domestic setting of the conflict and provide a basis for the chapters to follow. And second, they aim at examining the relationship between political division along ethnic lines and the generation of ethnic conflict. The following questions provide guidelines for the presentation and analysis of facts and events: What factors contribute to the maintenance and reinforcement of ethnic cleavages in a bicommunal society? Do political divisions along ethnic lines exacerbate ethnic conflict? Or do they contain and counteract ethnic differences? How likely is it that political and administrative institutions will be used for ethnic purposes in a biethnic state?

GEOGRAPHICAL AND HISTORICAL SETTING

Three geographic characteristics of Cyprus have determined much of its fate: location, size, and the fact that it is an island. It is located at a strategic position in the eastern Mediterranean, at the crossroads of three continents, and has an area of 3,572 square miles (9,851 square kilometres). Its strategic location, long exposed coastline, and small size always made it an attractive and easy target for outsiders.[1] Its historic and demographic records reflect the ebb and flow of peoples and powers in the region. In the course of its long history, Cyprus has

15

been conquered by most of the major powers that had interest in, or sought control of, the Middle East. The list of its successive rulers includes the Egyptians, Greeks, Phoenicians, Assyrians, Persians, Ptolemies, Romans, Byzantines, Franks, Venetians, Ottoman Turks, and British. It gained its independence from Britain in 1960.

Among these rulers only the Greeks and the Turks had a significant long-lasting demographic impact on the Cypriot society. The Greeks settled in the island during the second half of the second millennium BC. The Turks settled in Cyprus following the Ottoman invasion and occupation of the island in 1571. Under the Cyprus convention which was signed at the Congress of Berlin in 1878, the sultan ceded Cyprus to Britain which was to occupy and administer the island in exchange for a promise to help Turkey defend itself against Russian expansion.[2] In 1914, at the onset of the Second World War, and after Turkey had joined forces with the Central Powers, Britain declared the 1878 convention null and annexed Cyprus. With the 1923 peace treaty of Lausanne, Turkey officially recognized the annexation of Cyprus by Britain and the island was proclaimed a colony of the British crown in 1925.[3]

By 1878, when the British took control of the island, the bicommunal character of the Cypriot society had been formed and consolidated. During the eighty-two years of British rule no major demographic change took place on the island. In 1960, its population was approximately 570 000, consisting of roughly 80 per cent Greeks and 20 per cent Turks.[4] There were purely Greek, purely Turkish, and mixed settlements in all regions of the island. There are also small ethnic groups of Armenians, Maronites, and Latins living in Cyprus.[5]

The Greek Cypriots and the Turkish Cypriots have been divided along linguistic, ethnic, cultural, and religious lines. The Greek Cypriots speak Greek and identify with the Greek nation, Greek culture, and the heritage of classical Greece and the Byzantine Empire. Almost all of them are members of the Orthodox Church of Cyprus which is an autocephalous member of the Greek Eastern Orthodox Church. The Turkish Cypriots speak Turkish and identify with the Turkish nation, Turkish culture, and the heritage of the Turkish Ottoman Empire. Virtually all of them are Muslims of the Sunni sect.

Despite four centuries of coexistence and considerable physical intermingling, the two communities remained separate and distinct ethnic groups. (A partial physical separation of the two communities took place with the eruption of inter-communal violence in 1963. An almost complete separation came into effect after the Turkish invasion of Cyprus in 1974.) During the period of Ottoman and British rule, certain factors contributed to the preservation of the linguistic, ethnic, cultural, and religious characteristics of the two communities and the creation of a political cleavage along ethnic lines.

The Orthodox Church which maintained a dominant position among the Greek Cypriots helped them preserve their religious, ethnic, cultural, and political identity. When the Ottomans conquered Cyprus from the Venetians in 1571, they destroyed the Roman Catholic Church and elevated the Greek Orthodox Church to a position of supremacy in the island. The autonomy of the Orthodox Church was confirmed and the archbishop was recognized as the religious and political leader of the Greek Cypriot community.[6] For the Greek Cypriots, the church became a symbol of political and ethnic unity. Most of their political, social, cultural, and intellectual life was associated with religious activities and institutions. The church continued to be the dominant institution of the Greek Cypriots under British rule.[7]

The Ottoman *millet* administrative system distinguished the two communities on the basis of religion and ethnicity.[8] According to this system, which was applied throughout the empire, each religious ethnic group was treated as a distinct entity. Taxes were imposed on a denominational basis and administration was carried out with the help of the various religious institutions. The Ottoman conquerors restored the Orthodox Church of Cyprus with this aim in mind. The administrative separation of the Greek Cypriots and the Turkish Cypriots helped them maintain their ethnic identity, but it also contributed to the politicization of ethnicity. When the British took control over Cyprus, the *millet* system was not completely abolished.[9] A modern bureaucratic administration was established, but the two ethnic groups retained control over matters of religion, education, culture, personal status, and communal institutions.

The divisive educational system perpetuated ethnic distinctiveness by transferring conflicting ethnic values from generation to generation. The two communities had separate schools which were, to some degree, controlled by their respective religious institutions. Throughout the Ottoman period and the early years of British rule, Orthodox and Muslim priests were also schoolteachers. During the period of British rule, the curricula of the Cypriot schools were similar to those in Greece or Turkey. They placed emphasis on religion, national heritage, ethnic values, and the long history of Greek–Turkish rivalry.

The two Cypriot communities had antagonistic loyalties to Greece and Turkey. Each community honoured the national holidays, played the national anthem, and used the flag of its mother country. Cypriots from both ethnic groups fought as volunteers on opposite sides during the 1912–13 Balkan wars, the First World War, and the Greek–Turkish war of 1919–23. Attachment to two rival, and often belligerent countries promoted ethnic distinctiveness and served as an instrument for the transplantation of the wider Greek–Turkish confrontation into Cyprus.

The two ethnic groups held conflicting views about the political future of the island. Throughout the British period, *enosis* (union of Cyprus with Greece) was the most persistent and rigid goal of the Greek Cypriots.[10] It could be seen as part of the wider Panhellenic movement of *megali idea* (great idea) which aimed at reconstruction of the Byzantine Empire. On the Turkish side, the idea of *taksim* (partition of Cyprus into Greek and Turkish sections) was advanced as a counter force to *enosis*. Both movements were supported by Greece and Turkey respectively. Attachment to the conflicting goals of *enosis* and *taksim* led to a political polarization between the two ethnic groups.

The British colonial policy of 'divide and rule' maintained and reinforced the ethnic, administrative, and political separation inherited from the Ottoman period. The British administration made no effort to create a unifying Cypriot political culture. The two communities were treated as separate groups for administrative purposes and antagonism between them was stirred.[11] The maintenance of a psychological and administrative gap between the two ethnic groups was instrumental in securing British control over Cyprus.

The above factors – church dominance, *millet* system, fragmented ethnic education, antagonistic national loyalties, political polarization, and the British policy of 'divide and rule' – contributed to the preservation of the ethnic identity of the two Cypriot communities and the generation of a political schism between them. Four centuries of geographic proximity and physical intermingling did not produce inter-communal bonds strong enough to counteract the dividing effects of religious, administrative, educational, social, and cultural distinctiveness. Communal segregation was further reinforced by mutual suspicion, fear, and uncertainty 'for which one might coin the term "postjudices", since they are based upon close observation and not ignorant misconception'.[12]

It was on these fragmented historical and social foundations that an independent bicommunal Cypriot state was built in 1960. The institutional framework of the Republic of Cyprus reflected the divided past and antagonism of the two ethnic groups. It treated them as distinct self-contained political units and established political boundaries between them parallel to the ethnic cleavage. The political institutions of the state formalized and reinforced ethnic differences through political structures and practices. Ethnic fragmentation and political segregation of the two communities had a negative effect on the newborn republic. Political separation along ethnic lines prevented the two communities from participating and interacting in a common political arena. The coincidence of linguistic, ethnic, religious, cultural, and political cleavages eliminated any chance for cross-cutting political activities, overarching loyalties, and shared political culture supportive of the state. The two communities remained ethnically and politically distinct and looked upon each other as ethnopolitical antagonists, without distinguishing ethnicity from politics. Rather, ethnicity dominated politics and it was natural for both sides to seek to ethnicize the state in their favour. As a result, Cypriot politics were heavily coloured by ethnicity and turned into an implacable ethnic struggle, rather than a fair political game.

In sum, the ethnopolitical polarization inherited from the past, the structural inadequacies of the new state, the lack of experience in self-government, and the absence of a consensual political leadership that could transcend ethnic differences were the major factors which contributed to the generation of an open ethnic confrontation and the collapse of the Cypriot state in 1963, three years after its establishment. These factors are discussed in the following pages where the circumstances in the creation of the Republic of Cyprus are examined.

ESTABLISHMENT OF THE REPUBLIC OF CYPRUS

Britain granted independence to Cyprus in 1960, giving way to pressure coming from three different directions. First, there was a bloody Greek Cypriot anti-colonial revolt, which lasted from 1955 to 1959, causing much trouble for British authorities and making the administration of the island a difficult and costly task.[13] The revolt, which took the form of a guerrilla war, was spearheaded by the Orthodox Church under the leadership of Archbishop Makarios and the underground National Organization of Cypriot Fighters, EOKA (*Ethnike Organosis Kyprion Agoniston*), under the leadership of its founder General George Grivas Dighenis. The revolt was carried out in the name of *enosis* and had the support of Greece. Turkey and the Turkish Cypriots, on the other hand, were demanding partition. Some incidents of ethnic violence occurred and tension was generated between Greece and Turkey.[14]

Secondly, there was global pressure resulting from the internationalization of the Cyprus issue, especially at the UN, in the context of the broader anticolonial movement and decolonization process that were sweeping the world in the 1950s. The issue was taken to the UN General Assembly for five consecutive years, from 1954 to 1958.[15] Appeals to the UN were made by Greece, asking for application of the principles of equal rights and self-determination in Cyprus. The Greek appeals were supported by the Eastern bloc and the Third World countries. Greece also asked for *enosis* 'in view of the repeatedly and solemnly expressed will of the overwhelming majority of the people of Cyprus for union with Greece, which they regard as their mother country'.[16] The General Assembly made a recommendation for a peaceful solution of the Cyprus colonial problem in accordance with the principles of the UN Charter.[17]

Thirdly, there was American pressure applied to Britain, Greece, and Turkey to seek a solution to the Cyprus problem and heal the Greek–Turkish 'festering sore' within NATO. The USA was concerned with the mounting Greek–Turkish tension which threatened to paralyse the south-eastern flank of the Western alliance. American concern over Cypriot developments was manifested in unsuccessful initiatives taken in 1957 and 1958 aiming at a settlement of the problem within NATO.

As a result of the above pressures, a solution to the colonial problem of Cyprus was sought through diplomacy. Early in 1959, tripartite talks were held in Zürich between Britain, Greece, and Turkey and an agreement was reached for the establishment of an independent Cypriot state, the Republic of Cyprus. Final agreements were signed in London on 19 February 1959, by Britain, Greece, Turkey, and the two Cypriot communities, although the latter did not participate in the negotiations.[18] The problem was, in effect, settled on a bilateral basis between Greece and Turkey under British directorship. Factors and considerations emanating from the ethnic, historical, linguistic, cultural, and religious ties of the two Cypriot ethnic groups with their respective motherlands defined the context within which the settlement was reached.

THE LONDON AND ZÜRICH AGREEMENTS

The London and Zürich agreements consisted of a series of treaties which laid the foundations of the political structure of the new state. These treaties were: the Treaty of Establishment, the Treaty of Alliance, the Treaty of Guarantee, and the agreement on the basic structure of the Republic of Cyprus which contained the key provisions of the constitution which was drafted later. The treaties and the constitution were officially signed on 16 August 1960 in Nicosia and went into effect immediately.[19]

The Treaty of Establishment was aimed at safeguarding British military interests in Cyprus. It provided for two sovereign British military bases of 99 square miles (256 square kilometres).

The Treaty of Alliance was a defence pact between Greece, Turkey, and Cyprus. It provided for the permanent stationing of Greek and Turkish contingents in Cyprus, comprising 950 and 650 men respectively.

With the Treaty of Guarantee Cyprus undertook to 'ensure the maintenance of its independence, territorial integrity and security' and prohibit 'any activity likely to promote, directly or indirectly, either union with any other State or partition of the Island'.[20] Britain, Greece, and Turkey were named guarantor powers of the republic and were granted the right to take action, jointly or unilaterally, towards 'reestablishing the state of affairs created by the present Treaty'[21] in the event of its breach. The Treaty of Guarantee was primarily aimed at mutual abandonment of the conflicting ethnopolitical goals of *enosis* and partition.

The agreement on the basic structure of the Republic of Cyprus contained the key provisions of the constitution which was drafted later and put into effect when the republic officially came into being.[22] The constitution was based on communal dualism. It provided for the establishment of a bicommunal state and aimed at regulation and protection of the interests of the two communities as distinct ethnic groups. It identified and recognized the two communities with reference to their ethnic origin, language, cultural traditions, and religion.[23] It gave them 'the right to celebrate respectively the Greek and Turkish national holidays'[24] and to use 'the flag of the Republic or the Greek or Turkish flag without any restriction'.[25] The two communities were also granted the right to establish separate special relationships with Greece and Turkey on educational, religious, cultural, and athletic matters.

The constitution institutionalized communal dualism in all spheres of government activity. In the executive branch, it provided for a presidential regime, the president being Greek Cypriot and the vice-president Turkish Cypriot, elected separately by the two communities. The council of ministers was composed of seven Greek Cypriots and three Turkish Cypriots. The president appointed the Greek Cypriot and the vice-president the Turkish Cypriot ministers. Decisions by the council of ministers were taken by absolute majority, but the president and the vice-president had the right to veto, jointly or separately, decisions on foreign affairs, defence, and security. The frequent exercise of the veto right in the government led to disturbing controversies and immobilization of the entire governmental machinery with destructive effects on the functioning of the state and inter-ethnic relations.

According to the constitution, legislative power was exercised by the house of representatives and two communal chambers. The house was composed of thirty-five Greek Cypriots and fifteen Turkish Cypriot representatives, elected separately by the two ethnic groups.[26] The president of the house was Greek Cypriot and the vice-president Turkish Cypriot. Laws in the house were passed by simple majority, except in the cases of 'any modification of the Electoral Law and the adoption of any law relating to the municipalities and of any law imposing duties or taxes',[27] where a separate simple majority of the representatives of the two communities was required. The two communal chambers were independent legislative bodies elected separately by the two communities. They had exclusive legislative power in relation to their respective ethnic groups on the following matters: all religious matters; all educational, cultural, and teaching matters; personal status; administration of justice dealing with civil disputes relating to personal status and religious matters; and in matters where the interests and institutions were purely of communal nature, such as charitable and sporting institutions. The two chambers could also impose personal taxes and fees on their communities in order to finance communal activities and institutions. Division of the legislative branch meant, in effect, that each ethnic group could run its own affairs independently and in contrast to the interests of the other community.

Communal dualism was also institutionalized in the judicial system. The composition of the lower courts was determined by the communal membership of the disputants. If the plaintiff and the defendant belonged to the same community, the court was composed of judges belonging to that community. The supreme court was composed of a Greek Cypriot, a Turkish Cypriot, and a neutral judge. The neutral judge was the president of the court and could not be a citizen of Cyprus, Greece, Turkey, or Britain. The transplantation of ethnic fragmentation into the administration of justice, which was partly inherited from the colonial period, undermined the very concept of justice. In an ethnically and politically divided society, ethnic considerations could influence the operation of courts and result in undermining the administration of justice.

The constitution provided for the establishment of separate municipalities: 'separate municipalities shall be created in the five largest towns of the Republic...The Council of the Greek municipality in any such town shall be elected by the Greek electors of the town and the Turkish municipality in such towns shall be elected by the Turkish electors of the town'.[28] It is worth mentioning that despite the existence of Greek and Turkish quarters, there was some intermingling of the population in the five towns. Application of this provision could result in movement of populations. The Greek Cypriots looked on this provision with suspicion because it had partitionist connotations. Needless to say, the handling of the municipal affairs of a city by two councils would be, at the very least, impractical.

A disproportionate communal ratio of participation in the public service, the police, and the armed forces was fixed by the constitution. The public service and the police would be composed of 70 per cent Greeks and 30 per cent Turks. The ratio in the army was 60:40. (The ratio of the population was roughly 80:20.) The provisions for disproportionate participation of the Turkish Cypriots in all public sectors caused reactions among the Greek Cypriots. Moreover, serious problems arose because the Turkish Cypriots could not provide the number of qualified applicants needed to fill the positions reserved for them.

Finally, the constitution provided that provisions incorporated from the Zürich and London accords could not 'in any way be amended, whether by way of variation, addition, or repeal'.[29] All the constitutional features presented above were among the 'basic articles', and so were the Treaties of Alliance and Guarantee which were integral parts of the constitution. In other words, the political framework was not only awkward and unworkable, but also rigid and unalterable. It excluded any adaptation or evolutionary political process through which the two groups could negotiate, adjust their positions, and seek common ground for reconciliation and a settlement. As a political analyst put it, 'it was a constitutional strait-jacket precluding that adaptation essential to the growth and survival of any body politic'.[30]

The above presentation of the London and Zürich accords and the constitution shows that the Republic of Cyprus came into being as a result of international agreements which were reached in the absence of the Cypriot people. The constitution of the new state was imposed on the population; it was never submitted to a referendum. A series of treaties set limitations on the independence, sovereignty, and territorial integrity of the republic. Foreign powers were granted the right to station military forces on its territory and interfere in its domestic affairs.

In the sphere of communal relations, ethnic dualism was institutionalized in all sectors of public life. A political framework conducive to ethnic separation and antagonism was established. Although the conflicting ethnopolitical goals of *enosis* and partition were ruled out, no measures were taken to promote integrative politics cutting across ethnic boundaries. The political and administrative foundations of the new state were, to a great extent, based on the fragmented features and practices inherited from the past. The preservation and reinforcement of coinciding ethnic and political cleavages through institutionalization had a catastrophic impact on the state. Public institutions became the goals and means for the promotion of ethnic interests, thus eliminating any prospects for the building of a solid independent and sovereign state. Yet worse, ethnic controversies were injected into the state apparatus and public life, and crippled most vital organs and functions essential for a state and a society.

The right of intervention granted to foreign powers and communal separation could be viewed as measures aiming at protection of the Turkish Cypriot minority. More safeguards were given to the minority in the forms of disproportional participation in the public service, the police, and the army; veto right in the government on matters of security, defence, and foreign affairs; and separate majority vote in the parliament. The guarantees given to the Turkish Cypriots were 'more extensive, perhaps, than any ever written into a constitution for the protection of a minority community'.[31]

These extensive minority safeguards reflected the fears of the Turks and a compromise among the drafters of the founding treaties. To a great extent, they were also the result of the unequal distribution of bargaining power between Turkey and Greece. The superior negotiating power of Turkey in Zürich and London was due to the following three factors: first, Cyprus lies just 44 miles (70 kilometres) from the coast of Turkey and could be vulnerable in case of an open confrontation; secondly, Turkey, a country five times the size and population of Greece, had a military superiority which could be translated into negotiating power; and thirdly, Turkey was more important to NATO and Western security than Greece and, therefore, less susceptible to US and British pressure. Under these circumstances, Greece, which negotiated on behalf of the Greek Cypriots, gave in to Turkish demands and British pressure and accepted disproportionate rights for the Turkish Cypriots.

Finally, one should add that at the heart of the problem was the presence of ethnically coloured centrifugal forces in the society and politics of Cyprus. It was the release of these forces that destroyed the fragile constitutional construct and undermined the coexistence of the two communities in a united independent state.

THE PARALYTIC STATE

The Republic of Cyprus came officially into being on 16 August 1960. In the first presidential elections, which were held earlier, Archbishop Makarios and Dr Fazil Kutchuk, the Cypriot representatives who signed the Zürich and London agreements, were elected president and vice-president respectively. The political parties affiliated with Makarios and Kutchuk secured all seats in the parliament and the two communal chambers.

One of the primary tasks of the first government of the republic was to build the state institutions provided by the constitution. This, however, proved to be a difficult task. The Greek Cypriots were not enthusiastic about the implementation of some of the constitutional provisions which they regarded as unjust and unrealistic. The Turkish Cypriots, on the other hand, insisted on full implementation of the constitution, especially the provisions regarding their safeguards and privileges. A series of incidents revolving around 'basic articles' of the constitution undermined the entire process of state-building. After three years of simmering tension and fruitless efforts to establish constitutional order and a working state, a complete constitutional breakdown and eruption of violence occurred in December 1963. Some of the major sources of constitutional tension were the provisions for the 70:30 ratio in the public service, the separate majority vote in the parliament, the establishment of separate municipalities, and the right of the president and vice-president to veto decisions of the council of ministers and the parliament.

The 70:30 ratio in the public service was out of step with the 80:20 ratio of the population. The Greek Cypriots felt that this provision was arbitrary, unjust, and discriminatory, and therefore, it should not be implemented. The Turkish Cypriots, on the other hand, argued that the 70:30 ratio was restoring equity in the public service which had been dominated by the Greek Cypriots under the British administration. Efforts made by President Makarios and Vice-President Kutchuk to find a compromise solution failed and the issue was never settled. From 1960 to 1963, a large number of appointments in the public service were disputed on communal grounds and taken to court. The court, however, could not make any progress towards a settlement of the conflict because it was also paralysed by ethnic fragmentation and polarization. Its neutral president, German jurist Ernst Forsthoff, found himself caught amidst ethnically polarized factions and resigned in May 1963. Since the conflict was more ethnopolitical than legal in nature, the question of the 70:30 ratio was never resolved. As a consequence, the public service never became fully operational, and the state never functioned properly.

The provision for separate majorities in the parliament was another source of ethnic-based political tension. The Greek Cypriots felt that the provision violated democratic principles and gave the Turkish Cypriot minority a powerful obstructive weapon. The Turkish Cypriots argued that with the separate majority vote they could protect themselves from Greek Cypriot domination. The confrontation over the separate majority provision led to a communal polarization in the legislative process. As a result, basic laws badly needed for the smooth operation of the state could not be passed. This can be illustrated by the case of tax legislation. When the republic came into being, there was a need for legislation on income tax. The government introduced a bill on income tax in the parliament. The Turkish Cypriot representatives used their separate majority right to block it. They justified their position by referring to a delay in the implementation of other constitutional provisions, especially the 70:30 ratio in the public service and the establishment of separate municipalities. Finally, the two communal chambers intervened separately and passed communal laws imposing taxes on their respective ethnic groups. With this development, the two groups moved further apart and the unity of the state and the economy suffered a heavy blow. Taxes were, in effect, imposed on an ethnic basis and used to finance separate communal institutions, projects, and services. The lack of central control or regulation of public financial affairs led to chaos and disarray in the economic life of the new state. Economic paralysis in the public sector had, in turn, a negative impact on the economy and well-being of both communities.

The provision for separate municipalities also caused much trouble and problems which were never resolved. The Greek Cypriots criticized the provision as a first step towards partition, and resisted its implementation. The issue was brought to the parliament where separate majority votes confirmed the deadlock. Thereafter, the two sides followed different courses of action. The president, backed by the Greek Cypriot-dominated council of ministers, issued an executive order calling for the appointment of unified municipal boards. The Turkish Cypriot communal chamber responded by passing a communal law legitimizing separate Turkish municipalities. Both acts were ruled unconstitutional and void *ab initio* by the supreme court. In both instances the vote of the opposite communal judge decided the case. The two sides, however, insisted on their positions, and a settlement on the issue was never reached. The result was chaos and disarray in the municipal affairs of the five largest towns of the island.

The right granted to the president and vice-president to veto certain decisions of the government and the parliament led to a deadlock in the executive branch. A major crisis occurred when a decision was made by the council of ministers for the formation of an army on a mixed basis. The vice-president vetoed the decision and asked for the establishment of an army based on separate communal units. He argued that soldiers with linguistic, cultural, religious, and ethnic differences could not be quartered together, and therefore, the army should be ethnically separated. The president reacted by questioning the applicability of the right of veto of the vice-president in that particular case. Then, he went further to declare that under the circumstances there was no need for the creation of an army. The crisis in the government was never resolved and an army was never established as provided by the constitution. A destructive consequence of that deadlock was the emergence of underground military groups, a sort of 'private army', on both sides. These groups were largely controlled by aspiring political leaders who were not reporting to any authority. The emergence of private ethnic armies revived old fears, suspicion, and uncertainty among the two communities. Both sides began realizing that they could not rely on an inoperative state for their security and proceeded to take measures for their own protection.[32]

A PROPOSAL TO REVISE THE CONSTITUTION

Repeated ethnically coloured legal and political deadlocks caused severe tension which led to a breakdown of the Zürich and London settlement. The political life of the republic was polarized along ethnic lines and the state was headed for paralysis. Under these circumstances, President Makarios took the initiative for an amendment of certain articles of the constitution. In November 1963, he made a proposal of thirteen points to Vice-President Kutchuk for 'revision of at least some of those provisions which impede the smooth functioning and development of the State'.[33] Makarios argued that a revision of the constitution was necessary because 'one of the consequences of the difficulties created by certain Constitutional provisions is to prevent the Greeks and Turks of Cyprus from co-operating in a spirit of understanding and friendship, to undermine the relations between them and cause them to draw further apart instead of closer together, to the detriment of the well-being of the people of Cyprus as a whole'.[34] The proposed amendment mainly addressed constitutional deadlocks. The most important of them were the following: abolition of the veto right of the president and the vice-president; abolition of the separate majority votes in the parliament; establishment of unified municipalities; unification of the administration of justice; participation of the two communities in the public service in proportion to their population; and abolition of the Greek communal chamber.

Makarios' proposals were aimed at the establishment of a unitary state with majority rule. This would mean elimination of some of the privileges and safeguards of the minority. Vice-President Kutchuk rejected the proposals as completely unacceptable and of a sweeping nature aimed at the destruction of the republic and attainment of *enosis*. He insisted that Cyprus should remain a bicommunal state, or complete separation of the two ethnic groups should come into effect through partition of the island.

ETHNIC AND SOCIAL FRAGMENTATION

The legal controversies and political polarization which paralysed the state and the political process were merely the 'superstructure' of a similarly ethnically polarized and potentially explosive 'infrastructure' inherited from the past. Socially, the two ethnic groups remained largely divided. The epitome of their social segregation was the absence of intermarriage and the limited participation in joint social and cultural events. Greek and Turkish social activities were closely related to distinct religious beliefs and practices, ethnic holidays, and cultural traditions. Therefore, there was not enough common ground for social interaction. Intermarriage was extremely rare, since it carried with it a social and religious stigma. In effect, marriage of a Greek Orthodox with a Turkish Muslim was prohibited under the separate family laws of the two communities.

In the professional field and party organization, the two communities were largely self-sufficient and self-contained. They had separate political parties, professional organizations, and labour unions with mostly uni-ethnic membership. The major Greek Cypriot political parties at the time of independence were the pro-*enosis* Patriotic Front and the pro-independence communist party AKEL. The major Turkish Cypriot parties were the Turkish Cypriot People's Party and the National Front. Both held pro-partition views. The ethnic-based division of political parties was partly due to the ethnopolitical division provided by the institutional framework of the state. The lack of common parties and organizations articulating the economic interests of the two ethnic groups across ethnic boundaries further widened the gap between the two sides.

The segregation of education inherited from the colonial era was preserved and reinforced. The two communal chambers, acting separately and in accordance with the constitution, passed legislation that to a great extent established educational unity of the two communities with their motherlands. The curricula and textbooks used in Cypriot elementary and high schools were mostly imported from the two mainlands. Ethnic and political controversies also undermined early efforts for the establishment of a badly needed university. The state-supported University of Cyprus was established by law in 1989 and began operating in 1992. The limited communal interaction in the educational and intellectual fields sustained one-sided 'ethnic ways' of thinking among the two communities. The result was a growing gap in the perceptions held by the two sides about each other.

The two communities also had their own newspapers and other publications which were mostly presenting biased ethnic views and conflicting positions. Besides the local press, publications imported from Greece and Turkey emphasizing Greek–Turkish antagonism enhanced mutual fears and biased perceptions.

Despite the declaration of Cypriot independence, the two communities continued celebrating the national holidays of Greece and

Turkey which were mostly directed against each other. It should be remembered that the celebration of Greek and Turkish national holidays was allowed, if not encouraged, by the constitution. These celebrations – which as a rule included pompous parades, pageants, and flying of flags – cultivated mutually negative sentiments at the grassroots level. The Greek and Turkish national anthems and flags were used during these celebrations. (Cyprus has no national anthem of its own to the present day.) These ethnic celebrations quite naturally reminded the masses on the two sides of the ethnic line that their ethnic roots and loyalties extended to Greece and Turkey, and that the Cypriot state did not fulfil their national aspirations. As a result, any prospects for the development of a supportive political culture and mass legitimacy for the new state were undermined.

Perhaps the most destructive element in biethnic relations was the fact that the two communities failed to abandon their old conflicting ethnopolitical goals of *enosis* and partition. This was manifested in the attitudes of the communal elites who missed no opportunity to deliver intense patriotic speeches reaffirming their continuing commitment to the achievement of those goals. In effect, the creation of an independent state was viewed by the two sides as an interim phase for materialization of *enosis* or partition.

Finally, one could mention that some difficulties and misunderstandings were caused in intercommunal communication by language problems. Public documents and stationery were printed in Greek, Turkish, and English. Sessions of biethnic boards were conducted in English, but the problem of having participants incapacitated by linguistic inadequacy was not unusual. The most illustrative example was the cabinet where Vice-President Kutchuk (a Swiss-educated medical doctor) could not speak English, while President Makarios' knowledge of English was limited (he had studied theology in Boston for two years). The overall performance of the public service was also affected by similar problems.

FLARE-UP AND INTERNATIONALIZATION OF THE PROBLEM

Constitutional crises, political immobilization, ethnic passion, mutual mistrust, suspicion, fear, uncertainty, limited bicommunal interaction, and the emergence of underground military groups all paved the way for an open communal confrontation. The political and psychological setting was ripe for an open confrontation. Both communities had already begun stockpiling arms since the declaration of independence. The inevitable came in December 1963, when heavy fighting broke out in the capital city of Nicosia and soon spread to other parts of the island. The outbreak of hostilities brought about a breakdown of inter-communal relations. A process of physical separation of the two communities began in December 1963. The Turks moved into armed enclaves which emerged in various parts of the island. The Turkish Cypriot leadership and public servants withdrew from the government and set up a separate administration. The separation was completed in 1974 after the Turkish invasion of Cyprus. In the aftermath of the invasion, and because of it, two ethnic zones were created by forced movement of populations. The Turkish Cypriots have been living in the northern part of the island which is occupied by the Turkish army.

From 1960 to 1963 the Cyprus issue went through a transformation. The troubled colonial relationship with Britain came to an end and domestic ethnic conflict emerged as the dominant problem. The outbreak of violence in December 1963 marked the beginning of a new phase. Ethnic conflict took the form of an open armed confrontation and entered a course of internationalization. Certain factors were especially conducive to the internationalization of the problem in its new violent form.

Cyprus was now an independent state and, therefore, an autonomous unit within the international system. It could pursue its own foreign policy and interact directly with other states and international organizations. The young republic sought to establish itself in the international arena by becoming a member of international organizations and establishing relations with other countries. It became a member of the United Nations, the Council of Europe, the British Commonwealth of Nations, and other international organizations. It joined the Non-Aligned Movement and followed a foreign policy of non-alignment. It established diplomatic relations with Britain, Greece, Turkey, the United States, the Soviet Union, and other countries. Membership in the world community linked Cypriot developments to the web of international politics. Cyprus was no longer a colonial problem which could be contained within the jurisdiction of the imperial power. Outside parties could now interact directly with the new state and the parties involved in the conflict.

Ethnic ties between the two Cypriot communities and Greece and Turkey were also instrumental in causing foreign involvement in

Cypriot affairs. They provided the basis for the establishment of close relations between the two local ethnic groups and their mother countries. The Cypriots looked upon Greece and Turkey as their protectors and counted on their diplomatic, military, economic, and moral support. Greece and Turkey viewed the two Cypriot communities as parts of the Greek and Turkish nations and considered the Cyprus issue as their 'national issue'. Cyprus carried a heavy load of national pride and honour and had a great appeal in domestic Greek and Turkish politics. Geographic proximity and strategic considerations added another dimension to Greek and Turkish interests in Cyprus. The island is located 44 miles (70 kilometres) south of Turkey and 250 miles (400 kilometres) east of the Greek island of Rhodes.

The complicated treaty structure by which the Republic of Cyprus was bound at birth established also channels of external interference in Cypriot affairs. The Treaties of Establishment, Alliance, and Guarantee gave Britain, Greece, and Turkey the right to station forces in Cyprus and intervene, jointly or unilaterally, in Cypriot affairs. Any change of the status quo created by the London and Zürich accords could cause intervention from outside.

The Cyprus conflict presented a threat to regional stability, peace, and security and could not be kept within the jurisdiction of the parties directly involved. Other countries and organizations also had reasons to be concerned over the issue and to seek measures to protect peace and their interests. The United Nations which was created to 'save succeeding generations from the scourge of war'[35] had a primary responsibility in preventing an escalation of the armed conflict. NATO had a special interest in containing the conflict and averting an intra-alliance war between Greece and Turkey.

The power vacuum created with the British withdrawal from Cyprus was another factor conducive to the internationalization of the ethnic conflict. With the removal of British administration and the declaration of independence, Cyprus became a *terra nullius* in superpower politics. Both superpowers had the interest and the means to influence developments on the island. The United States could use its junior allies – Britain, Greece, and Turkey – to influence the course of events and seek a settlement safeguarding Western interests in Cyprus. The Soviet Union could use AKEL, the powerful Greek Cypriot communist party, to influence Cypriot politics and future developments. President Makarios had already established a political alliance with AKEL and friendly relations with Moscow. The outbreak of communal hostilities presented an opportunity and a challenge to both superpowers to fish in troubled waters and promote their goals.

The above factors – declaration of independence, cross-boundary ethnic ties, superpower concern and interests, the danger of war between two NATO allies, and the threat to regional and international peace and security – contributed to the internationalization of the Cyprus conflict after the flare-up in December 1963. The problem ceased to be a domestic Cypriot affair and became a major item in international politics and diplomacy. Its repercussions were felt far beyond the sea boundaries of Cyprus. It became a major source of friction between Greece and Turkey, and repeatedly brought the two countries to the brink of war. Greek–Turkish friction undermined the cohesion of NATO and threatened with paralysis the south-eastern flank of the Western alliance. The United States and the Soviet Union found themselves confronting each other in recurrent crises threatening regional and international peace and security. The United Nations intervened and played a major role by trying to contain the conflict, restore order, and resolve the problem. These and other international implications of the Cyprus problem are examined in the following chapters.

SUMMARY AND CONCLUSION

The roots of the ethnic conflict in Cyprus go back into history and deep into the bicommunal structure of the Cypriot society. Despite four centuries of coexistence, the two communities remained separate, distinct, and self-contained ethnic groups divided along linguistic, religious, and cultural lines. The ethnic cleavage was reinforced by political division and attachment of the two groups to their mother-lands. The lack of cross-cutting ethnic, social, or political ties prevented the development of a common Cypriot political culture and overarching loyalties among the two groups. With the establishment of the Republic of Cyprus, the ethnic and political divisions of the past were institutionalized and injected into the state apparatus and the political process. The coincidence of ethnic and political divisions had a mutually reinforcing effect. Politics were coloured by ethnicity and vice versa. Ethnicity was thus brought into the political arena and the political game was transformed into an ethnopolitical struggle.

The politicization of ethnicity, which was facilitated by the fragmented political framework of the state, enhanced the psychological distance and quest for political autonomy of the two ethnic groups. Furthermore, contradictions emanating from distinct and conflicting national, religious, ethnic, and cultural values and practices contributed to the transformation of the two ethnic groups into political conflict groups. Entangling of ethnics with politics, at both the elite and grassroots levels, mobilized individual and collective feelings of self-identification and group belonging. Thus, the two communities became distinct ethnopolitical rivals and their quest and exercise of political power became part and parcel of an ethnic rivalry.

The underlying dynamics of majority–minority relations added more trouble and barriers to inter-ethnic communication and reconciliation. The two groups were tempted to use the state institutions and political process at the expense of each other. The Turkish Cypriot minority made extensive use of its legal and political safeguards and avoided negotiations because it was in a weak bargaining position *vis-à-vis* the Greek Cypriots. Instead, it used intransigence as a measure of defence and sought political autonomy and secession.

It was in this setting of ethnic and political segregation, and against a historical and social background of unhealthy communal relations, that the domestic ethnic conflict in Cyprus was generated right after the declaration of independence in 1960.

Finally, the conclusion can be drawn from the analysis presented in this chapter that political differentiation of groups along ethnic lines can be conducive for the generation of ethnic conflict. This is especially true if in a bicommunal society there are no cross-cutting linguistic, social, and religious ties or other overarching loyalties, and the communal elites fail to co-operate in counteracting the centrifugal effects of ethnic and political fragmentation.

3 The Impact of Cross-Boundary Ethnic Ties

Nothing is ever done beautifully which is done in rivalship, nor nobly which is done in pride.

John Ruskin

OBJECTIVES

This chapter examines the implications that the ethnic conflict on Cyprus has had on the triangle of Greek–Cypriot–Turkish relations after the flare-up in 1963. The focus is on the role played by cross-boundary ethnic ties in generating and widening the conflict. Emphasis is placed on the spill-over effect that the presence of cross-boundary ethnic ties has had on Greek–Turkish relations.

The presentation, analysis, and interpretation of events revolve around the following questions: Do cross-boundary ethnic ties enhance the likelihood of external intervention in an ethnic conflict? Are they the primary causes and vehicles for such an intervention? Are local participants or outside parties more likely to use cross-boundary ethnic bonds to elicit or justify external intervention in a conflict? Whose purposes and interests are likely to be promoted by external intervention? Those of the rival ethnic groups or those of the intervening parties? Or some common goals dictated by shared ethnicity? What impact does the ethnic conflict have on the relations of outside parties involved? Does it have a spill-over effect that widens the conflict or does it encourage inter-state co-operation conducive for containment and resolution of the conflict?

HISTORICAL ANTECEDENTS

The involvement of Greece and Turkey in the internal affairs of Cyprus predates the establishment of the Republic of Cyprus in 1960. Greece had repeatedly expressed concern and interest in Cyprus

35

throughout the period of British rule from 1878 to 1960. It also supported the Greek Cypriot agitation for *enosis* while Turkey supported the Turkish Cypriots and their demand for *taksim*. It should be noted that the campaign for *enosis* and the revolt against the British in the 1950s were the culmination of a movement that spanned the entire period of British rule. As Hill wrote in 1948, 'Hardly a year has passed since the Occupation without the "Hellenic Idea" finding expression in some form or other.'[1] But the idea of *enosis* itself goes back to the years of the Greek war of independence (1821–29) and the establishment of an independent Greek state. Simply the change of rulers in Cyprus in 1878 revitalized pro-*enosis* feelings among the Greek Cypriots who were hoping that a Christian European power would be more considerate of their ethnic aspiration. Already on the day of his arrival in Cyprus on 22 July 1878, the first British Governor Sir Garnet Wolseley was told by the church leadership: 'We accept the change in Government inasmuch as we trust that Great Britain will help Cyprus, as it did the Ionian Islands, to be united with Mother Greece, with which it is naturally connected.'[2] The Turkish Cypriots, despite some initial positive feelings for the new administration,[3] repeatedly expressed their concern to the British rulers over the possibility of Cyprus becoming part of Greece.[4] As Purcell points out, 'The notion that the Greeks of Cyprus remained under British rule for many years without complaint is as groundless as the notion that the Turks were not antagonistic to *enosis*.'[5]

A turning point in Greek and Turkish involvement in Cyprus came with the Greek appeals to the UN General Assembly in the 1950s asking for *enosis*. The Greek appeals were based on the fact that 80 per cent of the Cypriot population were ethnic Greeks who had expressed their will to be united with Greece.[6] The justification for the Greek appeals to the UN, as it was presented in an explanatory memorandum, was that Greece and Cyprus had a 3000-year common history and shared ethnicity expressed in a common language, culture, and religion. 'Cyprus belongs to the Greek world; Cyprus is Greece itself', the memorandum added, and because of this, the Greek government, 'fully aware of the responsibilities of the past, present, and future of the Hellenic nation', called for the application of the principle of self-determination and the union of the island with Greece.[7]

Turkey reacted to the Greek appeal to the UN by intensifying its campaign for partition and by taking measures against the Greek community in Turkey. Turkish reaction manifested itself in massive anti-Greek demonstrations in Istanbul and other cities under the slogans 'partition' and 'Cyprus is Turkish'.[8] These demonstrations were encouraged by the government and resulted in violent attacks against schools, churches, shops, and houses in the Greek community, especially in Istanbul.[9] Other measures taken against the Greek community included confiscation of property and expulsion of thousands of people.[10]

The Turkish press contributed to the generation of ethnic passion and anti-Greek sentiment by headlining alleged atrocities against the Turks in Cyprus. (In the 1950s, there were some incidents of ethnic violence, but no significant inter-communal fighting took place on the island.) The Turkish newspapers also demanded the ousting of the Greek Orthodox Patriarchate from Istanbul which was allegedly supporting Greek claims on the island.[11]

On Cyprus, Turkey provided material and diplomatic support to Turkish Cypriots who were demanding partition. Arms and training were provided to TMT (*Turk Mukavemet Teskilati*, the Turkish Defence Organization), a Turkish Cypriot underground military organization created to fight for the partition of Cyprus.

At the UN, Turkey argued that Greece was pursuing a policy of territorial expansion under the cover of ethnic justification. The Turkish government demanded that in case of a change in the colonial status of Cyprus, a solution based on partition should be sought or the island should be given back to Turkey. The Turkish position was based on the fact that 'Cyprus was an island which had been part of Turkey for almost four hundred years, contained a large Turkish community, and was very important to Turkish security.'[12]

SETTLING THE COLONIAL PROBLEM

The General Assembly made a recommendation for a peaceful settlement of the Cyprus colonial problem in accordance with the principles of the UN Charter.[13] Eventually, a settlement was reached in 1959 through Greek–Turkish negotiations, but not in accordance with the UN principles of self-determination and sovereign equality of states. The Greek and Turkish governments negotiated the settlement under British directorship. Ethnic considerations and British interests determined not only the process through which the settlement was reached but also its content. The two motherlands and Britain appointed themselves guarantors of the newborn Republic of Cyprus and retained the right to maintain troops and intervene in the island, unilaterally or jointly, in the event of any change in the status quo created by the founding treaties.[14]

The internal affairs of the two communities were regulated by provisions based on the premise of historical, linguistic, cultural, religious, and educational unity with Greece and Turkey. The two communities were distinguished *vis-à-vis* each other with references to their Greek and Turkish origin, language, culture, and religion. They were granted the right to use the Greek and Turkish flags and celebrate the national holidays of Greece and Turkey. There was no provision for the creation of a Cypriot national anthem and, essentially, the Cypriots were left with the national anthems of Greece and Turkey. In all educational, cultural, religious, sporting, and ethnic related matters, the two communities were encouraged to establish and maintain separate 'special relationships' with their motherlands.

Quite illustrative, and ironically symbolic, of the internal and cross-boundary ethnic controversies surrounding the establishment of the Cypriot state was the flag given to the new republic. It had to exclude blue, red, and green as the Greek, Turkish, and Islamic colours. For similar reasons, crosses, stripes, stars, and crescents also had to be avoided. After long and resourceful thinking, the designers came up with the unique idea of a neutral orange map of the island on a white background.

The greatest irony, however, was that neither of the Cypriot communities nor their respective motherlands were asking for an independent Cypriot state. Nor was the principle of self-determination invoked for that purpose by any of the parties involved. Greece and the Greek Cypriots were asking for *enosis*, while Turkey and the Turkish Cypriots stood for partition. It was the dynamics of Greek–Turkish antagonism, external intervention, and cross-boundary ethnic alliances that shaped the settlement. The fettered independence granted to the island reflected a compromise aimed at neutralizing the conflicting ethnopolitical goals of *enosis* and partition. The two mainlands, in an effort to neutralize their mutual suspicion and rivalry, abandoned, at least on paper, their ethnic-based territorial claims on Cyprus. Moreover, the new republic undertook to maintain its independence and territorial integrity and not to seek *enosis* or partition under any circumstances.

It should be borne in mind that the attitudes and claims of Greece and Turkey on Cyprus were shaped in the context of an enduring and deep-rooted ethnic antagonism, reciprocal hatreds, and suspicion which go back in history and deep into the psyche of the Greek and the Turk. The conquest of Constantinople (Istanbul) by the Ottoman Turks in 1453 and the subsequent four-century Ottoman rule over Greece were deep wounds in Greek national memory and pride. Old frustration and strong ethnic sentiments revived with the creation of the modern Greek state in 1830, following nine years of brutal war with the Ottoman rulers. Rising Greek nationalism found expression in the movement of *megali idea* (great idea, that is, Greek irredentism of the Byzantine Empire), of which *enosis* could be seen as an integral part. The Greek–Turkish wars of 1897, 1912–13, and 1919–23 further reinforced old rivalries and hatreds. The Greek invasion of Anatolia in 1920 was interpreted by Turkey as indicative of a drive for territorial expansion at the expense of the decaying Ottoman Empire. The liquidation of the empire and the emergence of a new Turkish nationalism provided an impetus for the restoration of Turkish power and national prestige, especially *vis-à-vis* the Greeks.

It was against this background of conflicting claims and deep-rooted ethnic rivalry that the Greek and Turkish attitudes and goals on Cyprus were shaped and the 1960 settlement was reached. Turkey interpreted the agitation for *enosis* as part of the broader Greek drive for territorial expansion. Greece, on the other hand, interpreted Turkish intervention and support of partition as an attempt to reconquer the island. Thus, with the end of British colonial rule, Cyprus was caught between the ethnic-motivated policies and claims of two mainland rivals. Moreover, the attitudes and goals of the two countries were shared by their respective communities on the island. Greek Cypriot resistance against British colonial rule was carried out in the name of *enosis*, while the Turkish Cypriots demanded partition and co-operated with the British authorities in undermining the *enosis* movement. The creation of an independent Cypriot state represented the narrow middle ground between mutually exclusive ethnic policies and goals.[15]

CROSS-BOUNDARY ETHNIC BONDS

Besides the exclusion of *enosis* and partition, the establishment of an independent Cypriot state did not set any limitations on Greek and Turkish involvement in Cyprus. On the contrary, the removal of the colonial administration left the way open for the two mainlands to develop close relations with the newborn state, strengthen their bonds with the two communities, influence domestic developments, and seek promotion of their national goals on the island. Outside intervention along ethnic lines has been an important and influential factor in the society and politics of Cyprus since independence. Much of the friction and turbulence which led to the gradual disintegration of the bicommunal Republic of Cyprus which was created in 1960 can be attributed to Greek and Turkish interference. The geographic separation of the two communities and the unilateral declaration of independence by the Turkish Cypriots in November 1983 are the culmination of a series of developments largely shaped by outside ethnic intervention and the dynamics of Greek–Turkish rivalry and involvement in the conflict. Therefore, the role played by cross-boundary ethnic ties in shaping developments on Cyprus cannot be ignored.

After the declaration of independence in 1960, the ethnic ties and loyalties of the two Cypriot communities with their motherlands were maintained and reinforced. The major instruments used for the preservation and revitalization of cross-boundary ethnic bonds were education, religion, culture, language, history, and military ties.

In the educational field, harmonization of the educational systems of the two Cypriot communities with those of their motherlands came into effect after the declaration of independence. The political and legal barriers existing under colonial rule were removed and the two sides proceeded to strengthen cross-boundary ties along ethnic lines. Educational co-operation was also facilitated by the educational ties inherited from the colonial period and by constitutional provisions encouraging the establishment of separate cultural and educational relationships between the two ethnic groups and their motherlands. Since education in Cyprus was segregated, the two communities maintained separate schools in which teachers and textbooks imported from the motherlands were used to socialize the young Cypriots into Greek and Turkish cultural patterns, religious beliefs, social values, and ethnic ideals.[16] Religious instruction was a major part of the curricula. In the Greek Cypriot schools emphasis was placed on the history, culture, and glory of classical Greece and the Byzantine Empire. In the Turkish Cypriot schools the focus was on the grandeur of the Ottoman Empire and Turkish nationalism. In both communities, ethnic socialization was mainly directed against the other ethnic group. The youngsters were learning at school that besides language, religion, and culture, centuries of warfare and bloodshed separated them from the other side of the ethnic line. In the early years of independence, large numbers of high school graduates continued their education mostly at Greek and Turkish universities. Linguistic convenience, geographic proximity, ethnic affiliation, and the lack of a university in Cyprus, were the main reasons behind the large numbers of Cypriot students in Greece and Turkey.[17] (The University of Cyprus was founded in 1989 and began operating in 1992.)

Cross-boundary educational integration contributed to the maintenance and reinforcement of ethnic links and national loyalties between the Cypriots and their motherlands. Since education was a major instrument of ethnic socialization, it also served as an instrument for the transplantation of the broader Greek–Turkish antagonism into Cyprus. The result was a widening of the psychological gap and ethnopolitical controversies separating the two ethnic groups.

Besides education, religious bonds and practices contributed to the maintenance and reinforcement of ethnic and cultural links between the two Cypriot communities and their motherlands. The churches were centres of national indoctrination emphasizing the indivisibility of religion and ethnicity, and the necessity for attachment to the mainlands.[18] Catechism and ecclesiastic practices were aimed at keeping alive and reinforcing memories of common history and ancestral identification with the Greek and Turkish nations. Cyprus was never part of the modern Greek state, but the legacies of classical Greece and Byzantium, of which Cyprus was part, had a strong impact on the Greek Cypriot community throughout the centuries. Religious practices, cultural patterns, and social values were identical to those in Greece.

The Turkish Cypriots had similar attitudes and bonds with Turkey. The Ottoman rule, which lasted from 1571 to 1878, had a long-lasting impact on the Cypriot society. The Turkish Cypriots are the descendants of the Ottoman army that invaded and occupied the island in the sixteenth century. After the end of Ottoman rule, ethnic factors, geographic proximity, and a feeling of insecurity emanating from their minority status made the Turkish Cypriots look to Turkey for ethnic identification and protection.

It was the mission of the religious institutions on both sides of the ethnic line to maintain and strengthen ethnic legacies, national bonds, and loyalties with the mainland and preserve the ethnopolitical gap between the two ethnic groups. The creation of an independent state did not bring about any change in the role and attitude of the communal churches. Cross-boundary ethnic and religious affiliation continued to determine their orientation and activities. In other words, the churches remained organs of ethnic indoctrination and their contribution towards the creation of mutually negative predispositions and attitudes between the two communities has been a considerable one.

In the military field, close ties cutting across state boundaries began developing along ethnic lines with the dispatch of Greek and Turkish troops to the island under the 1960 Zürich and London accords. The 1960 Treaty of Guarantee provided for the permanent stationing of Greek and Turkish contingents on Cyprus, comprising 950 and 650 men respectively. The presence of Greek and Turkish troops had a symbolic meaning and substantive consequences for the island. Greek soldiers, for the first time in seven centuries, and Turkish soldiers, for the first time in nearly a century, were again setting foot on Cyprus, thus reviving national sentiments, bonds, loyalties, and hopes for ethnic unification. The two contingents co-operated with their respective ethnic groups and served as channels for the establishment of military ties. They also collaborated with the military groups which began emerging on both sides as a result of the failure to establish a unitary Cypriot army.

The national and cultural bonds of the two Cypriot ethnic groups with their motherlands were further strengthened through the celebration of common national holidays and the use of common symbols. The Cypriots used widely the flags of Greece and Turkey along with the ethnic-free flag of the Republic of Cyprus. Since the creation of an ethnic-free Cypriot national anthem proved an impossible task, they also played the Greek and Turkish national anthems. Thus, two of the more powerful symbols holding a state together were, to an extensive degree, dismissed and substituted by those of Greece and Turkey. It is also worth mentioning that Greek Cypriot celebrations culminated in the annual grand commemoration of the 1821 revolution against Ottoman rule which led to the establishment of the modern Greek state. The Turkish Cypriots, on the other hand, celebrated with equal ethnic fervor the Turkish national holidays. The central event in their celebrations was the annual commemoration of the 1923 victory over the Greek army and the subsequent expulsion of the Greeks from Asia Minor. National celebrations on both sides included parades of Cypriot war veterans, the mainland contingents stationed on the island, and high school students. The patriotic speeches delivered during these celebrations were, as a rule, eulogizing ethnic ideals and attachment to the motherlands.

The presence of cross-boundary ethnic, linguistic, educational, religious, cultural, and military ties between the Cypriots and their motherlands had a destructive impact on inter-communal relations. Attachment of the two ethnic groups to two rival states, which have been at sword's edge for centuries, prevented the generation of common patriotic bonds or overarching loyalties supportive of the newborn Cypriot state. Greek and Turkish social, religious, and cultural influence on the Cypriot society widened the gap between the two communities and contributed to the creation of mutually hostile ethnic sentiments. The 'suspicion syndrome' dominating Greek–Turkish relations and perceptions was also transplanted into Cyprus and eliminated any hope for constructive interaction between the rival ethnic groups. It was in this setting of national polarization and cross-boundary ethnic alliances that inter-communal violence erupted in 1963. The communal flare-up provided an opportunity for the mainlands to come in support of their local ethnic groups and seek advancement of their goals on Cyprus.

WIDENING OF THE CONFLICT

The first major external interference in the politics of the young Cyprus republic took place on ethnic and legal grounds. In late 1963, Turkey intervened on behalf of the Turkish Cypriots and rejected the thirteen constitutional amendments proposed by President Makarios. The Turkish government had previously warned the Cypriot president that it would not tolerate any changes in the constitution or 'cede one inch' of the rights of the Turkish Cypriots.[19] It is worth mentioning that the proposed amendments were referring to provisions of a domestic nature and did not affect the international status of the republic or the rights of the guarantor powers (that is, Greece, Turkey, and Britain). Turkey's reaction to Makarios' move could be interpreted as an expression of interest and concern over the Turkish Cypriots and as a signal to them not to enter into negotiations with Makarios on constitutional matters. Eventually, the Turkish Cypriot Vice-President Fazil Kutchuk, in consultation with the Turkish government, rejected the proposals as 'completely unacceptable', their 'ulterior intentions being to leave the Turks at the absolute mercy of the Greeks'.[20]

Turkey's intervention in the Cyprus constitutional and ethnopolitical crisis marked the beginning of a new phase of internationalization of the problem. Greece, in response to Turkey's reaction, came in support of the Greek Cypriots. External intervention along ethnic lines exacerbated the already tense situation on the island and communal violence broke out in December 1963. The Greek and Turkish contingents, which were permanently stationed on the outskirts of the capital city of Nicosia, left their camps and joined the fighting. As the hostilities were rapidly spreading and intensifying, Britain proposed the establishment of a joint peacekeeping force comprising British, Greek, and Turkish troops already stationed on the island. Although the British proposal was welcomed by all parties, the Greek and Turkish troops, which had already occupied strategic positions and were confronting each other, could not participate in the peacekeeping operation.

Further deterioration of the situation prompted the Turkish Cypriots, who were retreating with heavy losses before the superior numbers and equipment of the Greek Cypriots, to appeal to Turkey for military help. Turkey responded by moving troops, warships, and aircraft to the south coast and threatening to invade Cyprus.

The Greek Cypriots made a similar appeal to Athens. Greece criticized the Turkish government for its military preparations and let it be known that if Turkey invaded Cyprus, Greece would do likewise. Greece, however, proceeded to send a large number of troops and military equipment to Cyprus, in order to prevent a Turkish invasion. A joint decision was made by President Makarios and the Greek Premier George Papandreou in April 1964 for the secret dispatch of a division of the Greek army (approximately 10 000 men) to the island.[21]

The infiltration of Greek troops into the island and the creation of a conscript Cyprus national guard staffed by Greek officers and controlled by the Greek pentagon in Athens caused a major crisis and a severe deterioration in Greek–Turkish relations. Following Kutchuk's protest, and in co-operation with him, the Turkish government warned that the joint Greek and Greek Cypriot military build-up on Cyprus presented a threat to the Turkish Cypriots and, therefore, it was unacceptable. The danger of an all-out Greek–Turkish war became real and imminent when the Turkish national security council decided to invade Cyprus in early June 1964. Landing preparations were carried out in Turkey while Greece and the Greek Cypriots mobilized their forces for a full-scale confrontation on Cyprus as well as on the Thracian border. What seemed to be an almost certain military clash was averted at the last moment through the forceful intervention and adamant insistence of the American president, Lyndon Johnson, that there could be no war between NATO allies.

During another major crisis which developed two months later, the Greek and Greek Cypriot forces, fighting side by side, launched an all-out attack against the Turkish Cypriot enclave in the Tylliria region, the only one with access to the sea. Turkey was using that enclave to smuggle soldiers, arms, and supplies into Cyprus. The Turkish air force intervened by launching large-scale attacks on military and civilian positions in the region. The crisis reached its climax when President Makarios threatened to launch a merciless sweeping attack on all Turkish Cypriot settlements, and Greece publicly came in his support by declaring that 'if the action of the Turkish air force continues... Greece will assist Cyprus with its air force and every military means at its disposal'.[22]

The gravity of the situation and the imminent risk of a catastrophic war was epigrammatically stressed by the American representative at the Security Council who urged the parties involved to stop hostilities and show restraint, otherwise, 'in a matter of hours we will be over the brink and in the abyss – and none can see the bottom'.[23] Eventually, however, uneasy peace was once again restored through UN and US intervention. The 1963–64 crisis was the culmination of a gradually increasing Greek and Turkish involvement in Cyprus and the renewal of old ethnic animosities. With the eruption of communal violence and the active involvement of Greece and Turkey in the hostilities, the focus of the crisis began shifting from the domestic Cypriot setting to the imminent danger of a Greek–Turkish war. The following observations on Greek and Turkish involvement in the flare-up can be made:

First, Greece and Turkey intervened in the conflict strictly along ethnic lines. Ethnic affiliation and treaty provisions provided channels and justification for the participation of the mainlands in the conflict. External involvement in the hostilities exacerbated the crisis and made it more explosive and difficult to resolve.

Secondly, Greece and Turkey intervened in the inter-communal conflict with the primary aim of backing their respective ethnic groups in their struggle against each other. Intervention of the motherlands in support of their local kins was a matter of mutual and public expectation, and perceived to be in their common ethnic interests.

Thirdly, external intervention along ethnic lines led to direct confrontation of the two mainland powers. Despite the provisions of the 1960 Treaties of Guarantee and Alliance, calling for the military co-operation and common defence of Cyprus, Greece, and Turkey, conflicting ethnic goals and fanaticism prevailed and invalidated their contractual commitments. The result was an intensification and widening of the conflict across boundaries.

THE DIPLOMATIC FRONT

The establishment of ethnic-based alliances between the Cypriots and their respective motherlands was manifested not only on the military front, but also in the diplomatic and political fields. While the two mainlands were smuggling troops, arms, and supplies into Cyprus, their diplomatic services were fully mobilized to gain international support for their respective local ethnic groups. This was clearly illustrated during the numerous sessions of the Security Council which dealt with the repeated crises of the 1963–64 period. At the London conference, which was held under British chairmanship in January 1964 to negotiate a ceasefire and a political solution to the problem, the two sides participated as two competing ethnic blocs rather than as four parties. In the Geneva conference, which was held in August under UN auspices, Cypriot representatives were not present at all. Greece and Turkey negotiated on their behalf and in the interest of the two Cypriot communities.

Ethnic-based diplomatic alliances were made possible with the definition of identical goals and policies on the Cyprus issue by the two parties on each side of the ethnic line. After the eruption of violence and the internationalization of the problem through the UN and other international conferences, the Greek government and President Makarios officially dismissed *enosis*, which had been their explicit common goal until 1963, and adopted a policy of independence and non-alignment for Cyprus. This policy change on the Greek side could be attributed to several factors.

First, Greece and Cyprus had to abandon the pursuit of *enosis* for tactical reasons. The advocacy of *enosis*, which in effect meant annexation of Cyprus by Greece, had colonial connotations and was incompatible with the worldwide movement of self-determination and decolonization. Therefore, the Greek and Cypriot governments adopted a policy of self-determination and independence in expectation of gaining the support of Third World and Eastern bloc countries at international fora, especially the UN.

Secondly, *enosis* was excluded by the 1960 Zürich and London founding treaties, of which both Greece and Cyprus were signatories.[24] Pursuit of *enosis* in disregard of the above treaties would give Turkey an excuse to invade Cyprus.

Thirdly, there was a growing movement among the Greek Cypriots in favour of independence. This movement was spearheaded by AKEL, the local communist party which was a major political force on the island.[25] At that time, AKEL was the largest and most effective party, controlling about 35 per cent of the Greek Cypriot electorate. President Makarios relied heavily on AKEL's support and, therefore, he had to take into account its positions. AKEL was opposed to *enosis* on ideological grounds. It should also be borne in mind that, at that time, the communist party was outlawed in Greece, a member of the 'imperialist' NATO alliance.[26]

Fourthly, the abandonment of *enosis* could be partly attributed to personal factors. One could assume that President Makarios would not be so enthusiastic about giving up his temporal office as head of an independent state. After all, the ambitious celibate archbishop became president after long adventures and exiles, and his charismatic character made him a popular and trusted leader among the Greek Cypriots. Moreover, he had established himself as a leading figure in the movements of self-determination and non-alignment, the principles of which were incompatible with the spirit of *enosis*.[27]

The new official policy of Athens and Nicosia was outlined in widely publicized joint statements issued in Athens and Nicosia.[28] The main points of this policy were the following:

1 Greece supported the just struggle of the Greek Cypriots for independence through self-determination.
2 Greece followed a policy of peace, but in case of a Turkish military intervention it would go to war.
3 A solution of the Cyprus problem should be based on a unitary state with safeguarded minority rights for the Turkish Cypriots.
4 Makarios' termination of the 1960 Treaty of Guarantee was legal and merely confirmed reality. (The Cypriot president had unilaterally terminated the treaty after the dispatch of the UN peacekeeping force to Cyprus in March 1964 and the refusal of the Turkish contingent to return to its camp.)

One should mention, however, that despite the official dismissal of *enosis*, the *enosis* spirit remained very much alive among large segments of the population in Greece and Cyprus. Political leaders in both countries had to follow double-faced tactics in order to assure the pro-*enosis* groups that their long-established 'national aspiration' was not betrayed. This ambiguity on the positions of the Greek side had a negative impact on the prospects for a constructive communication with the Turkish side. The Turks interpreted the Greek tactics as manoeuvring aimed at misleading the Turks and world public opinion.

A coincidence of goals and policies also existed between the Turkish government and the Turkish Cypriot leadership. Those goals and policies could be summarized as follows:[29]

1 A solution of the Cyprus problem should be based on partitioning of the island, providing for the physical and administrative separation of the two communities.
2 The 1960 Treaty of Guarantee was valid and Turkey had the right to invade Cyprus to protect the Turkish Cypriots in the event of a breach of the treaty.
3 The Makarios government was unlawful because no Turkish Cypriots participated in it since the beginning of hostilities in December 1963.
4 The Turkish Cypriots were not an ordinary minority, but a distinct ethnic group, and should be treated as such.

The conflicting positions of the Greek and Turkish sides on Cyprus reflected the ethnopolitical gap between the two Cypriot communities, their alliances with the mainlands, and the broader rivalry between the Greek and the Turkish nations. The flare-up converged ethnic antipathies and policy goals both on Cyprus and the mainlands. This ethnic polarization was largely the consequence of the strong cross-boundary ethnic ties discussed above.

BRINKMANSHIP IN THE AEGEAN

Another major aspect of the ramifications which the Cypriot conflict had on Greek–Turkish relations was the deterioration of the bilateral relations of the two countries in other areas. During periods of tension, massive demonstrations took place in the major cities of both countries calling for support of their Cypriot kin and adoption of hard-line nationalistic policies towards the ethnic rival on the other side of the Aegean. The eruption of ethnic passions and the revival of old frustrations and hatreds had an overwhelming impact on the governments and policies of the two countries. The mood of the time and the people in that heavily electrified atmosphere were epigrammatically portrayed in the following celebrated statement of the Greek Premier George Papandreou: 'A war clash between Greece and Turkey would be madness, but if Turkey decides to enter the insane asylum, we shall not hesitate to follow her.'[30] The two governments were overwhelmed by blinding and deafening ethnic fanaticism to the extent that they were not even willing to listen to or consider each other's positions. In this atmosphere of ethnic hysteria, President Johnson failed to persuade the Greek and Turkish premiers to meet and talk about their differences during their simultaneous visits to Washington in June 1964. In the words of the Greek premier, that would not be 'a conversation but two monologues; two deaf men talking about different things'.[31]

Besides the conflicting official policy statements and mass manifestations of ethnic hostility, the two countries also took concrete ethnic motivated measures against each other. Turkey, in reaction to alleged oppression of the Turkish Cypriots, took a series of measures against the Greek community of Istanbul.[32] Those measures included hundreds of deportations, closing down of dozens of businesses, deprivation of work permits, and confiscation of property.[33] On the islands of Imbros and Tenedos (Bozcaada), whose population comprised mostly Greeks, several educational restrictions were imposed, including prohibition of the teaching of the Greek language. The Patriarchate of Istanbul was accused of collaboration with the Greek government in carrying out 'large scale subversive activities within the Greek community of a nature to jeopardize the prestige and security of Turkey'.[34] The Patriarchate was put under pressure and its printing house was closed down. Some of its bishops and priests were also prosecuted and expelled from the country. Furthermore, the Turkish government unilaterally terminated the Ataturk–Venizelos convention of 1930 which regulated matters of commerce and navigation between the two countries.

The Greek government reacted to the anti-Greek measures of the Turkish government by protesting to the Security Council and the signatories of the Treaty of Lausanne of 1923.[35] It argued that Turkey took those measures because it was 'disappointed in its plans over Cyprus' and that such actions were merely manifestations of Turkish nationalism directed against the Greeks.[36]

The ethnicization of most bilateral issues – political, economic, social, and cultural – badly damaged the relations of the two countries. The age-old 'suspicion syndrome' dominating the perceptions of the elites and masses on both sides was revived and reinforced, thus eliminating any prospects for the prevalence of goodwill and constructive spirit. Mounting ethnic tension and controversies destroyed almost all channels of substantive interaction and constructive communication across the Aegean. The relations between Athens and Ankara were, in effect, reduced to mere diplomatic representation.

Eruption of ethnic passions and lack of communication had, in turn, a devastating effect on the prospects for a negotiated settlement on Cyprus as well as on other bilateral issues.

Preoccupation with confrontational tactics not only prevented the two governments from practising bilateral diplomacy, but it also hindered mediation efforts undertaken by third parties. Thus, the mediation efforts undertaken by Britain during the first three critical months of the Cyprus crisis gave no results because they were undermined by the unwillingness of the two ethnic blocs to negotiate constructively. At the London conference, which was held in January 1964, the British chairman, Duncan Sandys, urged the parties involved to come to their senses and realize how dangerous and explosive the ethnic conflict was. He made it clear to the passionate contesters that Britain was not willing to 'go on acting as policeman in Cyprus indefinitely' by exposing British soldiers to the risks of an armed conflict dominated by ethnic fanaticism.[37] The two factions, however, showed no signs of co-operation. As a consequence, the British government, which was anxious to get rid 'of the onerous burden of keeping peace'[38] in an island torn by violence and destructive ethnic passions, gave up its mediating and peacekeeping roles and took the issue to the Security Council.

The American Under-Secretary of State, George Ball, who embarked on a peace mission after the British failure, was also faced with insurmountable difficulties in his efforts to reconcile the opposing sides and prevent a catastrophic war.[39] While engaged in shuttle diplomacy between Athens, Ankara, and Nicosia, the American envoy was frustrated by the intransigence of the governments involved and the ethnic passion dominating the peoples and their leaders. Reporting back to Washington, he informed President Johnson that the atmosphere in the troubled zone was not conducive for the practice of diplomacy, and 'that feelings were so high and passions so intense that a blow up is exceedingly possible'.[40]

In sum, Greek and Turkish involvement in Cyprus had a spill-over effect on most bilateral issues. In the form of an action–reaction process the two countries took mutually hostile measures pertaining to ethnic, political, social, and cultural matters. Rising national sentiments on both sides found expression in mass demonstrations and popular demands for assertive attitudes and policies on Cyprus. The ethnicization and intermingling of internal and external affairs led to a widening of the conflict and had a devastating effect on the relations of the two rival countries. Ethnic fanaticism caused an almost complete destruction of all forms of interaction and communication between Athens and Ankara. Ethnic polarization sharpened the conflict on Cyprus and drove the two sides further apart. Moreover, it reinforced the ethnic-based military, diplomatic, and political alliances of the Cypriot communities with their respective motherlands. In this context of confrontation and hostility, reconciliation of the two sides through bargaining in a give-and-take manner became inconceivable, although some unsuccessful mediation efforts were attempted by third parties.

THE 1974 CRISIS AND ITS AFTERMATH

The already tense Greek–Turkish relations deteriorated further with the ascent to power of a Greek nationalist right-wing military junta in 1967. The domestically unpopular and internationally isolated dictatorial regime explicitly abandoned the policy of independence for Cyprus and sought *enosis*.

Following a seven-year period of tension and hostility with Makarios, the military regime attempted to overthrow him.[41] In July 1974, the Greek forces on Cyprus and the Greek-staffed and controlled Cypriot national guard staged a bloody coup against the Cypriot president that brought to power an extremist pro-*enosis* puppet regime.

Turkey reacted fiercely to the military intervention of Athens by invading Cyprus and occupying 37 per cent of the island. The Turkish government justified its action on legal and ethnic grounds. It argued that the Greek coup was a step towards annexation which was prohibited by the 1960 Treaty of Guarantee. It also claimed that the Treaty of Guarantee had established a responsibility and a right for Turkey to intervene and protect the Turkish Cypriots. According to the Turkish argument, the nationalist policies and behaviour of the Greek junta posed a direct threat to the Turkish community on the island.

The coup and the invasion of 1974 once again brought Greece and Turkey to the brink of war and necessitated outside diplomatic intervention. The USA, deeply concerned over the prospects of a catastrophic escalation of the crisis, offered to mediate and prevent the 'unthinkable' from happening. Secretary of State Henry Kissinger dispatched Under-Secretary for Political Affairs Joseph Sisco to the troubled region two days after the coup, while Turkey was preparing for the invasion.[42] Upon his arrival in Ankara, he realized that the situation was out of control, and that there was no room for diplomacy. His plane was forced to land in a military base for security reasons as passionate crowds seething anger and demanding invasion had taken over the central streets in Ankara and around the airport. The Turkish government, in response to popular sentiment, the exhortation of the Turkish press, and the pressure of the military, rejected Sisco's mediation effort. Turkish Premier Bulent Ecevit cited earlier crises over Cyprus that resulted in Turkish humiliation and made it clear that the Turkish nation was in no mood for compromise this time. In Kissinger's words, 'Turkey was not interested in a negotiated solution; it was determined to settle old scores.'[43]

In Athens, Sisco was faced by an even more disappointing situation. While the Turkish invasion was in process, the military junta seemed determined to go to war with Turkey and refused to negotiate with the American mediator. The Greek government saw the crisis as a new phase in Greek–Turkish rivalry with no room for bargaining.[44] Eventually, it was the collapse of the military regime that prevented an escalation of the war across the Aegean. The Greek multiparty government of national salvation, which succeeded the military junta, proved prudent and avoided further military action. This is not to say that Greece gave up the Greek Cypriots, who were fighting side by side with Greek troops, at the moment they needed their motherland most. Indeed, the new civilian government was contemplating the dispatch of naval, air, and land forces to defend Cyprus, but the operation was dismissed strictly on military grounds.[45]

Following Sisco's failure to prevent the invasion, a second diplomatic initiative was taken by Britain to contain the crisis and its consequences. A peace conference was held in Geneva under the chairmanship of the British Foreign Minister James Callaghan. After two weeks of futile and fruitless talks between the two ethnic blocs, the conference broke down. Callaghan attributed the breakdown to the intransigence of Turkey which went to Geneva to accept the capitulation of the Greeks and not to negotiate.[46] Indeed, besides the sharp ethnic hostility and lack of understanding between the two sides, there was also an asymmetrical power relationship in favour of Turkey. Turkey's considerable superiority in bargaining power was due mainly to two factotrs: first, it had already gained a substantial military advantage on Cyprus; secondly, Greece and Cyprus were both in a state of political and military disarray because of abrupt changes in government.

The failure of the American and British mediating efforts proved, once again, that Greece and Turkey were incapable of overcoming their mutual hostility, and settling their differences through bargaining in a give-and-take manner. The conflict on Cyprus provided another opportunity for the two Aegean rivals to write one more chapter in their long history of confrontation and bloodshed. For Turkey, it was an opportunity to take advantage of its military superiority and promote its partitionist goals on the island.

The 1974 confrontation brought to Cyprus destruction and demographic changes unique in its history. Following the diplomatic failures of Sisco and Callaghan, Turkey launched a second massive attack on Cyprus, completing its control of 37 per cent of the island and bringing about an exchange of populations by force. The Greek Cypriots living in the north were forced to move to the south and the Turkish Cypriots living in the south were transferred to the north. This exchange of populations, which made one-third of the Cypriots refugees in their own country, brought into effect a physical separation of the two communities that had been living together for four centuries. The forcible creation of two separate ethnic zones demarcated by the heavily fortified 'Attila line' eliminated any interaction between the two sides. The unilateral declaration of independence by the Turkish Cypriots in November 1983 was another attempt by the Turkish side to undermine the bicommunal Republic of Cyprus which was created in 1960.

The Turkish Cypriot secessionist move drastically reduced the prospects for a peaceful settlement of the problem on the basis of a unitary Cypriot state. In their proclamation of independence the Turkish Cypriots made it clear that they had no intention of returning to the status quo of the Republic of Cyprus or any other similar form of joint government. They declared that each ethnic group should have 'the right to live and govern itself in its own territory in peace and security, and have the right to preserve its own national identity'.[47]

The Turkish government promptly granted formal recognition to the newly proclaimed 'Turkish Republic of Northern Cyprus' and asked other governments to take a positive position towards the new 'state'.

Greece and the Greek Cypriots, on the other hand, launched a co-ordinated worldwide campaign to reverse the Turkish Cypriot proclamation. The Greek President Constantine Karamanlis strongly condemned the unilateral declaration as an act of 'international piracy' and stated that Greece 'will never submit to Turkey's arbitrary actions' on Cyprus.[48] Prime Minister Andreas Papandreou urged all NATO members and the European Community to 'immediately take a stand over the unacceptable act of the Turkish Cypriots, to condemn it and proceed with protests to Ankara'.[49] The Greek ambassadors to all capitals were instructed to deliver similar requests to their host governments.

The Cyprus government accused Turkey of being exclusively responsible for the Turkish Cypriot declaration of independence and appealed to the Security Council for its reversal. The Greek Cypriots argued that the Turkish Cypriot secession was masterminded in Ankara and implemented by the occupation army which is the only source of power and authority in the northern part of the island. The Security Council adopted a resolution deploring the proclamation of independence as illegal and invalid, and called upon all states to respect the sovereignty, independence, territorial integrity, and non-alignment of Cyprus.[50] Similar resolutions condemning the unilateral proclamation of independence by the Turkish-occupied northern part of Cyprus were also adopted by the Council of Europe, the European Community, and the British Commonwealth summit conference which was held in New Delhi in November 1983. The vast majority of the states of the world, including the USA, the Soviet Union, China, Britain, and France, also deplored the Turkish Cypriot declaration of independence and called for its reversal. The 'TRNC' has not been recognized by any other country except Turkey.

The Cyprus crisis of 1974 and the subsequent restoration of democratic institutions and practices in Greece automatically led to the re-establishment of warm and cordial relations between the governments of Athens and Nicosia. The Greek civilian government, which succeeded the military junta seven days after the coup against Makarios and two days after the Turkish invasion, declared on the day of its formation that Makarios, who had been forced to flee the country, was recognized as the lawful president of Cyprus. Eventually, the archbishop returned to Cyprus via Athens and resumed his presidential duties in December 1974. Subsequent changes of government in Greece and the death of Makarios in 1977 did not affect the Athens–Nicosia relations which remain cordial to this day.

The relations between Turkey and the Turkish Cypriots have been consistently good since the declaration of Cyprus' independence in 1960. Because of their lack of international recognition the Turkish Cypriots let Turkey handle their affairs at the international level while providing them with military, economic, and political support. With the backing of the Turkish government and its occupation army on the island, the Turkish Cypriots have been able to consolidate themselves in northern Cyprus and impose a *de facto* partition of the island. The solid common front of Turkey and the Turkish Cypriots, and the changes brought about by the Turkish invasion of 1974, made the Greek Cypriots realize that they no longer have the upper hand. Consequently, they abandoned their policy of a unitary state and have agreed to negotiate on the basis of a bicommunal and bizonal federal state.[51]

The drastic changes which were brought about by the Turkish invasion have created a new reality and drawn a new bottom line for a solution to the problem. Whatever the new solution is going to be, it is more likely to be viable if it is the product of inter-communal consent and excludes external interference along ethnic lines in the future. If there is a need for external mediation and guarantees, it should be met through international organizations or other ethnic-free agencies and mechanisms.

SUMMARY AND CONCLUSION

After the declaration of independence in 1960, the colonial problem of Cyprus went through a transformation and turned into an ethnic conflict. The ethnic dispute, which turned into an open confrontation in 1963, had a destructive impact on the newborn bicommunal state. The presentation and analysis of events have shown that the cross-boundary ethnic ties between the two Cypriot communities and their motherlands served as a primary vehicle for Greek and Turkish involvement in Cyprus. These ties and loyalties were based on common language, a sense of ancestral identification, historical legacies, religious beliefs and practices, educational orientation, ethnopolitical ideals, and military co-operation.

The involvement of Greece in Cyprus took place exclusively on ethnic grounds. In fact, there are no other sources of Greek concern or interest in Cyprus. The island lies some 500 miles (800 kilometres) from the mainland and cannot be of any other particular interest. The repeated crises in the 1960s and 1970s showed that Cyprus, at that time, was logistically beyond the range of Greece's defence capability. Therefore, the conclusion can be drawn that ethnic constraints and considerations – especially the strong ethnic ties with the Greek

Cypriots and the age-old ethnic rivalry with Turkey – have determined the attitude, policy, and role of Greece on Cyprus.

Regarding Turkey's role on Cyprus, the conclusion can also be drawn that ethnic factors have been a primary cause and instrument for intervention. One should, however, add that strategic considerations have played an important role in shaping and implementing the Turkish policy. Ethnic and strategic factors have been congruent and mutually reinforcing in causing Turkish involvement in Cyprus, including the invasion of the island in 1974.

Co-operation between the two motherlands and their respective Cypriot communities has been close and constant, except during the period of military rule in Greece when the Athens–Nicosia relations suffered a setback. The strained relations between the Greek Cypriots and the military junta, however, were due to the general unpopularity and alienation of the military regime in both Greece and Cyprus.

Ethnic co-operation across boundaries took the form of tight alliances in the political, diplomatic, and military fields. The two motherlands became extensively involved in military operations on Cyprus while playing a major role in international diplomacy dealing with the ethnic conflict.

Greek and Turkish involvement in Cyprus led to a widening of the conflict across the Aegean and had a devastating effect on the bilateral relations of the two countries. The revival of old rivalry and animosity severely damaged Greek–Turkish relations in the economic, diplomatic, cultural, and social areas. Deterioration in bilateral relations and intermingling of ethnicized domestic and external politics had, in turn, an exacerbating effect on Cyprus. The overwhelming impact of ethnic tension and passion on the peoples and governments of the three countries hindered the practice of diplomacy and created conditions conducive for the use of force.

The devastating effect of ethnic rivalry was also reflected in the impediment of international diplomacy and mediation. The parties involved not only refused to talk to each other, but they also rejected or undermined initiatives undertaken by third parties for a peaceful settlement of the conflict through bargaining in a give-and-take manner. Despite the repeated efforts and appeals of outside 'honest brokers', the ethnic rivals never let diplomacy run its full course. Instead, they remained attached to old habits and tactics of passionate stubbornness and confrontation.

4 Ethnopolitics and Superpower Politics

> If a stone falls on the egg, alas for the egg. If the egg falls on a stone, alas for the egg.
>
> A Cypriot proverb

OBJECTIVES

In the two previous chapters, the nature and implications of the Cypriot conflict were examined in the context of ethnic rivalries and affiliations of the parties involved. It was shown that at both the domestic Cypriot level of inter-communal relations and the level of inter-state relations between Cyprus, Greece, and Turkey ethnic factors played a dominant role in determining attitudes and shaping developments. Regarding Greek and Turkish involvement in the dispute, cross-boundary ethnic ties proved instrumental in causing and channelling outside intervention in the strife-torn island.

In this chapter, the focus shifts to the triangle of US–Cypriot–Soviet relations. Although the analysis is still carried out at the state level, a new major element is introduced, that is, superpower politics. As was indicated in the first theoretical chapter, the USA and the Soviet Union were concerned over Cyprus because of their superpower status, their quest for influence and control on a global scale, and their conflicting interests in the region.

The primary goal of the chapter is to explore the causes, process, and consequences of superpower involvement in the Cypriot conflict especially in the 1960s and 1970s. During that period, the international system was dominated by Cold War confrontational politics. The presentation, analysis, and interpretation of superpower attitudes and policies revolve around the following questions: What were the sources of superpower concern in Cyprus? On what grounds, by what means, and with what goals did the superpowers intervene in the conflict? Were periods of crisis conducive or dissuasive to superpower involvement? Did superpower involvement have a containing or a ramification effect? Could the superpowers play a constructive mediatory role in the conflict?

SOURCES OF AMERICAN AND SOVIET CONCERN IN CYPRUS

It should be made clear at the outset that neither the USA nor the Soviet Union had any ethnic ties with Cyprus worth mentioning. Neither was the island itself of any actual or potential economic significance for the two superpowers. Rather, the sources of American and Soviet concern and interest in Cyprus lay in the strategic importance of the island and the foreign policy implications that the ethnic conflict had on the parties involved, that is, the two Cypriot communities, Greece, and Turkey, and their relations with one another and the two superpowers.

During the Cold War, as well as throughout history, Cyprus has been strategically important because of its location at the crossroads of three continents and the major routes connecting the West with the East. It is located 44 miles (70 kilometres) south of Turkey, 64 miles (103 kilometres) west of Syria, 130 miles (209 kilometres) north-west of Israel, and 240 miles (386 kilometres) north of Egypt and the Suez canal. More important, it is the only island in the utmost eastern corner of the Mediterranean basin.[1]

Because of its close proximity with the region, Cyprus can serve as a base of support for large-scale land, sea, and air operations in the Middle East. The joint British–French attack on Suez in 1956 proved its usefulness as a starting point for operations in the region.

Although Cyprus is located at the doorstep of the Middle East, it was not involved in the complexities of Arab nationalism, intra-Islamic rivalries, and Arab–Israeli confrontation. Therefore, it could be seen as a secure neutral ground with regard to the polemics scourging the major oil-producing region of the world.

The implications of the Cypriot ethnic conflict, seen in connection with the strategic significance of the island, were also a major source of concern for the two superpowers. Since the mid-1950s, the island has been a place of friction and violence caused by the clashing interests and claims of the two local communities and three NATO members – Britain, Greece, and Turkey.[2] Repeated crises and threats for an escalation of the conflict into a Greek–Turkish war made the island a symbol of Western disunity rather than a stronghold of Western defence. While the USA was trying to contain the conflict and keep Cyprus under Western control, the Soviet Union was using the opportunity to influence Cypriot politics and prevent 'NATOization' of the island.

The study of the interaction between superpower politics and the Cypriot conflict is carried out in this setting of US–Soviet rivalry in an economically and strategically vital region of the world, and in regard to the impact that the conflict could have on the East–West balance of power in the region.[3]

From the US viewpoint, the following interrelated and overlapping aspects and implications of the Cypriot conflict presented serious challenges to Western security interests:[4] first, the presence of strong ethnic ties between the two Cypriot ethnic groups and Greece and Turkey were conducive to the escalation of the local conflict into a Greek–Turkish confrontation. As was shown in the previous chapter, the fear of an ethnic-motivated military confrontation between the two US allies over Cyprus was well-grounded.

Secondly, it is not only ethnic ties that made the Cypriot conflict prone to internationalization and potentially explosive, but also the complicated treaty structure surrounding the island. According to the 1960 founding treaties – which reflected ethnic rivalries and compromises – Greek and Turkish troops were permanently stationed on Cyprus. Moreover, the Treaty of Guarantee gave the two motherlands the right 'to take action with the sole aim of reestablishing the state of affairs'[5] created on Cyprus by the 1960 settlement of the colonial problem.

Thirdly, Greek–Turkish friction and the risk of an armed intra-alliance war across the Aegean had a destabilizing effect on NATO. The Greek–Turkish 'festering sore' within the Western alliance theatened to undermine the operational utility of the south-eastern flank.

Fourthly, Britain has two large sovereign military base areas on Cyprus occupying 99 square miles (254 square kilometres), and an extensive network of support installations, training areas, and communication networks all over the island.[6] The British bases could be used by the USA and NATO to support operations in the Middle East.[7] All British military facilities, however, are heavily dependent on local supplies of power, water, labour, and transportation facilities. The maintenance of peace on the island is an essential requirement for their proper operation.

Like the USA, the Soviet Union linked its concern in Cyprus with broader regional interests. The goal of gaining access to warm Mediterranean waters had always been a driving force behind Soviet foreign policy. The importance of Middle East oil for the West's economic and military establishment was another major reason for Soviet concern in the region. Expansion of Soviet influence could seriously upset the world balance of power. Moreover, that vital and unstable region was adjacent to Soviet territory, a fact increasing Moscow's concern over developments in Middle East countries.[8]

Against the background of these geopolitical and strategic considerations, Soviet goals and interests in Cyprus could be seen as part of a broader drive for regional control and influence. Certain facts and circumstances pertaining to the island and the ethnic conflict presented opportunities for advancement of the Soviet goals at the expense of the West. The following factors in particular were especially important in determining Soviet attitudes towards the Cypriot ethnic conflict and the parties involved.[9]

First, Cyprus was a country with a likelihood of turning communist through normal democratic processes. The local communist party AKEL was by far the strongest political organization on the island. It was loyal to Moscow and held a pro-independence and anti-Western position on the Cyprus problem. It also advocated demilitarization of the island and dismantling of the British military bases.

Secondly, since independence, the Cyprus government had followed a policy of non-alignment and developed friendly relations with Moscow. President Makarios repeatedly appealed to Moscow for military and diplomatic help in order to counteract Western pressure and reject US plans for a pro-Western settlement of the ethnic conflict.

Thirdly, the major outside powers directly involved in the Cypriot conflict – that is, Greece, Turkey, and Britain – were members of NATO and could serve as a US leverage for the advancement of Western plans and goals on the island. It was, therefore, essential for the Soviet Union to be alert and prevent the imposition of a settlement securing Western control on the strategic island.

Finally, the Soviet Union looked upon the Cypriot ethnic conflict as a source of discord and instability within NATO. In this light, keeping the conflict alive was in agreement with the fundamental Soviet objective of undermining the unity of the Western defence system.

The above sources of American and Soviet concern and interest in Cyprus prompted the two superpowers to intervene in the conflict and seek advancement of their conflicting strategic and ideological goals. Superpower involvement and rivalry provided another channel for internationalization of the domestic conflict. It is the purpose of this chapter to explore the process and consequences of internationalization of the Cypriot conflict in the setting of US–Soviet antagonism for control and influence. In doing so, emphasis is placed on the actions and positions taken by the two competing global powers towards the conflict and the parties involved, and their reactions to each other's moves.

SUPERPOWER INTERVENTION

The eruption of inter-communal violence at Christmas 1963 marked the beginning of a course of internationalization of the Cypriot ethnic conflict. The outside powers to interfere first were Greece, Turkey, and Britain. The former two intervened to support their respective ethnic groups, and the latter to restore peace and protect its strategic interests on the island. The dangerous escalation of hostilities, coupled with Britain's inability to restore peace and reconcile the opposing ethnic factions, set the stage for superpower involvement.[10]

The USA intervened to take the place of Britain, and the Soviet Union took steps to counteract Western interference. Thus, the ethnic conflict became entangled in Cold War rivalry. The repercussions of this entanglement were felt in Cyprus and by the other parties involved in the conflict as well as in US–Soviet relations.

It is interesting to note that a similar scenario had unfolded seventeen years earlier when Britain could no longer bear the economic and military burden of safeguarding Western interests in Greece and Turkey. In the late 1940s, the two Aegean rivals were plagued by civil war and facing the prospect of a communist takeover. American intervention under the Truman Doctrine accompanied the onset of the Cold War and marked the transfer of Western leadership from Britain to the USA.[11] Similar shifts in global power and commitments involving glory and burden have been taking place throughout history with the rise and fall of empires, colonial powers, and superpowers. The American takeover of the British role in Cyprus was the result of the postwar decline of Britain and the emergence of the USA as a global power.

After the eruption of violence, American involvement in the Cypriot conflict mainly took the form of diplomatic intervention and occurred during periods of crisis in 1964, 1967, and 1974. The primary objectives of US diplomacy were to restore peace, contain the conflict, prevent a Greek–Turkish war, and advance a settlement safeguarding Western interests in the island and the region. Such a settlement would eliminate the causes of the conflict and establish a firm Western grip on Cyprus.

Soviet involvement in the issue culminated during the same critical years and took the form of diplomatic support for the Cypriot government and the independence, territorial integrity, and non-alignment of Cyprus. Moscow also offered substantial military aid to Cyprus and in 1964 threatened to use force against Turkey in the event of an invasion of the island.

The immediate objectives of American intervention in 1964 were, first, to bring about a ceasefire and prevent a military clash between Greece and Turkey. President Johnson intervened during the first days of fighting and urged the leaders of the two Cypriot communities and the governments of Greece and Turkey 'to end that terrible fraternal strife' and prevent an escalation of the crisis.[12]

Secondly, the USA wished to prevent involvement of the UN and the Soviet Union in the issue. The view from Washington was that internationalization of the conflict through the UN would give 'the Communist countries leverage in that strategically placed island'.[13]

Thirdly, the USA sought a permanent peaceful solution of the Cyprus problem within a Western setting securing Western strategic interests. This goal was clearly reflected in US diplomatic initiatives.

The advancement of the above goals was assigned to two prominent American diplomats: Under-Secretary of State for Political Affairs George Ball and former Secretary of State in the Truman Administration Dean Acheson. The recruitment of Acheson, who was called back from retirement, was a well-calculated move. The veteran diplomat had a strong and forceful personality, and was an almost legendary figure in Greece and Turkey. He was the man behind the Truman Doctrine through which the two countries had received generous US aid to fight communism in the 1940s.

Ball embarked on his peace mission to the troubled zone with clearly defined goals. In his words, 'the issues were clear enough. Cyprus was a strategically important piece of real estate at issue between two NATO partners: Greece and Turkey. We needed to keep it under NATO control.'[14]

In January 1964, amidst mounting tension and military preparations on both sides of the Aegean, Ball proposed the dispatch of a 10 000-man NATO peacekeeping force to Cyprus and the appointment of a Western mediator. Makarios rejected the proposal outright and insisted that the Cypriot government would only accept an international peacekeeping force under the Security Council. He also rejected the idea of Greek–Turkish negotiations on Cyprus.[15]

In a last effort to change the archbishop's mind, Ball threatened that if the Turks were to use their unilateral right to invade Cyprus 'neither the US nor any other Western power would raise a finger to stop them'.[16] Despite the joint Anglo-American pressure and the constant threat of a Turkish invasion, Makarios remained adamant. He disregarded American mediation and threats, and appealed to the Security Council asking for help against aggression and intervention in the internal affairs of Cyprus. His firm opposition to American pressure was made possible by staunch Soviet support. The Cypriot president had already received assurances from Moscow that the Soviet Union would back him in his confrontation with the West. Such assurances were conveyed through the Soviet ambassador in Nicosia and statements in *Pravda, Isvestiya,* and TASS.[17] The first Soviet arms also began arriving in the island in early 1964.[18] The culmination of Soviet support came in an austere lengthy letter from Khrushchev to Johnson condemning the American initiative as 'aiming at actual occupation by NATO forces of the Republic of Cyprus which adheres to a policy of nonalignment with military blocs'.[19] The Soviet leader accused the USA and other Western powers of trying to impose a solution on Cyprus despite the expressed will of the Cypriot government to seek a settlement through the UN. Khrushchev went on to explain in his blunt note that the 'Soviet Union, although it does not border directly to the Republic of Cyprus, cannot remain indifferent to that situation which is developing in the area of the eastern Mediterranean – an area not so distant from the southern borders of the USSR, especially if one considers how the notion of distance has changed in our time'.[20]

Soviet support for the Cypriot government was also manifested in a similar tone at the open forum of the Security Council where Cyprus became an issue of Cold War polemics. The Soviet representative, Nikolai Fedorenko, in line with the Cypriot representative, claimed that the causes of inter-communal discord were to be found in the unequal 1960 Zürich and London treaties which were imposed on Cyprus by Western powers. These treaties, Fedorenko explained, provided for the military presence and intervention of NATO powers in Cyprus with the ultimate goal of bringing the island under NATO control. Commenting on the recent American diplomatic initiative and the NATO plan, Fedorenko stated that 'the dangerous actions of the NATO Powers in Cyprus are aimed with cynical frankness at nullifying the independence of the Republic of Cyprus, tying Cyprus to NATO and converting it into one of their military bridgeheads'.[21]

The American representative Adlai Stevenson, in complete contrast to the joint Soviet–Cypriot position, defended the Zürich and London treaties and claimed that the three Western guarantor powers had a legitimate right to intervene in Cyprus, jointly or unilaterally, under the Treaty of Guarantee.

The Cypriot president, with the backing of the Soviet Union, won the first battle in his confrontation with the USA. The Security Council adopted resolution 186 of 4 March 1964, calling upon all states to refrain from any interference in Cyprus. It also recommended the establishment of a UN peacekeeping force and the appointment of a UN mediator on Cyprus. The same resolution reconfirmed that Cyprus – and not any outside power – was responsible for the restoration of law and order on the island.

Makarios' stubbornness, hostility towards the West, and alignment with the Kremlin alarmed Washington. But US officials proved stubborn and tough as well. They disregarded the Cypriot president and tried to bring Greece and Turkey to the negotiating table. They also urged the Greek government to use its influence to stop Makarios from flirting with Moscow and Khrushchev. When the Greek and Turkish premiers Papandreou and Inonu were called to Washington to confer with President Johnson, their host reminded them of the Soviet 'threat' and the need for cohesion within NATO. In the name of 'the union and harmony of free nations', the American president urged his guests to transcend ethnic differences and 'stand steadfast against the threat of Communist aggression'.[22] He asked them to approach the Cyprus problem in the broader context of East–West confrontation. But in Ball's view, the two elderly men 'seemed incapable of comprehending the larger issues'[23] of worldwide ideological antagonism; they remained attached to the ethnic aspects and consequences of the conflict and refused even to talk to each other.[24]

THE ACHESON PLAN

Similar attitudes and positions were held at the Geneva conference in August 1964 where Acheson tried to resolve the ethnic conflict by advancing his so-called 'double *enosis*' plan. That plan provided for the dissolution of the Republic of Cyprus and distribution of the island between Greece and Turkey. Its main provisions were the following:[25]

1 Cyprus to be united with Greece.
2 Turkey to be given a sizeable military base on the island which would be an indispensable part of mainland Turkey.
3 Cyprus to be divided into eight cantons with the Turkish Cypriots controlling two of them.
4 Greece to cede the tiny island of Kastellorizo (Meis), lying off the Turkish shore, to Turkey.

Turkey accepted the Acheson plan as a basis for negotiation, but Greece, at Makarios' instigation, insisted that a solution to the problem should be sought under the UN Charter, guaranteeing 'full and unrestricted independence that will afford the Cypriot people the right to decide freely on its future'.[26] The Cypriot government refused even to attend the Geneva conference. Makarios, commenting on Acheson's role, explained in a derogatory remark that although he greatly respected the UN mediator Sakhari Tuomioja, there were also in Geneva 'certain other self-invited mediators who have worked out unacceptable plans for solution of the Cyprus problem'.[27]

Acheson's plan reflected US concerns and objectives on Cyprus. It aimed at satisfying the conflicting national goals of *enosis* and partition, and eliminating the sources of Greek–Turkish friction. With the dissolution of the Cypriot state, Makarios and AKEL with their pro-Soviet policy would also be eliminated from the Cypriot political scene. (It should be remembered that in both Greece and Turkey, the communist parties were outlawed at that time.) Moreover, the fundamental American objective of bringing Cyprus under NATO control would be achieved.

Regarding the Makarios–AKEL connection, one should bear in mind that it is doubtful whether the Cypriot president could stay in power without the solid support of the powerful communist party. The archbishop, who had no formal affiliation with any party, managed to govern as a 'nonpolitical national leader' by balancing conflicting party interests and using the exceptional power deriving from his ecclesiastical office.[28] During the seventeen years of his presidency, he enjoyed, at one time or another, the support of all major political parties. AKEL, however, proved his strongest supporter throughout most of this period. This peculiar alliance between the Orthodox prelate and the communist party which maintained close relations with Moscow, was the corollary of a common policy for an independent, united, and non-aligned Cyprus.

Makarios, once again, stood firm against the American initiative and rejected outright Acheson's plan. He was in no mood for negotiating the independence, territorial integrity, and non-alignment of Cyprus. Nor would he allow others to negotiate and decide on the future of the island. In Acheson's words, who made no secret of his hostility towards the 'political priest with considerable gifts of demagogy and ruthlessness', the Cypriot president 'did not go out of his way to be helpful. He threw a monkey wrench into the machinery'.[29]

It is interesting to note that while Acheson was trying to advance his plan (August 1964), the Turkish air force, for the first time (and with American toleration), was vehemently bombarding Cyprus. The Turkish action was in harmony with the American objective of bringing Makarios to his knees and making him receptive and conciliatory to Western proposals. The State Department completely mistrusted the 'Castro of the Mediterranean', as Makarios was known in Washington, and believed that the only way to deal with him was through pressure, threat, and coercion. As Stevenson put it to Ball, the only way to deal with Makarios was by 'giving the old bastard absolute hell'.[30] Ball went a step further by stating: 'that son of a bitch (Makarios) will have to be killed before anything can happen on Cyprus'.[31]

Once again, however, the State Department officials miscalculated. With the dropping of US-made napalm bombs over Cyprus, a hell was indeed created, but the Orthodox archbishop found his way out of that too. Following tactics of Byzantine manoeuvring and tightrope international diplomacy, he appealed openly and formally to the Kremlin asking for military assistance to protect the independence of his country. Such an appeal was welcomed in Moscow and received a positive and quick response. The Soviet fleet, which had made its appearance in the Mediterranean earlier that year, sailed ostentatiously towards Cyprus. Khrushchev sent a harsh message to Inonu warning him of 'the responsibility which Turkey is assuming in carrying out an armed attack on the Republic of Cyprus'.[32]

At the Security Council, the Cypriot and Soviet delegates had a lot in common to say in blaming the USA and NATO for the Turkish assaults. Fedorenko claimed that the Turkish action was 'essentially part and parcel of NATO policy',[33] while the Cypriot representative argued that Turkey had 'obtained the full consent of NATO Headquarters for the air attacks'.[34] Both also agreed that the new crisis was part of a Western plot aimed at turning 'the island into an armed base – a kind of "unsinkable aircraft carrier", as they call it, anchored in the eastern Mediterranean'.[35]

THE KHRUSHCHEV WARNING

At the same time, large quantities of Soviet arms, including heavy artillery, tanks, torpedo boats, and anti-aircraft began pouring into the island.[36] A formal agreement for Soviet military aid was signed in Moscow where Makarios hastily sent his ministers of foreign affairs and commerce. As it was stated in the agreement, the Soviet aid was given to Cyprus to protect its freedom and territorial integrity 'against the aggressive actions and intrigues of certain NATO countries'.[37] Soviet support for the Cypriot president and his anti-Western attitude, once again, culminated in the personal intervention of Khrushchev, who in an especially harsh speech at Frunze (in the Soviet Republic of Kirghiz), reiterated that the Soviet Union 'cannot and will not remain indifferent to the threat of an armed conflict near our southern borders'.[38] The Soviet leader warned Turkey that it could not drop bombs on Cyprus with impunity, because such actions may have a 'boomerang effect'. Regarding the role of the USA and NATO, the furious Khrushchev had the following to say:

Of course, every right-thinking man will understand that without somebody's blessing Turkey would never have embarked on this dangerous military adventure. Turkey is a member of NATO and is in practice completely under the influence of those forces which determine the policy of that aggressive bloc. There is no getting away from the fact that the Turkish armed forces which carried out the attack on Cyprus are a constituent part of the armed forces of NATO, and that the bombs dropped on the peaceful Cypriots bear NATO markings.

Everything therefore indicates that the secret threads of the imperialist conspiracy against Cyprus, and the attack on Cyprus, lead to Washington and London. Arguments to the effect that the armed attack by Turkey on Cyprus was carried out because the government of Cyprus does not provide the Turkish Cypriots with good enough living conditions do not fit the facts. Something else is involved here.

If the situation becomes more strained and it comes to invasion of Cypriot territory, the Soviet Union will not remain on the side-lines. In answer to the request of the government of Cyprus and the personal request of President Makarios, the Soviet government hereby states that if there is an armed foreign invasion of Cypriot territory, the Soviet Union will help the Republic of Cyprus to defend its freedom and independence against foreign intervention.[39]

Eventually, there was no need for further Soviet intervention as Turkey ended its air strikes and a truce came into effect. Beyond the restoration of uneasy peace, however, no progress was made towards a political settlement of the problem. The whole issue fell into a limbo of oblivion which was eventually disrupted in 1967 and 1974 when Cyprus again became a flashpoint on the international scene.

With regard to the Soviet role and its connection to Cyprus, special reference should be made to AKEL. It was one of the strongest communist parties in the non-communist world and well-represented in the parliament.[40] It is also worth mentioning that AKEL was always loyal to Moscow and never suffered a serious doctrinal split. As was mentioned earlier, Makarios' political supremacy in Cyprus was largely based on the constant support of AKEL. The maintenance of close ties between the Cypriot government and Moscow was also facilitated by the close bonds between AKEL and the Kremlin. By the mid-1960s, Soviet–Cypriot relations had expanded considerably and covered a broad range of activities, including exchange of high-ranking government officials, economic and military aid, commercial agreements, participation in conferences and trade fairs, friendship societies, and granting of scholarships.[41] Quite illustrative of the close Soviet–Cypriot political connections is the fact that during the critical year 1964 the Cypriot foreign minister visited Moscow three times to ask for economic, military, and diplomatic support.

The fraternal ideological bonds between AKEL and the Communist Party of the Soviet Union (CPSU) were undoubtedly a major factor behind the Soviet attitude towards Cyprus. These bonds were manifested in regular meetings of delegations of the two parties, mutual attendance at party congresses, and statements of reciprocal support in the Cypriot and Soviet press. Regarding the Cyprus issue, the common line followed by Moscow and AKEL called for support of the Cypriot government and its anti-Western policy.[42]

US–Soviet intervention and confrontation in Cyprus during the repeated 1964 crises revealed that the two superpowers approached the issue and defined their goals and policies in the broader context of

East–West polarization and antagonism. Washington and Moscow hardly showed any interest in the ethnic nature and aspects of the domestic ethnic conflict itself. Rather, they expressed concern over the implications that the conflict could have with regard to the local and regional balance of power.

The USA saw the ethnic conflict as a threat to Western unity and strategic interests and intervened to resolve it through quiet diplomacy. In doing so, it took diplomatic initiatives aimed at restoring peace and establishing Western control over Cyprus.

For the advancement of these goals, the USA tried to use its junior allies Greece and Turkey, but ethnic hostility undermined the utility of the two countries as agents of American influence in the region. At the domestic Cypriot level, the USA exercised considerable pressure on the Cypriot government, mostly through threat and coercion, but without effect. The policy and goals of the Cypriot government were in sharp contrast to those of the State Department and, therefore, there was no middle ground for the search for a mutually accepted settlement.

The Soviet Union saw the conflict as an opportunity for expansion of its influence on Cyprus. Soviet intervention took the form of diplomatic and military support for the government of Cyprus which was confronting American goals and tactics. The Soviet–Cypriot alliance proved an effective instrument in neutralizing American interference and objectives. The counterbalancing effect of superpower confrontation became a major factor in the Cypriot conflict, the ethnic aspects of which were overshadowed by strategic and ideological considerations in Washington and Moscow. Superpower interference and transformation of the conflict into a Cold War dispute added another dimension to the issue and further complicated local and regional ethnic controversies. The result was an increased complexity and intermingling of ethnic and ideological antagonism that made the conflict more difficult to resolve.

THE 1967 CRISIS

The two superpowers were again challenged to interfere in the Cypriot conflict during the short but sharp November 1967 crisis. While the crisis was reaching boiling point and a Greek–Turkish war seemed imminent, the USA urgently intervened diplomatically to manage the crisis and prevent a catastrophic war and disruption within NATO.

President Johnson hastily dispatched former Secretary of Defense Cyrus Vance to the troubled region with the succinct instruction: 'Do what you have to, to stop the war. If you need anything let me know.'[43]

The American envoy was successful in resolving the crisis by exercising pressure on the Greek military junta, which was largely responsible for the crisis, and satisfying most of the Turkish demands.[44] Among the Turkish demands met were the withdrawal of the 10 000 Greek troops which had infiltrated into Cyprus and the removal of General Grivas, commander of the Cypriot National Guard. As it was indicated by some commentators, Vance's formula was to delay Turkish action and 'provide the weaker side with a ladder it can climb down'.[45]

But while it was easy for Vance to deal with the weak – domestically unpopular and internationally isolated – Greek military junta, the Soviet-backed Makarios again proved a hard nut to crack. The archbishop refused to dismantle the Cypriot National Guard, which was largely equipped with Soviet arms, although he raised no objection to the removal of Grivas and the Greek troops who were controlled by the hostile right-wing military regime of Athens.

Soviet intervention in the crisis followed the same pattern as in 1964, with one exception: besides the USA and NATO, Greece rather than Turkey was the target of the Kremlin. This change could be attributed to the Turkish–Soviet *rapprochement* which began in 1965 and the seizure of power in Greece by a fanatic anti-communist military junta. The US-backed Greek regime had launched a merciless persecution against the communists in Greece and against Makarios and his policy of independence and non-alignment.[46] The Cypriot president was regarded in Athens as 'a traitor of *enosis*, a red priest who flirted with the local communist party and championed nonalignment, and consorted with such dubious Third World figures as Tito of Yugoslavia and Nasser of Egypt, not to mention his friendliness with Moscow'.[47] Regarding Cyprus, the NATO-minded colonels were actively pursuing a policy of NATOization of the island through double *enosis*.

Moscow once again intervened to back the Cypriot president, called for 'restraint and common sense', and warned that any 'maneuvering' against the Cypriot government and its policy would not be tolerated.[48] Strong Soviet support for Makarios was again manifested at the Security Council where the exchange of accusations and counter-accusations between the US and the Soviet delegate was carried out with Cold War rhetoric in an atmosphere reminiscent of the 1962

Cuba crisis. Moscow's view was that the crisis was caused by Greek military action in which Greek troops took part 'under the command of General Grivas, the henchman of the reactionary militaristic circles of Greece'.[49] But the Greek action, according to Fedorenko, would not be possible 'without the influence and support of the US inasmuch as Greece itself is firmly in the grip of the US military bases'.[50]

The US delegate rejected the Soviet accusations although it is no secret that Washington was trying to undermine Makarios and his anti-Western policy. Regarding Grivas' role and his US connection it suffices to cite a paragraph from Ball's memoirs:

> Meanwhile, our intelligence had reported the growing antipathy between Makarios and General Grivas, the famous leader of EOKA. Though Grivas was, of course, a passionate advocate of *enosis*, he might, I thought be easier to work with than Makarios... Meanwhile, Grivas returned to Cyprus with a plan for *enosis* that provided protection for the Turkish Cypriots remaining on the island and compensation for those wishing to leave. The fact that the plan called for the ousting of Makarios enhanced its attractiveness.[51]

It should be remembered that Grivas, a Cyprus-born officer of the Greek army, was an anti-communist known for his persecution of communists in both Greece and Cyprus.[52]

The 1967 crisis was eventually resolved, but again a settlement of the broader ethnopolitical conflict never came within sight. The USA could exercise considerable influence on Greece and Turkey, but that was not enough for the promotion of a final solution. Makarios, with the Kremlin on his side, showed no interest in negotiating such a settlement with Western powers. Therefore, the problem remained and so did the prospects for another flare-up and more bloodshed.[53] As President Johnson put it in his welcome address to Vance, 'peace has emerged victor in the crisis. But the basic problems of Cyprus remain.'[54]

Once again, the conclusion can be drawn that at the superpower level the ethnic aspects of the conflict were overshadowed by strategic and ideological goals pursued in a Cold War mentality. The USA expressed concern over the destructive implications that a deterioration of the conflict could have on the Western defence system, while the Soviet Union approached the 1967 crisis as an 'imperialist conspiracy' aimed at bringing Cyprus under NATO control.

THE 1974 SEQUEL

The Cold War strategic doctrines which provided guidelines for US and Soviet policies towards Cyprus during the 1960s came into play again during the 1974 crisis. The primary US goal remained the NATOization of Cyprus the way it was conceived in the Acheson plan. The Soviet objective was the maintenance of a non-aligned Cyprus with a pro-Soviet government. At the centre of these two conflicting policies was Makarios practising tightrope diplomacy balancing conflicting Greek and Turkish claims, and East–West tactics and goals. In this setting of contesting parties, interests, and goals, the Cypriot president pursued a policy aimed at the establishment of an independent, unitary, and non-aligned Cyprus with majority rule which would favour the ethnic majority. At the peripheral level, the dramatic improvement in Soviet–Turkish relations and the establishment of cordial relations between the USA and the Greek military regime became important elements in the constellation of relationships and contesting ethnic and strategic interests on Cyprus.

The strong antipathy for Makarios shared by Athens and Washington provided the impetus for a new round of violence and bloodshed. The bloody coup which the Greek junta staged against the Cypriot president on 15 July 1974, upset the delicate balance of power on the island. Interestingly enough, though not surprisingly, the USA did not condemn the coup and was indeed the only country besides Greece that tilted towards recognition of the puppet dictatorial regime that came into power in Nicosia. The American ambassador to Nicosia, Roger Davies, who was shot and killed in his embassy a month after the coup during a Greek Cypriot demonstration, was the only foreign ambassador received by the foreign minister of the coupist regime. In Washington, Henry Kissinger, after chairing two meetings of the WSAG (Washington Special Action Group, composed of top officials of the State and Defense Departments, the CIA, and the National Security Council) stressed 'that the US would do nothing to jeopardize its air and sea bases in Greece'.[55]

As a result of the coup, Makarios fled the country and the Soviet Union lost its leverage on the island. The succession of events after the coup was quick and 'logical'.[56] Turkey invaded Cyprus under the pretext of seeking protection for the Turkish Cypriots. The Soviet Union strongly condemned the Greek coup as a new American plot against Cyprus and called for Makarios' return. The Soviet ambassador in Ankara gave assurances to the Turkish government that the

Kremlin was 'supporting those fighting against insurgents'[57] while a sharp Soviet note was delivered to Athens warning that Greece would bear the responsibility for the consequences of the coup. Throughout the long sessions of the Security Council, from 16 July to 15 August 1974, the Soviet delegate kept blaming the Greek junta, the USA, and 'certain NATO circles' for trying to liquidate the Cypriot state and turn the island into a military base. He also made repeated statements in support of Makarios and the independence of Cyprus, but not a single word from his long speeches was directed against Turkey. Not even after the completion of the second phase of the Turkish invasion that resulted in the occupation of 37 per cent of the island. Quite accurately and meaningfully, the British delegate told him: 'not once did you see fit to mention the word Turkey, not once did you see fit to mention the present advance of the Turkish army in Cyprus'.[58]

The sharp contrast in the Soviet attitude towards Turkey between 1964 and 1974 can be explained with reference to the Soviet–Turkish *rapprochement* and regional strategic considerations linked to East–West rivalry. At the heart of the change in the Soviet attitude was the impressive improvement in Soviet–Turkish relations. By 1974, close political and economic ties were established between Moscow and Ankara, while US–Turkish relations were becoming more and more strained.[59] In fact, the Soviet–Turkish *rapprochement* was largely the corollary of increasing deterioration in US–Turkish relations which began in 1964 because of Cyprus. The Kremlin fruitfully took advantage of Ankara's growing belief that the USA was insensitive to Turkey's regional interests, security, and economic development. The ultimate Soviet goal was detachment of Turkey from NATO and undermining of the extensive American military installations in the neighbouring country. A relevant Soviet objective was the assurance of unimpeded access through the Straits. It should be remembered that the Soviet fleet in the Black Sea and the Eastern Mediterranean expanded considerably after the 1967 Arab–Israeli war.

It was on the basis of these considerations that the Soviet Union said nothing and did nothing to offend Turkey when its army was advancing on Cyprus. Moreover, with the overthrow of Makarios and the imposition of dictatorial rule, there was no active Soviet proxy on Cyprus. The island was in the grip of the anti-communist Greek junta and its micro-puppet in Nicosia. More important, a military clash between Greece and Turkey would blow up the south-eastern flank of NATO and give great satisfaction to Moscow.

The US attitude also was conducive to the Turkish invasion of Cyprus. Although Washington expressed concern over the frightening possibility of a destructive Greek–Turkish war, it did nothing to prevent either the coup or the invasion. On the contrary, Makarios' overthrow brought great relief to the State Department. Commenting on the incident in an elegantly backhanded way, Secretary of State Kissinger, who was a leading member of the anti-Makarios chorus, referred to the archbishop 'as a man who is much too big for so small an island'.[60]

The overall mood in the State Department was reflected in a celebrated incident where a senior official, on learning that Makarios was not killed at the bloody coup, exclaimed: 'How inconvenient!'[61]

A similar attitude towards the Turkish invasion was held in the State Department where a wait-and-see policy was adopted. While the invasion was in progress, Kissinger, speaking at a press conference, defined the US goals as follows:[62] first, to prevent a Greek–Turkish war from erupting; secondly, to keep open the possibility of a settlement of the Cyprus issue along constitutional lines; and thirdly, to prevent further internationalization of the conflict. Responding to a relevant question, Kissinger said that the USA gave no warning to Turkey for a cut-off in military aid, but a Greek–Turkish war would not be fought with an open American supply line.[63]

Kissinger justified the US policy of tolerance towards Turkey by stating that 'only the threat of American military action could have prevented a Turkish landing on the island; that was an impossibility'.[64] Indeed, US influence on Turkey was limited and any forceful intervention would push Turkey closer to the Soviet Union. As a Turkish diplomat put it, 'unlike 1964 and 1967, the United States leverage on us was minimal in 1974. We could no longer be scared off by threats of the Soviet bogeyman.'[65] The Turkish Prime Minister Bulent Ecevit made it clear to the American envoy Joseph Sisco that Turkey was determined to seize the golden opportunity and settle old scores with the Greeks on Cyprus. As for the other motives behind the US position during the 1974 crisis, the similarities between the 1964 Acheson plan and the consequences of the coup and the invasion speak for themselves.

The point can be made here that Turkey was the big fish for which the two superpowers were contesting. The Turkish government exploited this contest to neutralize any possible superpower objection to an invasion of Cyprus. In fact, both Washington and Moscow tilted towards Turkey as a tactic to maintain or expand their influence over that sizeable and very strategic country. The result was a change in US and Soviet attitudes towards Turkey that had prevented an invasion in 1964 and 1967. Therefore, the conclusion can be drawn that superpower rivalry over Turkey created conditions encouraging Turkey to invade Cyprus, and determined the outcome of the conflict between Greeks and Turks in 1974. The intermingling of superpower concerns and interests with the ethnic conflict played a major role in determining the behaviour and actions of the ethnic disputants and the outcome of the conflict. In this light, the findings of this chapter and the previous one, which focused on the impact of cross-boundary ethnic ties, should be linked to provide a broader basis for an understanding of the dynamics and consequences of the Cypriot conflict in an international context.

Another implication of the 1974 crisis indicative of the far-reaching consequences that a domestic ethnic conflict may have across boundaries was the mobilization of the Greek-American community in support of Greece and the Greek Cypriots. This ethnic-motivated mobilization was spearheaded by the Greek-American lobby in Washington and was aimed at influencing American foreign policy in favour of the Greeks.[66] Intensive lobbying contributed to the imposition of a US arms embargo on Turkey that came into effect in February 1975. It cannot be claimed that the Greek lobby was solely responsible for the embargo, but its ethnic-based attitude on a crucial foreign policy matter illustrated the political implications that ethnicity may have across boundaries.[67]

Although the gradual lifting of the embargo began a year later and was completed in 1978, its impact on US–Turkish relations was devastating. Turkey responded to the suspension of US military aid by shutting down all American military installations on its territory, including air bases, naval facilities, early warning radar stations, and intelligence gathering facilities directed towards the Soviet Union.[68] This development greatly alarmed Washington, while causing satisfaction in Moscow where *Pravda* was quoting the Turkish foreign minister saying: 'US bases in Turkey represent an additional risk to us. We were prepared to accept this given further arms supplies. But now that arms supplies have been cut off, all that is left is the additional risk.'[69] In late 1978, when the arms embargo was completely lifted, Turkey allowed reactivation of the US military installations. By that time, however, anti-American feelings were sweeping Turkey and irreparable damage had been done to US–Turkish relations. In 1979, when the USA sought to relocate its monitoring stations ousted from Iran after the fall of the Shah, the Turkish government rejected American overtures outright.

The corollary of the deterioration in US–Turkish relations was a further improvement in Soviet–Turkish relations. This improvement was manifested in extensive economic co-operation that culminated in a 1979 agreement for the Soviet construction of energy-related projects in Turkey worth $3.8 billion.[70] Former Turkish Premier Ecevit (who had ordered the invasion of Cyprus), commenting on the dramatic improvement in Soviet–Turkish relations precipitated by the US embargo, noted that 'even if the US embargo is lifted, we cannot rely on the US for our security beyond certain limits'.[71]

One should mention, however, that the arms embargo had no effect whatsoever on the Cypriot conflict and the status quo created by the 1974 Turkish invasion. Turkey refused to withdraw its troops from the island and no progress was made towards a settlement of the problem. Meanwhile, other problems had arisen with the Greek withdrawal from the military command of NATO. The impact of the Greek withdrawal from the Western alliance and other issues pertaining to the Cypriot conflict and Western security are the focus of the following chapter.

SUMMARY AND CONCLUSION

The exploration of the causes, process, and consequences of American and Soviet involvement in the Cypriot conflict has shown that the role played by the two superpowers in shaping developments on and around Cyprus was a significant one. It should be clarified, however, that the USA and the Soviet Union intervened in the conflict after its implications began spreading beyond the island. The superpowers were not directly associated with the generation of the ethnic conflict, although their reaction and involvement in it were quick and substantive.

The two superpowers, preoccupied by considerations emanating from their global political, military, economic, and ideological objectives and responsibilities, found themselves contesting for control and influence over Cyprus and the region. The US attitude reflected the containment doctrine that was the driving force behind American foreign policy since the Second World War. As a Cold War protagonist, the USA intervened to prevent expansion of Soviet influence and protect vital Western security interests in the region. The main American goals were to bring Cyprus under Western control and protect the unity of NATO by preventing a Greek–Turkish war.

The Soviet Union, thinking and acting along similar lines, intervened to counteract American policy and goals, and benefit from the conflict that involved American allies. The undermining of Western strategic interests through NATO disruption and the maintenance of a pro-Soviet independent Cyprus were Moscow's basic goals.

In carrying out their policies, the two superpowers took initiatives of their own or attempted to use local and regional proxies directly involved in the conflict. Despite some fluctuations in their attitudes and relations towards these proxies, Washington and Moscow remained attached to the promotion of strategic and ideological goals.

Intervention by diplomacy, threat, coercion, and military aid were the major means used for the pursuit of their goals. The USA turned to its junior allies, Greece and Turkey, and sought to resolve the conflict through quiet diplomacy, but because of ethnic hostility the two Aegean rivals did not prove instrumental in promoting US objectives. The Soviet Union, on the other hand, sided with the Cypriot government to which it provided a staunch support through diplomacy and military aid.

Superpower involvement in Cyprus was manifested during periods of crisis. In fact, superpower interference came in response to the development of crises. The threat of an escalation of the conflict was especially alarming for the USA, while the Soviet Union expressed concern over the possibilities of a pro-Western settlement of the problem by diplomacy or by force. The resolution of repeated crises could be largely attributed to superpower intervention in the form of mediation or balancing confrontation, but efforts undertaken by one superpower aimed at a permanent solution of the problem were undermined by the other. It should be clarified that the resolution of crises was not the result of superpower co-operation, but rather it was largely the product of American intervention aimed at containment of the conflict. The ever-present possibility of Soviet intervention and exploitation of the dispute could be seen as a factor conducive to the settlement of the crises through US mediation.

A parallelism can also be made here with the balancing effect of superpower confrontation at the global level which sustained an equilibrium and a relative order in the bipolar world system during the Cold War, but nevertheless it was not conducive for the permanent settlement of conflicts connoting East–West rivalry.

Regarding the impact of the ethnic conflict on US–Soviet relations, the transformation of Cyprus into a Cold War dispute led to a sharp confrontation between Washington and Moscow, and precipitated changes in the relations of the two superpowers with regional actors. However, despite some adjustments in superpower attitudes dictated by the complexity of conflicting local, regional, ethnic, strategic, and ideological interests involved in Cyprus, both the USA and the Soviet Union steadily pursued tactics and goals reflecting their global rivalry and the bipolar nature of the world system.

5 Ethnic Rivals vs NATO Allies

> Identity of interests is the surest of bonds whether between states or individuals.
>
> Thucydides

OBJECTIVES

In the three previous chapters, the impact of the Cypriot ethnic conflict on states and inter-state relations was examined in three different settings. On Cyprus, the conflict had a disintegrating effect that led to the undermining of the biethnic state which came into being in 1960. The conflict also had a spill-over effect on Greek–Turkish relations which deteriorated dangerously as the two countries intervened in support of their respective communities. The USA and the Soviet Union found themselves confronting one another over Cyprus, while pursuing goals emanating from their superpower status and concerns. In this chapter, the focus shifts to the impact that the ethnic conflict had on NATO and the reaction of the alliance to the conflict.

The notion of alliance is as central to international politics as is conflict and co-operation among states.[1] An alliance is basically an instrument of collective defence against common external enemies. Its formation and maintenance require common security-related objectives, and reciprocal confidence and co-operation among states in the military field. According to Robert Osgood, an alliance reflects a 'latent war community, based on general cooperation that goes beyond formal provisions and that the signatories must continually cultivate in order to preserve mutual confidence in each other's fidelity to specified obligations'.[2]

NATO was formed in 1949 as a result of the post-Second World War deterioration in East–West relations.[3] The manifested intention of the Soviet Union to expand its sphere of influence westward prompted the Western nations to establish a collective defence system. The signatories of the North Atlantic Treaty agreed that 'an armed attack against one or more of them in Europe or North America shall be considered an attack against them all'.[4]

The fear of Soviet expansion secured endurance of NATO, but the unity and smooth functioning of the alliance were repeatedly threatened by intra-alliance disputes. Political strains and crises among Western allies were mainly caused by discrepancies in national policies in areas other than the central purpose of the alliance.[5] Cyprus has been the source of one of the most serious and protracted internal problems facing NATO. This chapter explores some of the aspects and consequences of that problem.

EARLY SIGNS OF TROUBLE

Greece and Turkey had been difficult, but important countries for NATO before they joined the alliance in 1952. Originally, they were left out of the Atlantic defence pact because by strategic definition they were not Atlantic, and their internal economic and political problems would make them a burden rather than an asset for the pact. Eventually, membership in NATO was extended to the Aegean countries essentially on political grounds in order to commit them to an anti-communist alliance and eliminate any chances for further southward Soviet intrusion in the Mediterranean.

Greek and Turkish membership in NATO, however, created new problems for the Western alliance. The main source of these problems was the ethnic rivalry of the two countries over Cyprus. In contrast to NATO's fundamental goal of promoting collective security through political and military co-operation, Greece and Turkey, acting under ethnic constraints, overlooked their collective commitments and sought promotion of their national goals in a way jeopardizing Western security interests in the region.

In the 1950s, Britain, Greece, and Turkey were at odds over the settlement of the Cypriot colonial problem. Deterioration in Greek–British and Greek–Turkish relations culminated in awkward diplomatic crises involving the recall of the Greek ambassador to London and the withdrawal of Greek personnel from the NATO command at Izmir (Turkey).[6]

These early warnings about the potential dangers of Greek–Turkish rivalry over an independent Cyprus prompted NATO officials to intervene and seek a solution of the colonial problem that would eliminate the sources of the ethnic conflict.[7] NATO proposals ranged from the establishment of NATO bases and Cypriot membership in NATO to the transformation of the island into a 'NATO trust territory'.[8] The internationalization of the Cypriot colonial problem through the UN, however, undermined the NATO initiatives and resulted in bilateral Greek–Turkish negotiations that led to the Zürich and London agreements.

These agreements were hailed as reconciling conflicting Greek and Turkish claims on Cyprus and resolving a thorny problem for NATO. President Eisenhower, expressing the relief felt within the alliance, called the settlement of the colonial problem 'an imaginative and courageous act of statesmanship which cannot fail to strengthen and encourage the whole NATO alliance'.[9]

The euphoria and optimism generated in NATO capitals by the creation of the Republic of Cyprus were short-lived. Three years after the declaration of independence, Cyprus, once again, became a place of strife, Greek–Turkish confrontation, and NATO concern. Independence might have solved the colonial problem, but it did not wither away the age-old ethnic controversies and claims dominating Greek–Turkish relations in connection with Cyprus.

Ironically, some of the provisions of the 1960 founding treaties contributed to the generation and expansion of the domestic ethnic conflict which erupted in 1963. Such provisions were those providing for the permanent stationing of Greek and Turkish military forces on the island, and granting the two mainlands the right to intervene, jointly or unilaterally, to protect their respective ethnic groups. At the heart of the problem, however, were the strong cross-boundary ethnic ties which, as was shown in chapter 3, proved instrumental in causing and channelling Greek and Turkish intervention in Cyprus.

THE 1963 CRISIS

Throughout the repeated crises that developed on Cyprus since 1963, Greece and Turkey acted as uncompromising rivals rather than members of the same political–military alliance. Their confrontation and the dangers involved were manifested in the military as well as the diplomatic fronts.[10]

Already in the first week of inter-communal violence that erupted in December 1963, the Greek and Turkish contingents stationed on the island moved out of their camps and joined the fighting. This was the first time in NATO's history that troops from two member states were fighting one another. Greek and Turkish military involvement in the conflict expanded rapidly and dangerously with the secret dispatch of more troops and arms from the mainlands, especially on the Greek side.[11] In 1964, Greece dispatched an entire division to Cyprus to provide a defensive force in case of a Turkish invasion. As Andreas Papandreou explains, the Greek forces were sent to Cyprus to prevent 'the Turks from being able to "promenade" to Cyprus, and strengthen the Greek government's bargaining position in Washington and New York'.[12] A full-scale military invasion did not take place that year, but Greek and Turkish forces became involved in a large-scale bloody confrontation in August 1964 when the Turkish air force carried out extensive bombardments of the island. It is worth mentioning that, as documented at the Security Council, the Turkish airplanes and other equipment used during the air attacks bore NATO markings and were intended for NATO purposes.[13]

Besides their involvement in hostilities on Cypriot soil, Greece and Turkey caused panic within NATO with the mobilization and massing of troops on the Thracian border. The ethnic rivals made it clear in Athens and Ankara that they were preparing for the worst. The south-eastern flank of NATO was further weakened with the sailing of the navies of the two countries towards Cyprus. The Turkish fleet left the strategic Straits and sailed to the ports of Iskenderum and Mersina opposite Cyprus, while the Greek fleet stood by between the islands of Rhodes and Crete some 250 miles (400 kilometres) west of Cyprus.

THE NATO PEACE PLAN

It is interesting to note that deterioration of the situation on and around Cyprus came after an attempt at mediation and interference by NATO that had failed. The alarming military developments in the eastern Mediterranean had caused great concern for NATO. Already in January 1964, following emergency sessions of the Council in Brussels, the NATO Commander in Europe, General Lyman Lemnitzer, rushed to Athens and Ankara to warn the two governments of the grave consequences that a Greek–Turkish war would have for the south-eastern flank and the security of the region. Following Lemnitzer's mission, which was credited with preventing a unilateral Turkish intervention in Cyprus, a comprehensive NATO plan was proposed for the restoration of peace and the promotion of a political settlement of the problem.[14] Although the plan was basically an Anglo-American product, it did reflect a broader concern within the alliance.[15] As George Ball explained, the ethnic conflict in Cyprus 'threatened the stability of one flank of our NATO defenses and consequently concerned all NATO partners'.[16]

The main provisions of the NATO plan were the following:[17] first, a peacekeeping force of no less than 10 000 men drawn from NATO countries would be dispatched to Cyprus to restore law and order. The Greek and Turkish contingents (950 and 650 men respectively) already stationed on the island would be integrated into the force. Secondly, Greece and Turkey would undertake not to intervene in the troubled island as long as the NATO force was in place. Thirdly, the force would receive political guidance from an intergovernmental committee including representatives of the participating countries. The Cyprus government would not be represented in the committee. Fourthly, a mediator from a NATO country other than the three guarantor powers (Britain, Greece, and Turkey) would be appointed to seek a peaceful settlement of the ethnic dispute.

The British government provided the following two reasons for the creation of a peacekeeping force drawn from NATO countries: 'First was that these countries had forces close at hand and immediately available. The second was that all NATO members had a direct interest in stopping an intercommunal conflict in Cyprus which, if allowed to develop, could all too easily lead to a clash between two NATO allies.'[18]

The NATO plan reflected fears held in Western capitals about the disintegrating effect that Greek–Turkish confrontation over Cyprus might have on the alliance, especially the south-eastern flank. More so, it reflected an effort on the part of NATO, especially Britain and the USA, to resolve the problem by intervening and playing an active peacekeeping and mediating role. The fundamental objective of the NATO plan was to eliminate the conflicting Greek and Turkish roles and establish a unifying NATO grip on the island. It was with this purpose in mind that the Greek and Turkish contingents would be absorbed by the NATO force and the two mainlands would waive their right of joint or unilateral intervention under the 1960 Treaty of Guarantee.

The size of the proposed force was also indicative of the intention of the sponsors of the plan. A peacekeeping force exceeding 10 000 was, by any standards, too large for the island.[19] At that time (February 1964), neither of the opposing ethnic factions had a regular army or any other sizeable force. The police, small groups of irregulars, and the mainland contingents (which would be neutralized by becoming part of the NATO peacekeeping force) were the only combatants involved in the hostilities. Apparently, the presence of such a large NATO military force on an island the size of Cyprus would have an effect and implications beyond the restoration and maintenance of peace. This prospect was further reinforced by the fact that the NATO force would have no accountability to Cypriot authorities. This raised questions and suspicion in Cyprus where such a peace mission was seen as amounting 'to an actual occupation of Cyprus by NATO'.[20]

President Makarios rejected outright the NATO plan and insisted that only a UN peacekeeping force would be acceptable. In his words, 'it is necessary that any force stationed in Cyprus should be under the Security Council, which is the only international organ created for and entrusted with the preservation of peace'.[21] In rejecting the NATO proposal, the Cypriot president had the backing of the Greek government. In Athens, it was made clear that any proposal for a settlement of the ethnic conflict should be subject to the approval of the Cypriot government. Meanwhile, the mere proposal of a NATO plan aroused strong anti-Western (especially anti-American and anti-British) feelings in Greece and Cyprus. Massive anti-NATO demonstrations took place in the major Greek cities expressing solidarity with the Cypriot government and the Cypriot people. In Cyprus, US and British citizens were evacuated after bombs exploded outside the American embassy and American- and British-owned cars were set on fire. In Ankara, the NATO proposal was accepted in principle and subject to further negotiations. Turkey, however, expressed concern over the security of the Turkish Cypriots and wished to increase its contingent as well as retain its right to intervention. But Makarios' rejection of the plan left no room for further bargaining and the issue was taken to the UN.

The attempt at NATO intervention in Cyprus also caused a strong Soviet reaction that strengthened Makarios' and Greece's position *vis-à-vis* Turkey.[22] This was another blow at NATO's unity and principles. The Kremlin accused the Western alliance of 'flouting the principles of the UN Charter and generally accepted norms of international law'.[23] The Soviet position was that the Western initiative on Cyprus represented 'an attempt to place this small neutral state under the military control of NATO'[24] and impose a settlement on the government and people of the island. Soviet interference in support of Greece and the Greek Cypriots was intended to counterbalance NATO pressure, widen the gap between the two ethnic factions, and undermine NATO unity.

THE JOHNSON LETTER

In the meantime, the situation in Cyprus was reaching boiling point and in June 1964 Turkey decided to invade Cyprus. While final landing preparations were carried out and an intra-alliance war seemed imminent, the USA, in its capacity as senior NATO member, forcefully intervened to prevent a military clash that would blow up the south-eastern flank. President Johnson, in a celebrated letter to the Turkish Premier Inonu, which Ball has characterized as 'the most brutal diplomatic note I have ever seen',[25] called for restraint and warned of the grave consequences that a unilateral Turkish action on Cyprus would have. The American president urged Turkey to consult fully in advance with the USA before taking any action involving the use of military force. Regarding the far-reaching consequences that such an action would have on NATO, Johnson had the following to say:

I must call to your attention, also, Mr Prime Minister, the obligations of NATO. There can be no question in your mind that a Turkish intervention in Cyprus would lead to a military engagement between Turkish and Greek forces. Secretary of State Rusk declared at the recent meeting of the Ministerial Council of NATO in The Hague that war between Turkey and Greece must be considered as 'literally unthinkable'. Adhesion to NATO, in its very essence, means that NATO countries will not wage war on each other. Germany and France have buried centuries of animosity and hostility in becoming NATO allies; nothing less can be expected from Greece and Turkey. Furthermore, a military intervention in Cyprus by Turkey could lead to a direct involvement by the Soviet Union. I hope you will understand that your NATO allies have not had a chance to consider whether they have an obligation to protect Turkey against the Soviet Union if Turkey takes a step which results in Soviet intervention without the full consent and understanding of its NATO allies.[26]

Johnson's letter caused grief and frustration in Ankara. Inonu responded with an equally blunt letter in which he accused the USA for not siding with Turkey which is on the 'right side' in the intra-alliance dispute with Greece. With respect to the American warning that NATO would not come in support of Turkey in case of a Soviet attack, Inonu indicated that on this point 'there are as between us wide divergence of views as to the nature and basic principles of the

North Atlantic Alliance'.[27] The Turkish premier claimed that an attack on a NATO member, under any circumstances, imposes an obligation for the alliance to come to its support, otherwise 'the very foundations of the Alliance would be shaken and it would lose its meaning'.[28]

But the foundations of the Western alliance had already been shaken before a Greek–Turkish war or a Soviet military intervention might possibly take place. In Washington, where the Greek and Turkish premiers were summoned to confer with Johnson, any spirit of solidarity or collective security was completely lacking. The American president stressed the common interests, bonds, and principles uniting the Western world and emphasized the necessity for a strong front against communism. He reminded his guests that for this reason 'we have marched together in arms. We stand together as partners in NATO.'[29] But the ethnic rivals stood steadfast on their ethnic goals and commitments and disregarded appeals for respect and attachment to the NATO principles and objectives. Turkey had already indicated that it was considering withdrawal from NATO,[30] while the Greek premier, in a conversation with Ball, was expressing his disappointment over the US inability to restrain Ankara in the following words: 'Would the United States sit back and let a NATO member, armed and financed by NATO, attack a NATO ally? If this is the case, what was the nature of alliance?'[31]

Along with the breakdown in Greek–Turkish relations, a phase of severe deterioration in Greek-American and Turkish–American relations began that further weakened NATO. In Ankara, Johnson's letter had already caused a reappraisal of Turkey's foreign policy that eventually led to the Soviet–Turkish *rapprochement* discussed in the previous chapter.

In Athens, the Greek government, expressing popular demands and anti-NATO sentiment, which were sweeping the country, interpreted the US request for dedication to NATO and moderation on Cyprus as an insult to the Greek nation and its history. The tactic of pressure and threat used by the American government did not gain any results either. When Secretary of Defense McNamara threatened that in case of a Greek–Turkish war the USA would not intervene 'to save' Greece from a military devastation, the Greek premier responded: 'In 1940 we were asked to surrender or face attack. The Greek nation said no to fascism then. We regret deeply that in 1964 we must also say no to democratic America, for the choice you offer us is no different than that offered to Greece by Mussolini.'[32] Papandreou went as far as to declare that in the event of a Greek–Turkish war over Cyprus, Greece was counting on Soviet military action against Turkey. As he put it to McNamara, 'Turkey neighbors on a country that has a much more powerful Air Force. It is more than likely that this Air Force would be drawn into the conflict were the Turks to attack.'[33] (As was mentioned in the previous chapter, during the 1964 crisis the Soviet Union was contemplating the use of force against Turkey.)

It is worth mentioning that while the south-eastern flank was in a state of disarray, other NATO members were also divided over Cyprus and the role NATO should play in resolving the ethnic conflict. France and West Germany considered the Cyprus question as one of Britain's post-colonial problems and did not want to become involved. In response to the proposal for the dispatch of a NATO peacekeeping force, West Germany clarified that German troops would land on Cyprus only with the approval of the Cypriot government.[34] France maintained a pro-Greek position and refused 'to become involved in an operation based on the Zürich statute, in whose elaboration she did not participate, and which moreover does not seem to her to be capable of lasting forever'.[35] Besides the USA and Britain, only Belgium and The Netherlands agreed to participate in the force but on the condition that the NATO plan was approved by all interested parties.

THE NATO FAILURE

The failure of the NATO initiative on Cyprus did not come as a surprise. The prospects for a successful NATO peace operation were slim from the very beginning. The following factors were especially unfavourable for a constructive and effective interference by the Western alliance:

First, Greece and Turkey put their national goals and commitments above those of NATO. The two countries were not even willing to use NATO as a forum for negotiations. This was especially true for Greece which was afraid that Turkey, because of its vital importance for NATO, would get more support from other NATO members. A similar scenario had evolved in reaching the 1960 settlement, the memories of which were still fresh in Athens and Nicosia. In Washington nobody made a secret of the view that 'the overriding criterion for any permanent solution on Cyprus should be its effect on the Western alliance. In the interests of NATO and world peace, Greece and

Turkey again must abandon their extreme views on Cyprus, as they did in 1959, and cooperate to bring about a new, workable detente.'[36] Secondly, the conflict involved an independent country which was not a member of NATO. Makarios was not willing to accept NATO intervention, to lose control of the situation, and to eliminate his chances of drawing support from the Eastern bloc and Third World countries. As an observer put it, 'this time Makarios could not be bullied into accepting an agreement reached by others. This time he held some high cards.'[37] Thus, the NATO proposal precipitated a Cypriot appeal to the UN and a request for help from the Soviet Union.

Thirdly, NATO had been unpopular in Greece and Cyprus since the colonial period. In the 1950s it was regarded as an obstacle to the application of self-determination on the island. The new NATO initiative was interpreted as an effort to liquidate the Cypriot state and turn Cyprus into a military bridgehead. The Greek and Cypriot governments, in response to popular demand, had, therefore, to oppose it.

Fourthly, the proposed NATO plan was, in effect, prejudging the political settlement of the Cypriot conflict. It provided for negotiations between NATO members under a NATO mediator, while the situation on the island would be under NATO military control. It should be remembered that the 1960 Zürich and London agreements, which caused so much grief and trouble in Cyprus, were negotiated under similar conditions. Greece and Cyprus, which considered the 1960 Zürich settlement unfair, would rather resort to the UN this time for purposes of peacekeeping and mediation.

Fifthly, the NATO plan was, in essence, an Anglo-American product which the other NATO members were reluctant to adopt. The alliance did not, and probably could not, act with cohesion and effectiveness on an issue that did not affect directly all its members. Consequently, the proposal did not enjoy the support of the Western pact as a whole. In this regard, Philip Windsor has argued and reasonably supported the view that 'an open intervention by the Alliance was in fact more likely to split the Alliance itself than to calm the situation on the island'.[38]

The unsuccessful NATO initiative on Cyprus was the first and last attempt by a regional military organization to intervene in the ethnic conflict. Right after NATO's failure, the issue was taken to the UN where it became a major item on the agendas of the Security Council and the General Assembly. A UN peacekeeping force has been on the island continuously since March 1964. Repeated unsuccessful rounds of inter-communal talks and bilateral Greek–Turkish negotiations for the settlement of the problem have also been carried out under the UN or in the name of the UN. To a great extent, UN involvement accounts for the lack of further attempts at substantive NATO interference in the Cypriot conflict after 1964.

In this light, another observation can be made with regard to the limited role NATO played after 1964. Although the USA and Britain did intervene to manage the crises that developed later in 1964, 1967, and 1974, they did so without involving NATO directly. Britain became involved in its capacity of a guarantor power and with the aim of protecting its military interests on the island. The USA intervened in its capacity of a superpower, although it did try to use NATO bonds to exercise influence on Greece and Turkey.

The two leading NATO members, which had major interests in Cyprus and the region, realized that the Western pact could not be used as an instrument or channel for intervention in a non-aligned country. Such a tactic could backfire and give results opposite to the ones desired. The fact that Greece and Turkey have ethnic ties with Cyprus would not make NATO intervention legitimate in the eyes of other countries in the West or the East. On the contrary, other Western countries wanted to avoid involvement in the conflict through NATO. The Eastern bloc would rather see the conflict deteriorate and undermine the Western defence system.

THE PROBLEMS CONVERGE

The 1974 crisis on Cyprus caused new problems to NATO, more serious than the ones in the 1950s and 1960s. The danger of an all-out Greek–Turkish war, once again, became real and imminent as the two countries fully mobilized their forces and showed by word and action that they were ready to settle their differences on the battlefield. The fact that they were both members of the same military alliance did not seem to have any impact on their attitude.

As was mentioned in previous chapters, it was the downfall of the Greek military junta, the political and military disarray in Greece and Cyprus, and the military superiority of Turkey that prevented an escalation of the crisis into a catastrophic war across the Aegean. Although the Greek contingent stationed on Cyprus became involved in a fierce battle with the invading Turkish forces, the new Greek civilian government did not implement the idea of an attack on the Thracian border which had been entertained by the military regime. Plans made in Athens for the dispatch of sizeable military reinforcements from Crete to Cyprus did not materialize because of logistical reasons and the great risks involved in such an operation.[39] Eventually, the 1974 confrontation was resolved by force in favour of Turkey with the occupation of the northern part of the island and the forced exchange of populations.

The role played by NATO during the 1974 crisis was minimal, if any, although the consequences were grave for the Western defence system. It was, instead, the USA and Britain who intervened by diplomacy to manage the crisis. They did so on a unilateral basis, without entangling NATO. Both countries, however, failed to establish a bridge of communication between Greece and Turkey. Assistant Secretary of State Joseph Sisco was given the cold shoulder in both Athens and Ankara. The Turkish Premier Ecevit, responding to Sisco's request for a 48-hour postponement of the invasion, explained that in previous cases 'the United States and Turkey both have made mistakes – the United States by preventing Turkish military action and Turkey by accepting. We should not make the same mistakes.'[40] At the Geneva peace conference, the British Foreign Minister James Callaghan tried in vain to find some common ground to reconcile the opposing ethnic factions.

To some extent, the lack of NATO involvement in the crisis could be attributed to UN involvement. The Cypriot government immediately took the issue to the Security Council and tried to shift the centre of diplomacy from Western capitals to the UN. The motives behind the Cypriot preference for the UN are discussed in detail in the next chapter.

Although NATO did not become directly involved in the crisis, the motives and objectives of the British and American initiatives were aimed at protecting NATO unity. The two countries were acting separately, but yet with some co-ordination and common goals. The following statement by Secretary of State Kissinger summarizes the tactics and objectives of Anglo-American intervention:

> Our effort throughout was that this was an issue affecting NATO, affecting Western Europe, in which we should work in the closest cooperation with our allies and particularly with Great Britain, which had a relationship as one of the guarantors of the Zurich agreement. Throughout the period as I pointed out

Saturday, there has been a complete unanimity as to objective and very substantial agreement between the United Kingdom and the United States in every facet of the diplomatic process and complete coordination on our efforts. The United States concentrated on getting the cease-fire; the United Kingdom concentrated on getting the negotiating process started after the cease-fire. The attempt has been made to get a cease-fire established and then have the United Kingdom invite Greece and Turkey to a meeting.[41]

Indeed, a meeting between Greek and Turkish representatives took place in Geneva under British chairmanship. Some talks took place after the first phase of the Turkish invasion was completed and a ceasefire had been arranged. Despite Anglo-American pressure, however, the two sides failed to conduct any constructive negotiations on any substantive matters. As a result, the Geneva conference broke down and Turkey proceeded to a second massive attack on Cyprus that resulted in the occupation of 37 per cent of the island. In the meantime, Greece made a formal appeal to NATO Secretary-General Joseph Luns to convene a meeting of the NATO Ministerial Council and exercise pressure on Turkey to show restraint on Cyprus. Luns refused to convene such a meeting or intervene actively in the conflict.[42] Greece responded by withdrawing from the military wing of NATO.[43] In an official statement issued in Athens following a meeting of a war council, it was explained that 'after the Atlantic Alliance demonstrated its inability to prevent Turkey from creating a state of conflict between two allies, the Prime Minister ordered that the Greek armed forces should be withdrawn from NATO. Greece shall remain a member of the Alliance only in connection with its political aspect.'[44]

To make things worse, the Greek minister of defence summoned the ambassadors of the five permanent members of the Security Council and handed them notes warning that Greece would go to war unless Turkey was willing to stop advancing on Cyprus. As mentioned above, however, eventually Greece did not take any military action and Turkey was left to complete its 'Attila operation'.[45]

With the withdrawal of the Greek armed forces from NATO, the south-eastern flank suffered a heavy blow. The operational utility of the alliance in the region was further undermined when the Turkish government, in response to the imposition of a US arms embargo, closed down the extensive network of American military installations in Turkey. Moreover, in early 1975 Turkey proceeded to form the so-called

'Aegean army', deployed along the west coast, not far from the Greek islands. Quite interestingly, and for obvious reasons, this army was equipped with landing craft and independent of the NATO command.[46]

The above developments led to the virtual destruction of the south-eastern flank and the defence system of the Straits and the Aegean. Under these conditions, it is doubtful whether a Soviet expansionist move in the region would meet any Greek or Turkish resistance. In sum, Greek–Turkish rivalry over Cyprus deteriorated to the point that the two countries lost any sense of alliance or collective security and caused the disintegration of one of NATO's vital flanks.

The outcome of the 1974 crisis also demonstrated that NATO was unable to play a mediating role in the Greek–Turkish conflict where two of its members were seeking the promotion of conflicting national goals. The age-old ethnic rivals showed in a clear fashion that considerations of national interest, especially ethnic-based objectives, superseded their contractual commitments to a regional political–military organization.

In 1980, after six years of Greek military absence from the Western defence system, an agreement was reached between the Rallis conservative pro-Western government and NATO for the return of Greece to the military branch of the alliance. The agreement, known as the 'Rogers plan' (named after the NATO Supreme Commander Bernard Rogers) provided for increased national control over Greek forces compared to the pre-1974 arrangement. Soon after the agreement was reached, however, the Greek socialist party under Andreas Papandreou came to power and partially suspended the Rogers plan. Papandreou also demanded the renegotiation of the treaties under which the USA maintains NATO-linked military bases in Greece. A new provisional bilateral defence and economic agreement was reached in July 1983 providing for increased US aid to Greece and the suspension of the operation of the American bases in an emergency, if the Greek national interest was at stake. Eventually, following the collapse of the Soviet Union and the end of the Cold War, problems pertaining to Greek–NATO and Greek–American relations were settled, although no settlement came within sight on Cyprus.

SUMMARY AND CONCLUSION

The outbreak of inter-communal violence on Cyprus in 1963 marked the beginning of a disintegrating process of the south-eastern flank of

NATO which culminated in the Greek withdrawal from the alliance in 1974. Greece and Turkey, acting under ethnic constraints and pursuing conflicting national goals, intervened in Cyprus to support their respective ethnic groups. In doing so, the two mainlands demonstrated attachment to ethnic commitments and insensitivity to commitments deriving from their membership in NATO. Ethnic factors rather than NATO bonds and principles proved the determinants of their objectives and attitudes.

Greek–Turkish confrontation over Cyprus was manifested in both the military and diplomatic fronts and repeatedly brought the two countries to the brink of war. The possibility of an all-out war across the Aegean and the destruction of the Western defence system in the region greatly alarmed NATO. By and large, however, it was the USA and Britain – the two leading NATO countries having major interests in Cyprus and the region – which were disturbed over the developments on and around Cyprus. In response to the well-grounded likelihood of a blow-up of the south-eastern flank, the two countries tried to 'drag' NATO into the conflict as an instrument of peacekeeping and mediation. Beyond the immediate task of peace restoration, NATO intervention was intended to pave the way for the establishment of a lasting Western control over Cyprus and the elimination of the sources of Greek–Turkish friction over the island.

The Anglo-American initiative failed because it did not receive any support from within or outside NATO. Other NATO countries were reluctant to participate in a NATO operation prescribed by the USA and Britain in a non-aligned country. Cyprus rejected intervention by a regional military alliance with whom it had no affiliation, and opted for the UN. The Soviet bloc and Third World countries supported the Cypriot appeal to the UN. In sum, the abortive attempt at NATO intervention showed that the Western alliance could not play a constructive role in containing or resolving the ethnic conflict.

6 The Role of the United Nations

Give me but one firm spot on which to stand, and I will move the earth.

Archimedes

OBJECTIVES

This chapter deals with the internationalization of the Cypriot ethnic conflict through the UN. Since the eruption of inter-communal violence in 1963, the world organization has been involved in the conflict in various ways and settings. Cyprus has repeatedly been on the agendas of the Security Council and the General Assembly, while the Secretary-General has been actively involved in efforts to resolve the problem. A more evident manifestation of UN involvement in the issue has been the uninterrupted presence of a UN peacekeeping force on the island since 1964.

The primary objective of this chapter is to explore the circumstances under which the UN became involved in an issue that at first appeared to be a domestic ethnic dispute. The implications and consequences of UN involvement will also be examined in the light of further developments that culminated in the Turkish invasion and occupation of the northern part of the island.

The UN was created in 1945 to pursue the functional tasks of peace maintenance and socioeconomic development worldwide.[1] But as an organization of sovereign states competing over wealth, values, and power, it has been entangled in conflicts inherent in international politics. The politicization of the UN has, in fact, become a major feature of the modern world system. As a public forum for the practice of international parliamentary democracy and conflict resolution, the world organization is increasingly turning into an instrument of national policies. It is functioning as 'a center of intense, competitive, oblique diplomacy and equally intense open propaganda'.[2] States are using and abusing it in many ways and for a variety of political purposes, such as a platform for political debate or propaganda, a means for the mobilization of world opinion and concern, an arena for diplomatic manoeuvring, a lever for exercising political pressure, and an instrument of collective legitimization and support.[3] The exploration of the Cypriot case illustrates how the world organization can become involved in an ethnic conflict and be used for purposes other than and beyond peace maintenance and conflict resolution.

FLARE-UP AND EARLY UNITED NATIONS INVOLVEMENT

For the first time, Cyprus became a major issue at the UN in the 1950s. From 1954 to 1958, Greece appealed five times to the General Assembly asking for the termination of colonial rule and application of self-determination on the island. The Greek appeals were aimed at internationalization of the issue and the exercise of global pressure on Britain to withdraw from Cyprus.[4] The settlement of the colonial problem reached in 1960 providing for the establishment of the Republic of Cyprus was partly the result of pressure deriving from the internationalization of the problem through the UN.

Following a five-year interval, the world organization again became involved in Cyprus after the eruption of inter-communal violence in 1963. The island was now beset by problems deriving from domestic ethnic rivalry and external intervention along ethnic lines. On 26 December 1963, four days after the flare-up, and while the situation was rapidly and dangerously deteriorating, the Cypriot government, which was headed by Makarios and controlled by the Greek Cypriots, took the issue to the UN. The Makarios government resorted to the Security Council asking for help against 'acts of aggression and intervention in the internal affairs of Cyprus by the threat and use of force against its territorial integrity and political independence'.[5] In the view of the Cypriot government, the declared intention of Turkey to intervene in Cyprus by force threatened the sovereignty and political independence of Cyprus and was in direct violation of the UN Charter. Therefore, the Greek Cypriots argued, it was 'in the vital interests of the people of Cyprus as a whole, and in the interest of international peace and security'[6] that the Security Council takes measures to remedy the situation.

It is interesting to note that UN intervention was requested by invoking articles 1(1), 2(4), and 24(1) of the Charter. Article 1(1) defines the maintenance of international peace and security as the primary goal of the UN. Article 2(4) calls upon all states to 'refrain in their international relations from the threat or use of force against the territorial integrity or political independence of any state'. Article 24(1) recognizes the Security Council as the primary organ responsible for the maintenance of international peace and security.

Eventually, the Cypriot resort to the UN proved an abortive one as the Makarios government agreed, after a short session of the Security Council, to attend the London peace conference.[7] As Purcell points out, Makarios 'came round to the point of view that it was better to let the [London] conference fail slowly rather than refuse to attend. Besides, under article 33 of the UN Charter it was desirable to exhaust all possible alternative solutions before having direct recourse to the Security Council.'[8] Indeed, the Cypriot president made it clear that his ultimate intention was to take the issue to the UN.[9] At the press conference where he announced his decision to attend the London conference, he stated that if his objective of an independent unitary Cypriot state free of external intervention was not achieved in London, he would seek a settlement through the UN.[10]

As expected, after the collapse of the London conference, Cyprus reactivated its appeal to the Security Council. The reasons cited for the reactivation were again a threat to international peace and security and the 'obvious and imminent' danger of a Turkish invasion which threatened 'the independence, sovereignty and territorial integrity of a small country by a stronger neighbouring Power in direct violation of the Charter'.[11]

INTERNAL STRIFE AND EXTERNAL THREAT

The first observation to be made with regard to Makarios' recourse to the UN is that for the Greek Cypriots the real problem was not the internal communal strife, but the likelihood of a Turkish invasion in support of the Turkish Cypriots. What Makarios had in mind by involving the UN was to prevent Turkish intervention, and protect and strengthen the sovereignty and political independence of Cyprus. In order to identify and assess the political motives and objectives of the archbishop's move at the UN, we have to examine the circumstances under which he acted.[12]

As it was mentioned and discussed in some detail in chapter 2, the newborn Republic of Cyprus was beset by two major ethnopolitical controversies pertaining to the 1960 Zürich and London settlement. At the domestic level, the constitution proved inapplicable, and the two communities failed to reach a compromise and set up a working state. With regard to the international status and external relations of Cyprus, a sharp ethnopolitical controversy arose over the limitations imposed on the sovereignty and political independence of the new republic. The self-appointed guarantor powers granted themselves the right to station troops on the island and intervene in its internal affairs. The Treaty of Guarantee provided that in the event of a breach of the 1960 settlement, the three guarantor powers could, jointly or unilaterally, take action to re-establish the status quo created by the Zürich and London agreements.

The two ethnic factions held different views on the validity and utility of the Treaty of Guarantee. President Makarios made no secret of his intention to get rid of it and gain real and unfettered independence for Cyprus.[13] In his view, the treaty was in direct contrast to the UN principles of non-intervention and sovereign equality of states and, therefore, it became void when Cyprus became a member of the UN.

The Turkish Cypriots argued that the treaty, which was an integral part of the constitution, was valid and could not be unilaterally abrogated. The right of Turkey to intervene was seen by them as a major deterrent to Greek Cypriot domination.

It was against the background of this ethnopolitical deadlock and simmering tension that President Makarios took the initiative for a constitutional reform in November 1963. Not surprisingly, his proposal for a thirteen-point constitutional amendment marked the onset of ethnic violence and external intervention in Cyprus. The situation deteriorated rapidly as Greece and Turkey became actively involved in the hostilities, and the two superpowers, along with Britain, interfered to protect their own interests.

HEADED FOR THE SECURITY COUNCIL

In this setting of military and diplomatic confrontation involving local and regional actors, and conflicting ethnic, political, and strategic interests, Makarios took the issue to the UN. Looking at the Cypriot president's move from a purely local perspective, it would be difficult to explain his request for UN intervention. The Greek Cypriots, because of their superior numbers and equipment, were in a commanding position to control the situation on the island. The Turkish Cypriots, because of their numerical inferiority and the fear of retaliation, and acting on instructions of their leadership, moved into military enclaves, and their representatives withdrew from the government. Virtually the entire government, state institutions, and economy fell into the hands of the Greek Cypriots. In sum, the local balance of power was in favour of the majority, and the Makarios government would have no problem coping with the outnumbered minority if external intervention was excluded.[14] But for Makarios, the real problem was Turkey's determination to play a major role in Cyprus, and the hostile (pro-Turkish) Anglo-American attitude. The archbishop first tried to counteract Turkish and Anglo-American pressure by appealing for help to Greece and the Soviet Union. The military and diplomatic support he received from Athens and Moscow proved crucial, but the Cypriot president believed that UN involvement would strengthen considerably his diplomatic position *vis-à-vis* the Turks and the Anglo-Americans. From Makarios' viewpoint, an appeal to the UN was especially tempting for the following reasons:

First, the international organization could be used to strengthen his government, the legality of which was questioned by Turkey and the Turkish Cypriots. According to the constitution, three out of ten ministers and fifteen out of fifty members of the parliament had to be Turkish Cypriots.[15] But after the outbreak of hostilities, the Turkish Cypriots holding public positions withdrew and began setting up a separate administration. This gave rise to questions about the constitutionality of what had seemingly remained a Greek Cypriot government. Makarios could try to extract a resolution from the UN recognizing, directly or indirectly, his government as the only legitimate source of authority on the island.

Secondly, an appeal to the UN could help Makarios counteract the strong Anglo-American pressure and initiatives aimed at a settlement of the conflict in a Western setting. The archbishop had experienced similar pressure during the 1960 settlement when Greece and Turkey, acting under Anglo-American pressure, settled the fate of Cyprus over the head of the Cypriots. Three years later, Makarios was the head of an independent state and determined to play the role of a protagonist in the new act of the Cypriot drama. His appeal to the UN would give him room for manoeuvring in the broader stage of international diplomacy and enable him to take advantage of non-Western forces favouring Cyprus' complete independence from Western powers. A presentation of the problem in the light of foreign intervention and 'neo-colonialism' would gain him the support of the Afro-Asian and

Eastern bloc countries. For the Soviet Union, which had already expressed a staunch support for Makarios, the UN would be the place for a face-to-face confrontation with the Anglo-Americans.[16]

Thirdly, what Makarios needed most at the UN was a ratification of his effort to revise the 1960 settlement. He had already made it clear that he would like to abrogate the Treaty of Guarantee, but Turkey and Britain insisted that the treaty could not be abrogated unilaterally. The Cypriot president had also tried to initiate an amendment of the constitution, but the mere proposal of a constitutional modification had caused a severe reaction from the Turkish side and precipitated ethnic violence. A UN declaration confirming the invalidity and abrogation of the 1960 treaties would greatly strengthen Makarios' position *vis-à-vis* the Turks and free his hand to reshape the internal political structure and external relations of Cyprus.

A fourth major goal of the Cypriot government at the UN was to get a peacekeeping force under the Security Council. Meeting the need for a peacekeeping force through the UN was in agreement with Makarios' political and diplomatic objectives for the following reasons:

First, the British troops, which began patrolling the first ceasefire, were considered hostile by the Greek Cypriots. As the *Economist* wrote, 'through no fault of their own, the British forces have lost the trust of the Greek Cypriots, who appear to be firmly convinced that they are conniving at the de facto partitioning of the island by the Turks'.[17] After all, these were the same forces against which the 1955–59 war of independence was fought. Makarios saw the British troops as an instrument of Turkish policy and a bargaining card in the hands of an unfriendly guarantor power.

Secondly, the Cypriot government was hoping that the presence of a UN force on the island would serve as a deterrent against external military intervention; a kind of shield protecting the Greek Cypriots from a Turkish invasion. The threat of an invasion was the most powerful weapon Turkey had in its confrontation with Makarios. By taking that weapon away from Turkey, the Cypriot president was expecting a considerable improvement of his position in the military and diplomatic fronts.

Thirdly, by having a UN force on Cyprus, Makarios could easily neutralize Anglo-American pressure and effectively eliminate any prospects for the dispatch of a strongly undesirable NATO peacekeeping force. The Anglo-Americans had already submitted a NATO plan for peacekeeping, which Makarios adamantly resisted.[18] The archbishop was afraid that a NATO force would become a powerful leverage in the hands of unfriendly Western powers holding pro-Turkish positions.

In sum, the Cypriot president needed a UN peacekeeping force to counteract external military and diplomatic pressure and keep the situation on the island under his control.

It was with these goals in mind that Makarios took the issue to the UN. Basically, he wanted to use the Security Council (and later the General Assembly) as a forum for political debate on what he presented as an issue of external intervention. The political gains he expected from such a debate would enhance his position domestically and internationally, and enable him to resolve the Cyprus problem by revising the 1960 settlement.

MAKARIOS SCORES THE FIRST VICTORIES

In fact, Makarios had already scored two major political victories by managing to take the issue to the Security Council. His first victory was over the Turkish side and reinforced the legitimacy of his government. Vice-President Kutchuk complained to the UN that the Greek Cypriot representative who filed the appeal to the Security Council did so without obtaining the decision of the biethnic council of ministers and the concurrence of the vice-president, which, in Kutchuk's view, were necessary under the constitution. Therefore, Kutchuk argued, the representations of the Greek Cypriot delegate at the Security Council were 'illegal and unconstitutional'.[19] To Makarios' great satisfaction, however, Kutchuk's complaint remained without effect and the Greek Cypriots secured the significant political and diplomatic advantage of exclusive representation of Cyprus at the UN.[20] The rejection of Kutchuk's complaint was also an indirect recognition of the legality and constitutionality of Makarios' 'Turkish free' government. Makarios scored his second political victory against the Anglo-Americans who insisted that the ethnic conflict should be resolved among the guarantor powers. During the early diplomatic confrontations between the Cypriot president and the West, the likelihood of a Cypriot recourse to the Security Council became a hot issue. The American Under-Secretary of State, George Ball, who had tried in vain to persuade Makarios to accept a NATO peace plan in lieu of UN intervention, provides the following account of a relevant illustrative incident:

I can describe the afternoon session only as 'bloody'. The Archbishop was unrelenting in repeating a litany he knew I would never accept. The matter must be submitted to the UN Security Council; and the United Nations must guarantee the political independence and territorial integrity of Cyprus. That meant, as I told my British colleague later, that Makarios' central interest was to block off Turkish intervention so that he and his Greek Cypriots could go on happily massacring Turkish Cypriots. Obviously we would never permit that.[21]

But Ball had more in mind than 'saving' the Turkish Cypriots by trying to prevent Makarios from involving the UN in Cyprus. In his words, 'involving the United Nations risked giving the Communist countries leverage in that strategically placed island'.[22] And that is what really bothered the Americans: the prospect of international politicization of the issue and the likelihood of a Soviet–Cypriot alliance at the Security Council where the Soviet veto could become an insurmountable political weapon at the disposal of the 'Castro of the Mediterranean', as Makarios was known in the State Department.

Ball tried further to move the stubborn archbishop by threatening that a UN appeal would inevitably cause the Turks to invade and 'neither the United States nor any other Western power would raise a finger to stop them'.[23] The forceful American diplomat also warned Makarios 'by quoting chapter and verse that the UN in previous actions has usually favored the maintenance of partition as a solution'.[24] But the Orthodox prelate had his own 'chapter and verse' to quote, and he was determined to do it at the UN with the expectation of major political benefits.

Eventually, the controversy over UN involvement ended with a diplomatic triumph for Makarios and an embarrassing irony for the Anglo-Americans. On 15 February 1964, Britain, in its capacity of a guarantor power, and in co-operation with the USA, filed a separate request for a meeting of the Security Council two hours before the Cypriot government reactivated its appeal of 26 December 1963. The British government characterized its move as 'pre-emptive action' aimed at shifting the attention of the Security Council to the restoration of internal security on Cyprus.[25] The British appeal stressed that the problem had its 'origin in a dispute between the two communities and the inability of the Government of Cyprus'[26] to co-operate with the guarantor powers in restoring law and order. By focusing on the immediate goal of internal security, and by blaming Makarios for the continuing bloodshed, the Western powers were trying to undermine the Greek Cypriot position at the UN and 'get priority over Council consideration of the Archbishop's ultimate political goals'.[27]

THE ACRIMONIOUS DEBATE

The three-week-long discussion at the Security Council turned out, as expected, to be a political debate between two blocs advancing distinct positions on the nature of the problem and the way it should be resolved.[28] One bloc included Turkey, Britain, and the USA which argued that the problem was basically one of internal conflict and disorder for which the Makarios government was largely responsible. As the Turkish representative put it, the cause of the problem was Makarios' attempt to bring about changes in the political structure of the Cypriot state at the expense of the Turkish Cypriot minority. With regard to the motives behind the Greek Cypriot appeal to the Security Council, the Turkish view, which was also shared by Britain and the USA, was that Makarios was using the UN as a political instrument for the abrogation of the 1960 settlement and the creation of a new status quo. What the Greek Cypriots were seeking in New York, the Turks claimed, was a 'UN resolution which they could pretend to interpret as though international treaties had been abrogated'[29] so that they could proceed undisturbed to implement their plans.

The British position was complementary to the Turkish view: the 1960 treaties were valid and the guarantor powers had the right and the duty to intervene in Cyprus to restore peace and settle the conflict. The British delegate emphasized that 'the Treaty of Guarantee is of particular importance as the linchpin'[30] of the 1960 settlement and it should be thoroughly respected. He clarified that Britain was not willing to go on carrying alone the burden of peacekeeping on the island, but he insisted that any action by the Security Council should be consistent with the 1960 treaties and be taken in co-operation with the guarantor powers.

The Western point of view was rounded off by the American representative who emphatically declared that the Treaty of Guarantee 'or any international treaty cannot be abrogated, cannot be nullified, cannot be modified either in fact or in effect by the Security Council of the UN'.[31] The common position held by Turkey, Britain, and the USA reflected their effort to undermine the political objectives of Makarios at the UN. The Western powers were afraid that if the

Treaty of Guarantee was abrogated, the Cypriot president would get a licence to bring about changes in the domestic and external affairs of Cyprus in a way harmful to the Turkish Cypriots and Western interests. The treaty was seen by the West as a means for keeping a tight rein on the 'red priest'.[32]

A completely different view on the issue was advanced by the Greek Cypriots who received the full support of Greece and the Soviet Union. The Cypriot Foreign Minister, Spyros Kyprianou, in his long speeches repeatedly argued that the problem facing Cyprus was one of circumscribed independence and external intervention. The cause of all trouble, he claimed, was the unfair 1960 settlement which was imposed on Cyprus by outside powers. As he explained, the parties to that settlement were 'in an unequal bargaining position and the Greek Cypriot side did not give its consent freely...making the doctrine of unequal, inequitable, and unjust treaties relevant'.[33] Moreover, the Cypriot minister argued, the Treaty of Guarantee was conflicting with the UN Charter which prohibits the unlawful use of force. Therefore, he concluded, the treaty was void, his government intended to abrogate it, and the Security Council had the responsibility to affirm and protect the political independence of Cyprus.

The Greek Cypriots also had a different opinion from the Anglo-Americans and the Turks on how to bring peace to the strife-torn island. While the Anglo-Americans suggested the guarantor powers had the primary responsibility for the restoration of peace and the political settlement of the problem, the Makarios government stubbornly argued that it was the Security Council's responsibility to protect the island from external intervention and help the two communities settle their differences in accordance with UN principles. With regard to the creation of a peacekeeping force, the Greek Cypriots made it clear that they would only accept one drawn from countries other than the guarantor powers, and controlled by the Security Council.

Soviet rhetoric and arguments at the Security Council added another dimension to the issue. In an eyeball-to-eyeball confrontation with the Anglo-Americans, the Soviets claimed that Cyprus was the target of an imperialist conspiracy aimed at 'de facto subjugation of this small neutral State Member of the United Nations to the military control of NATO'.[34] In line with the Greek Cypriots and Greece, the Soviet Union blamed the 1960 'inequitable agreements' for the internal problems of Cyprus and declared total support for the island in its quest for 'independent political development' on which it embarked after liberation from 'colonial administration'.[35]

The common position advanced by the Greek Cypriots, Greece, and the Soviet Union reflected the fundamental political objectives of Makarios. The Security Council was asked to reconfirm the political independence of Cyprus, declare null the 1960 treaties, and prohibit external interference. Once these objectives were achieved, and a UN force was in place to protect the island from a Turkish invasion, the archbishop could proceed to bring into effect the changes necessary for the establishment of a truly independent unitary Cypriot state with majority rule.

THE WILD CARD RESOLUTION

The long acrimonious debate at the Security Council ended with a victory for the Cypriot president. The Council unanimously adopted a resolution endorsing most of his claims.[36] It made reference to the 'sovereign Republic of Cyprus' in conjunction with article 2(4) of the Charter and urged all parties to respect 'the territorial integrity and political independence' of the island. Commenting with satisfaction on the resolution, Makarios said: 'We have secured a resolution in the first phase of our struggle in the international field. Turkey cannot threaten intervention in the future by invoking the Treaty of Guarantee.'[37] The United Nations Force in Cyprus (UNFICYP) was created to preserve 'international peace and security', and to co-operate with the government of Cyprus in restoring law and order. The resolution also recommended the appointment of a UN mediator to promote a 'peaceful solution and an agreed settlement of the problem confronting Cyprus in accordance with the Charter of the United Nations'. Although no direct reference was made to the validity or invalidity of the 1960 treaties, the recommendation for a new settlement based on UN principles substantiated Makarios' claim for a revision of the 1960 settlement. In sum, with the adoption of the resolution, Makarios achieved a major political goal at the UN. As Stegenga points out, the archbishop secured international ratification for a 'political revolution' at home by using 'the United Nations as an instrument to attain the next goals in the continuing struggle for real and complete independence that had been interrupted and upset by the disappointing and bizarre settlement of 1960'.[38]

Some attention should be directed to the fact that the USA and Britain did not veto the resolution which was jointly sponsored by Brazil, Bolivia, Ivory Coast, Morocco, and Norway. The two leading Western powers, which for weeks were steadfastly resisting the notions advanced by the resolution, felt that blocking any action by the Security Council could be more harmful to their interests than the active involvement of the UN in the issue. As the *Economist* put it in an editorial, for the West 'the risks of United Nations involvement in the smoldering island were still less than the risks of delay in getting a peace there'.[39] The most vital and urgent goal of Anglo-American policy was to restore peace and prevent an escalation of the crisis that would have a catastrophic impact on Western security interests in the region. As was shown in previous chapters, all signals coming from the countries involved clearly indicated that the likelihood of a military confrontation threatening to engulf the region in flames was not far from certainty. Repeated Western mediating efforts (Sandys, Lemnitzer, Fulbright, and Ball) had failed to give any results and the governments of Athens and Ankara left no doubt about their intentions to resolve their ethnic differences on the battlefield. Ball was informing President Johnson from Nicosia that the Greek Cypriots 'seemed determined to put Cyprus to flames if they could not get it on their terms',[40] while the State Department was trying to persuade the parties involved 'that the important, the imperative, the urgent thing to do is to restore order and communal tranquillity – and do it quickly before peace in the eastern Mediterranean is endangered'.[41]

Britain had additional urgent reasons for letting the Security Council assume the peacekeeping role in Cyprus. Ethnic violence was directly affecting its extensive military installations on the island, including two vital bases. Moreover, the former colonial power had been trapped in shouldering alone 'the onerous burden'[42] of peacekeeping, and now it was looking for a way out. As the British delegate put it to the Security Council, his country was not willing to go on policing Cyprus alone 'for a day longer than is necessary. It is, to put it mildly, neither easy nor pleasant.'[43] As it was reported from Cyprus in less diplomatic language, 'the position of the British troops is almost intolerable'.[44]

The Anglo-Americans were the ones most concerned about the grave consequences of an escalation of the crisis, but there was no doubt in anybody's mind that what started as a domestic ethnic conflict was about to turn into a broader confrontation with worldwide consequences. As discussed in previous chapters, the three guarantor powers and the two superpowers were intimately involved in the conflict and no prospect for a peaceful settlement was within sight. In the words of a commentator expressing the anxiety and frustration of those involved in futile peacemaking efforts, 'this fairy-tale island threatens world peace in the nuclear era, while statesmen of the world scramble for solutions and a few excitable politicians on Cyprus, concerned only with local issues and overwhelmed with the world attention being paid them, throw monkey wrenches in the peace machinery'.[45] Intensive hostilities and military preparations on and around Cyprus were accompanied by threats, charges, and counter-charges coming from Nicosia, Athens, Ankara, London, Washington, and Moscow. The *New York Times*, commenting editorially on the imminent danger facing international security, wrote that Cyprus was threatening 'to embroil Europe, the United States, and even the whole world in its petty communal strife. The Cyprus issue could become the classic example of how internal conflicts become world conflagrations. Cyprus is like a vortex sucking more and more nations into its center.'[46]

The threat to international peace was, indeed, real and imminent, and as such was it perceived by all participants in the debate at the Security Council. Despite the sharp differences the opposing parties had on other aspects of the problem, they all agreed that something had to be done before it was too late. The speedy dispatch of UNFICYP to the strife-torn island, 'where madness is catching',[47] was the corollary of a widely held view within and outside the UN that developments in the troubled zone 'are serious in themselves and also have very special implications for international peace and security'.[48]

In sum, the assumption of the peacekeeping and peacemaking role by the UN was the *sine qua non* of a general assessment that Cyprus presented a threat to international peace and security under the UN Charter.

A point should be made here with regard to the explosive nature of the conflict, the threat it was presenting to international peace, and Makarios' use of the UN as a forum for diplomatic manoeuvring. The Cypriot president, who was a master of international diplomacy and 'an extremely shrewd and purposeful politician of the first order',[49] calculated that the Anglo-Americans were sitting 'over a barrel' in Cyprus and they would rather see him benefiting from UN involvement than the barrel exploding. Moreover, the archbishop, with his open appeals for help to Moscow, made the British and American governments realize that UN exclusion from Cyprus would not impede Soviet involvement in any way. To the contrary, the quick development of close Soviet–Cypriot ties in the diplomatic and military fields made the opposite appear more likely. With the West feeling the pressure of a dangerously deteriorating crisis and increasing Soviet involvement, it was easy for Makarios to manipulate 'voting behavior' in the Security Council and extract the very significant (for him) resolution of 4 March 1964.

The Security Council resolution became a political wild card in Makarios' hands. At home, he used it to justify the creation of a conscript Greek Cypriot army, which was not provided by the 1960 constitution. His answer to Turkish protests was that Cyprus was a sovereign country (the Security Council had affirmed that) and the Cypriot government had the right and the responsibility 'to take all additional measures necessary' to restore law and order (the Security Council had recommended that).

Turkish threats of military action also lost much of their weight after the dispatch of the 6500-man UN force to Cyprus.[50] Turkey had to think twice before invading an island protected by contingents from Austria, Canada, Denmark, Finland, Ireland, Sweden, and Britain. (In 1974, when the invasion took place, inter-communal relations were peaceful and UNFICYP had been reduced to 2000.)

THE PLAZA REPORT

In his confrontation with the West, Makarios used the resolution to back his renunciation of Anglo-American involvement in the search for a peaceful political settlement. Thus, Cyprus refused even to attend the Geneva conference in August 1964 where Acheson advanced his 'double *enosis*' plan. The Cypriot president explained that the American envoy was a self-invited mediator trying to remove the issue from the UN.[51] The appointment of a UN mediator earlier that year (in implementation of the Security Council resolution) left no room for argument with Makarios on this point.

The final blow against Western plans and mediating efforts came with the submission of the 'Report of the UN Mediator on Cyprus to the Secretary General', in March 1965.[52] The Ecuadorian mediator, Dr Galo Plaza, after a year of talks and consultations with the parties concerned, endorsed most of Makarios' views. He criticized the treaties and the 'constitutional oddity'[53] of 1960 as unworkable, and recommended self-determination and direct negotiations between the two communities under UN auspices. In his 66-page document, which contained frequent references to the UN Charter and principles, Plaza also recommended the establishment of a truly independent unitary Cypriot state with majority rule and safeguarded proportional rights for the minority. With regard to the controversial issue of guarantees, Plaza suggested abolition of the 1960 treaty arrangement and added:

> The possibility could be explored, I believe, of the United Nations itself acting as the guarantor of the terms of the settlement. It might prove feasible, for example, for the parties to agree to lay before the United Nations the precise terms of the settlement and ask it not only to take note of them but also to spell them out in a resolution, formally accept them as the agreed basis of the settlement, and request that any complaint of violation or difficulty in implementation be brought immediately before it. Such a role for the United Nations would, I believe, be in full accordance with the letter and the spirit of the Charter.[54]

Plaza's recommendations were in complete agreement with Makarios' political objectives and conception of a settlement of the problem. Turkey reacted furiously to what seemed to be an escalating 'conspiracy' between the Cypriot president and the UN. The Turkish government accused Plaza of exceeding his mandate and authority as a mediator, and rejected not only his report but also the notion of a UN mediator.[55] Apparently, the Turks were irritated over the successful utilization of UN forums, agents, and principles by the 'cunning priest', as Makarios was known in Ankara.

RESORT TO THE GENERAL ASSEMBLY

While Turkey and the West were trying to contain UN involvement in Cyprus, Makarios was seeking further involvement of the world organization. In a move of oblique diplomacy, he took the issue to the General Assembly where he presented it as a problem of continuing colonialism and self-determination. As he explained, 'since the establishment of the UN forty-nine new countries emerged to independence and joined the organization. For all, except Cyprus, the right of self-determination under the Charter was applied.'[56] It was further clarified in the Cypriot appeal that the 1960 treaties, which deprived Cyprus of its sovereignty and independence, were used by foreign powers (especially Turkey) to serve 'neo-colonialist purposes alien to the interests of the Cypriot people, whether of Turkish or Greek origin'.[57] Finally, the Greek Cypriots, by invoking UN principles and the Declaration on the Granting of Independence to Colonial Countries and Peoples,[58] asked the General Assembly to call for respect for the sovereignty, unity, independence, territorial integrity, and non-alignment of Cyprus.

Makarios' resort to the General Assembly was a well-calculated political move. Apparently, he felt confident that the large group of newly independent former colonies would support his request for a resolution reaffirming the independence of another former colony.

The recent Congo crisis (1960–64) had also shown that the idea of secession, for obvious reasons, was not seen favourably by the states of the world, most of which are multiethnic. The universal condemnation of Tshombe's attempt at secession of the Katanga province, and the dispatch of UN troops to restore the unity of the Congo, reflected a worldwide disapproval of secessionist tendencies.[59] The newly born – mostly fragmented and with less developed unifying political, economic, and political structures – Afro-Asian countries were especially sensitive to the notion of secession, and Makarios expected them to condemn the Turkish Cypriot demand for partition and any external intervention favouring a settlement based on the dissolution of the Cypriot state. Certainly, the *Economist* was right when commenting that 'there is little doubt that President Makarios had the Congo operation in mind when evolving his present tactics'.[60] And the *Times* (London) was stating the obvious in an editorial predicting that Makarios would be successful in persuading governments facing restless minorities 'to see the Turkish Cypriots as a lot of Tshombes, bent on secession, to be brought to heel by an outraged international community'.[61]

Under these circumstances, the Afro-Asian support given to the Cypriot appeal, and the adoption of resolution 2077 (XX) of 18 December 1965, by the General Assembly endorsing Makarios' anti-colonial claims did not come by surprise. The common viewpoint held by the arithmetically powerful Afro-Asian bloc called for protection of the unity of Cyprus and the observance of the principles of sovereign equality, self-determination, and non-intervention. Summing up this position before the plenary session of the General Assembly, the Indian delegate stated: 'As we have all seen, partition creates new problems, we, therefore, view with the utmost sympathy the efforts of the Government of Cyprus to maintain the unfettered sovereignty, independence, and unity of the State of Cyprus.'[62]

The resolution confirmed that Cyprus 'is entitled to and should enjoy full sovereignty and complete independence without any foreign intervention or interference' and called upon all states 'to respect its sovereignty, unity, independence and territorial integrity'.[63] It was adopted by a vote of forty-seven in favour, five against, and fifty-four abstentions. A closer look at the vote clearly shows that the General Assembly functioned as a political forum, and the votes of the individual states were determined by considerations of national interest, and political affiliations and sympathies. The five countries which voted against the resolution were Turkey, the USA, Iran, Pakistan, and Albania. The USA was the leading supporter of Turkish views on Cyprus for reasons explained earlier. Iran and Pakistan were traditional Islamic friends and allies of Turkey in CENTO, the counterpart of NATO in the Middle East. Albania was at odds with Greece over minority issues.

The forty-seven votes cast in favour of the resolution came mainly from the Afro-Asian countries which approached the issue in the context of self-determination and anti-colonialism. With their vote, they reconfirmed their support for the culminating anti-colonial movement, and expressed their solidarity with a former colony, 'a new-born infant left on the world's doorstep',[64] facing internal problems and external threats in the first years of its independent life.

The fifty-four abstainers included the Western nations and the Soviet bloc. Abstention could be interpreted as a gesture aimed at avoiding Turkish irritation. For the Western nations, this was a natural policy towards an important ally. For the Soviet Union and its satellites, it was the corollary of the Soviet–Turkish *rapprochement* that had begun a year earlier.

The large number of abstentions gave rise to some questions about the political significance of the resolution. A commentator went as far as to characterize it 'a classic example of hollow voting victory'.[65] Elimination of the word 'classic' could give some validity to this characterization, but still, the resolution had a considerable weight because only five states voted against it, and it was supported by a cohesive bloc of forty-seven states including countries such as Nehru's India, Tito's Yugoslavia, and Nasser's Egypt. But despite some arithmetical inadequacy, there is no doubt that the resolution represented another major diplomatic victory for Makarios, who successfully used the General Assembly as a means for the articulation, channelling, and publicization of international support for his position.

The point to be made here is that the Cypriot president managed to utilize the General Assembly as a platform for political debate where the concurrent opinions of a large number of nations supporting his views could be expressed and heard publicly by the world community. It is, indeed, doubtful whether any other forum could so effectively aggregate and spread the voices of so many countries in such a uniform and resounding fashion. Needless to say that putting those voices together on the record of the world's parliamentary assembly and 'sanctifying' them under the label of a formal resolution increased their political significance and utility. For Makarios, this was another political triumph made possible through the use of a UN organ as a ground for diplomatic manoeuvring, as a channel for communication, and as an instrument for mobilizing collective concern and support.

PILING RESOLUTIONS

The significance attached by the Cypriot government to the use of the General Assembly as an instrument of national policy is shown by the fact that similar appeals were repeatedly made to the Assembly, and similar resolutions were adopted until 1983. Apparently, the Greek Cypriots, who appear indefatigable in practising open diplomacy at the UN, believe that keeping their cause in the frontlines and piling resolutions is helpful. After all, the UN provides an ideal and inexpensive place for getting the attention, and keeping the interest undiminished, of other governments in Cyprus. The repeated adoption of resolutions consistently pointing in the same direction establishes a pattern reiterating collective support and reinforcing their political legitimacy. The analogy can be made here with the strengthening effect which repetition and consistency in state behaviour has on customary rules of international law.

The main objective, however, of the repeated Cypriot appeals to the General Assembly was the reinforcement of the political foundations of the resolutions by getting more countries to vote for them. The increasing number of independent Afro-Asian countries was helpful on this point. But it was not until after the 1974 Turkish invasion that the Greek Cypriots won their most impressive political victory in the General Assembly by extracting a resolution with a truly universal support directed against Turkey.[66] The resolution – which was adopted by 117 votes in favour, none against, and no abstentions – expressed grave concern over the alarming developments threatening world peace in the region, called for the withdrawal of all foreign armed forces from the island, and urged all states to respect the sovereignty, independence, territorial integrity, and non-alignment of Cyprus.

The unanimous adoption of the 1974 resolution was not accidental. The use of force by Turkey against a small neighbouring country irritated friends and foes who wanted to show their disapproval (at least in public) of military aggression. Certainly, no country wanted to present itself before the world's public opinion as an advocate of the use of force. Even Turkey voted for the resolution for face-saving purposes. In similar resolutions adopted in 1975 and 1976, calling again for the withdrawal of foreign troops and reconfirming the independence and unity of the Cypriot state, Turkey was the only country that cast a negative vote.

STRONGER WORDS BUT NO ACTION

The Cypriot government also sought to enhance the cumulative impact of the General Assembly resolutions through stronger wording and tone. Thus, the resolutions became increasingly peremptory and specific in demanding compliance by the states concerned. Resolution 37/253 (1983), for example, was austere and explicit in stating that the General Assembly 'demands the immediate withdrawal of all occupation forces from the Republic of Cyprus'.

Although the resolutions of the General Assembly do not have a legal binding force on states, and Turkey did not comply with the resolutions on Cyprus, the Greek Cypriots and the Republic of Cyprus derived great political benefits from them. The resolutions of the supreme political organ of the UN are not just 'pseudo-agreements'[67] representing mere paper victories. They rest upon the prevailing will of the international community and embody political norms that create constraints which no country can completely disregard. In particular, resolutions repeatedly adopted by a large majority, including the most powerful states, carry with them a heavy load of political and moral authority. They delineate the 'rules of the game' for the quest and exercise of power among states. In this regard, they are influential factors in the process of international politics, which 'is not merely a struggle for power, but also a contest over legitimacy'.[68]

It is in the light of this contest over legitimacy – that is, the approval of the international community – that the UN resolutions came into play in support of the Greek Cypriots. Since 1974, Turkey has been in commanding control of the situation in Cyprus and in a position to dictate forceful demographic and administrative changes. But it failed to gain any international ratification for the *faits accomplis* created by force. The military occupation of 37 per cent of the island and the forced exchange of populations have remained an illegitimate *de facto* situation deprived of a *de jure* status. The creation of the 'Turkish Federated State of Cyprus' in 1975 and the unilateral declaration of independence of the 'Turkish Republic of Northern Cyprus' in 1983 were both stigmatized and universally condemned as illegal and invalid.

The lack of international support for the Turkish attempts at legalization of the partition of Cyprus is largely due to the successive condemnations of the General Assembly and the Security Council. Apparently, no country has been willing to take the political and moral risks involved in the recognition of a situation created by force and repeatedly condemned by the 'world organization [which] has come to be regarded, and used, as a dispenser of politically significant approval and disapproval of the claims, policies, and actions of states'.[69]

In this regard, the Greek Cypriots have managed to turn the UN into a powerful and effective political weapon and use it against the Turks. As a result, the Greek Cypriot government – which is internationally recognized as the only legitimate authority on Cyprus – succeeded in gaining a dominant supremacy in the international political and diplomatic scene.

The Turkish Cypriots, on the other hand, have fallen into a limbo of international political, diplomatic, and economic alienation, and total dependency on Turkey. The Turkish occupation army has become the only source of authority in northern Cyprus where 'despite the sense of security the Turkish Cypriots now enjoy, a virtual isolation from the world has spawned a new kind of insecurity – economic stagnation and the denial of identity and real independence'.[70] In the words of the Turkish Cypriot leader Rauf Denktash, 'we have never been heard anywhere... This is what the Greeks have done to us. They are trying to squeeze us dry.'[71]

Denktash is probably right in one sense, but a clarification is needed. The Greek Cypriots would have not been able to 'squeeze them dry' without the skilful use of the UN as an instrument of

national policy. The key to their success lies in the effective utilization
of the UN, especially the General Assembly, as a means for the
mobilization of world public opinion and as a lever for the exercise
of global political pressure.

SUMMARY AND CONCLUSION

The UN has been involved in the Cypriot ethnic conflict since the
eruption of violence in 1963. The Security Council and the General
Assembly have been especially influential factors throughout the various phases of the problem. Concern and involvement of the world
organization have been mainly directed towards the restoration of
peace, the containment of the conflict, and the search for a settlement
of the dispute by pacific means.

Political motives and objectives coupled with diplomatic expediency
prompted the Greek Cypriots to request UN intervention and seek
internationalization of the problem through UN institutions. The
explosive nature of the conflict and its potentially dangerous implications for world peace have also been major factors behind the active
involvement of the world organization in the dispute.

The Greek Cypriots used the Security Council and the General
Assembly to strengthen their diplomatic position and gain international support for their positions on the issue. In doing so, they placed
emphasis on the international aspects of the problem, especially the
threat and use of force by Turkey against the independence, unity,
and non-alignment of Cyprus. Since the international political environment was favourable to the notions advanced by the Greek
Cypriots, the Cypriot government managed to turn the UN institutions into instruments of national policy. In this regard, the UN
provided a ground for diplomatic manoeuvring, a platform for political debate, and a means for mobilizing foreign governments and
world public opinion in support of the independence, unity, and
non-alignment of Cyprus.

The presentation of the problem in the context of foreign interference brought into play the UN principles of self-determination, equal
sovereignty of states, and non-intervention. Consequently, the attachment of the states of the world to these principles was transformed
into political support for the Greek Cypriots who denied the right of
intervention to foreign powers. As a result, the overwhelming global
condemnation of Turkish policies favouring external intervention,

resort to force, and partition of Cyprus proved crucial for the Greek Cypriots, especially after the 1974 Turkish invasion and the forcible partition of the island. The lack of international approval for the *faits accomplis* created by force in contradiction to UN principles and the expressed will of the world community, played a prominent role in preventing the legitimization of the *de facto* partition of Cyprus. Thanks to UN involvement, and the use of UN forums and principles for the expression, articulation, and communication of the will of the states of the world, the Greek Cypriots can still hope for a negotiated settlement of the problem on the basis of a unified federal republic with two ethnic zones.

Summing up, the violent character of the Cypriot ethnic conflict and the prospect of its escalation through external intervention paved the way for UN involvement. UN interference was requested by the side that was more likely to benefit from the use of the world organization as a global political institution.

As the Cypriot case has shown, the effectiveness of the UN as a guardian of peace, or as an instrument of national policy, is limited because of its inability to implement its resolutions. It can, however, play a very important role in the process of world politics as a dispenser of collective political and moral approval or disapproval of the policies and actions of states.

7 The European Union and the Cyprus Problem

We are not building a coalition of States but a union of peoples.

Jean Monnet

OBJECTIVES

In broad terms, the post-colonial problem of Cyprus can be divided into two phases.[1] The first phase covers the period from 1960 to 1974, and the second one the period from 1974 and thereafter. Until 1974, the main elements and parameters of the problem were defined by the failure of the 1960 London–Zürich settlement of the colonial issue and the subsequent inter-communal conflict in which external powers became involved. Following the 1974 Turkish invasion, the Cyprus problem entered a new phase the dominant elements of which have been the continuing *de facto* division of the island and the military occupation of its northern part by Turkey.

Although the Cyprus problem is still the major source of concern and interest in Cypriot politics, the island's European orientation and its efforts to become a member of the European Union (EU) are now getting considerable attention. Not surprisingly, Cyprus' prospects of joining the EU have occasionally been mired in the continuing impasse in efforts to resolve the political problem.

The purpose of this chapter is to examine the prospects of Cyprus joining the EU and becoming part of 'the process of creating an ever closer union among the peoples of Europe'.[2] The discussion will revolve around the following questions: Is Cyprus eligible and ready to join the EU? When is that going to happen? Is the settlement of the Cyprus question a precondition for accession? And can Cyprus' prospects of joining the EU help in the search for a settlement on the island?

EARLY EUROPEAN ORIENTATION

Cyprus first expressed interest in becoming an associate member of the European Economic Community (EEC), after Great Britain's

116

initial EEC application in 1962.[3] Cyprus' heavy dependence on exports to Britain and the prospect of losing the preferential Commonwealth tariff rate prompted the government to seek an institutionalized arrangement with the EEC. Following the withdrawal of the British application in 1963, Cyprus' interest remained dormant until 1971 when it was reactivated almost simultaneously with Great Britain's renewed efforts to join.

On 19 December 1972, an association agreement was signed between Cyprus and the EEC. It went into effect on 1 June 1973. The agreement provided for the gradual elimination of trade obstacles for industrial and agricultural products between Cyprus and the EEC. The elimination of customs and other restrictions on trade would lead to a customs union after a ten-year transitional period which was divided into two stages. The first would be completed by June 1977 and the second by 1982.

The Turkish invasion of Cyprus in 1974, however, and its disastrous consequences for the economy of the island led to a delay in implementation of the association agreement. After successive extensions of the first stage, a protocol for the implementation of the second stage of the association agreement was signed in 1987 laying down the terms for the gradual establishment of a customs union.[4]

Under the protocol, the customs union will be implemented by the year 2001 or 2002 at the latest. Both Cyprus and the EEC (now the EU) are required to eliminate all tariff and quantitative restrictions on all manufactured goods and a number of agricultural products (mainly potatoes, citrus and other fruit, vegetables, and wine). Cyprus will progressively adopt the common customs tariff of the EU, completing the transition by the end of 1997.

APPLICATION FOR MEMBERSHIP

The close relationship established between Cyprus and the EEC with the signing of the 1987 customs union agreement, coupled with other developments in Europe and the European Communities (EC), encouraged the government of Cyprus to apply for full membership in 1990.[5] This was, of course, facilitated by the impressive bouncing back of the Cypriot economy from the setback caused by the Turkish invasion and occupation.[6]

It should be noted that the government of the Republic of Cyprus submitted the application for membership on behalf of the entire population of the island. The application was challenged by the Turkish Cypriot leadership, who 'rejected the right of the government of the Republic of Cyprus to speak for the whole of Cyprus in such an approach'.[7] The Turkish Cypriots argued that under the 1960 treaties and the constitution, they had the right to veto decisions on foreign policy issues, and Cyprus could not join an international organization in which Greece and Turkey are not members. The EC, however, rejected the Turkish Cypriot argument and 'following the logic of its established position, which is consistent with that of the United Nations where the legitimacy of the Government of Cyprus and non-recognition of the "Turkish Republic of Northern Cyprus" are concerned, felt that the application was admissible and initiated the procedures laid down by the Treaties in order to examine it'.[8]

Three years later, on 30 June 1993, the European Commission issued its *Opinion* on Cyprus' application, confirming the island's European character and vocation and concluding 'that the Community considers Cyprus as eligible for membership and that as soon as the prospect of a settlement [of the Cyprus question] is surer, the Community is ready to start the process with Cyprus that should eventually lead to its accession'.[9]

The *Opinion*, however, stated also that there were problems resulting from the *de facto* division of the island that needed to be addressed. It pointed out that 'the fundamental freedoms laid down by the [EEC] Treaty, and in particular freedom of movement of goods, people, services and capital, right of establishment and the universally recognized political, economic, social and cultural rights could not today be exercised over the entirety of the island's territory. These freedoms and rights would have to be guaranteed as part of a comprehensive settlement restoring constitutional arrangements covering the whole of the Republic of Cyprus.'[10]

The *Opinion* went a step further to suggest 'that Cyprus' integration with the Community implies a peaceful, balanced and lasting settlement of the Cyprus question – a settlement that will make it possible for the two communities to be reconciled, for confidence to be re-established and for their respective leaders to work together'.[11]

On 4 October 1993, the Council of the EU endorsed the *Opinion* and welcomed its positive message, reconfirming that Cyprus is eligible to become a member. The Council also supported the Commission's proposal for close co-operation with the Cypriot government in order to facilitate the economic, social, and political transition aiming at eventual integration of the island into the EU. To this end, the

Council invited the Commission to 'open substantive discussions forthwith with the Government of Cyprus to help it to prepare for the accession negotiations to follow later on under the best possible conditions'.[12]

In November 1993, substantive talks between the Commission and the government of Cyprus started. They continued until 1995 when they were successfully completed. The substantive talks, primarily at the technocratic level, covered a broad range of issues and their primary objective was to help the Cypriot authorities familiarize themselves with all the elements of the *acquis communautaire*, that is, the treaties, laws, rules, regulations, policies, and practices of the EU.[13]

In June 1994, the Corfu European Council, at which Cyprus–EU relations were examined, concluded that an essential stage in Cyprus' preparations for accession could be regarded as completed and that the next phase of enlargement of the EU will include Cyprus and Malta. This positive message was included in the *Conclusions* of the [Greek] Presidency as follows:

> The European Council welcomes the significant progress made regarding the application of Cyprus and Malta for accession to the European Union and considers that an essential stage in the preparation process could be regarded as completed.
>
> The Council asks the Council and the Commission to do their utmost to ensure that the negotiations with Malta and Cyprus with a view to the conclusion of the fourth financial protocols, intended in particular to support the efforts of Malta and Cyprus towards integration into the European Union, are brought to a rapid conclusion. The European Council notes that in these conditions the next phase of enlargement of the Union will involve Cyprus and Malta.[14]

The Corfu decision was reconfirmed by the European Council at its meetings at Essen (December 1994), Cannes (June 1995), Madrid (December 1995), and Florence (June 1996). At Cannes, it was also reaffirmed 'that negotiations on the accession of Malta and Cyprus to the Union will begin on the basis of Commission proposals, six months after the conclusion of the 1996 Intergovernmental Conference and taking the outcome of that Conference into account'.[15] It is also interesting to note that at the European Council meeting at Madrid, it was decided that Cyprus and Malta, together with the associated countries of Central and Eastern Europe, 'will be briefed regularly on the progress of discussions [at the Intergovernmental

Conference] and will be able to put their points of view at meetings with the Presidency of the European Union'.[16] The Intergovernmental Conference started in March 1996 and it is expected to last until the end of 1997.

In the meantime, at the meeting of the Council of General Affairs on 6 March 1995, and at the nineteenth meeting of the Cyprus–EU Association Council on 12 June 1995, it was decided that a pre-accession structured dialogue at various levels will be established between Cyprus and the EU. At the March meeting, Greece lifted its veto and agreed to a customs union established between the EU and Turkey beginning 1 January 1996.[17] At the same meeting, Greece also lifted its veto and allowed for the implementation of the fourth EU–Turkey financial protocol which provides for considerable financial aid to Turkey. According to the resolution, which was adopted at the association council meeting in June:

> the purpose of the [structured] dialogue will be to help to achieve the objective of Cyprus' accession, which both parties consider will benefit both of the island's communities and contribute to civil peace and reconciliation. In this connection the Council hereby renews the invitation made to the Commission to establish the necessary contacts with the Turkish Cypriot Community, in consultation with the Government of Cyprus, which will remain the European Union's sole interlocutor in the structured dialogue.[18]

The EU Council of General Affairs, at its meeting of 17 July 1995, confirmed the establishment and institutionalization of the structured dialogue, which will cover a broad range of issues, including home and justice affairs, and common foreign and security policy.

At the meeting of the Cyprus–EU Association Council in June 1995, the fourth financial protocol between Cyprus and the EU, which amounts to 74 million European Currency Units (ECUs), was also signed. It is interesting to note that the protocol has a pre-accession character and aims 'to facilitate Cyprus' economic transition with a view to its accession to the European Union'.[19] The protocol, which expires on 31 December 1998, contains the following important provision: 'Should Cyprus accede to the European Union during the period covered by this Protocol, arrangements will be negotiated to ensure a harmonious transition as regards financial aid from the system for the associate countries to that of Member States.'[20]

The European Parliament has also expressed its interest and support for Cyprus' accession to the EU. This support was clearly stated in a resolution passed in January 1995 confirming that Cyprus' 'membership is of importance to all Member States' and reiterating the island's 'vocation and its eligibility for membership of the Union'.[21]

The above presentation of developments in Cyprus–EU relations shows that Cyprus is on its way to becoming a full member of the EU and facing one of the biggest challenges it has been presented with since independence. Joining the fifteen-member European club is a challenge accompanied by both privileges and burdens which the eastern Mediterranean island seems ready and able to face successfully.

FACING THE CHALLENGE OF ACCESSION

Any country that seeks membership of the EU must meet several conditions and criteria. Among these are European identity, democratic institutions, respect for human rights, an open market economy, satisfactory level of economic development, and the ability to adopt the *acquis communautaire*, including the Maastricht Treaty.[22]

Cyprus has no problem in meeting any of these conditions. This was confirmed by the 1993 *Opinion* of the Commission which clearly states that the EU considers Cyprus eligible for membership, although reference is made to the need for a settlement of the political problem. Subsequent decisions of the Council, the European Council, and the European Parliament have also repeatedly confirmed that Cyprus is on its way to becoming a member of the EU.

In the Commission *Opinion* it was also stated 'that Cyprus' integration with the Community implies a peaceful, balanced and lasting settlement of the Cyprus question'.[23] This, however, seems no longer to be the position of the EU in the light of the decisions of the European Council taken at Corfu, Essen, Cannes, Madrid, and Florence which confirm that Cyprus will be included in the next phase of enlargement and accession negotiations will start six months after the conclusion of the Intergovernmental Conference. In these summit decisions, no reference is made and no link is implied between accession to the EU and settlement of the Cyprus problem.

As far as European identity and vocation is concerned, there is no doubt that historically and culturally Cyprus is an inalienable part of Europe. All aspects of life on the island – political, economic, social, and cultural – are based on and reflect its European heritage, values, and orientation. Nowhere else is this stated as clearly as in the *Opinion* of the Commission which points out the following:

> Cyprus' geographical position, the deep-lying bonds which, for two thousand years, have located the island at the very fount of European culture and civilization, the intensity of the European influence apparent in the values shared by the people of Cyprus and in the conduct of the cultural, political, economic and social life of its citizens, the wealth of its contacts of every kind with the Community, all these confer on Cyprus, beyond all doubt, its European identity and character and confirm its vocation to belong to the Community.[24]

When it comes to democracy and human rights, Cyprus subscribes to the same fundamental principles and values as the EU and its member states. This is evidenced by the stable democratic multiparty system of government which guarantees an open and fair political process to individuals and organized groups. The political parties on the island represent and reflect a broad range of views and positions covering the entire ideological spectrum. It can also be stated that one of the main characteristics of the political culture of the island is the overarching loyalty and commitment to democracy shared by all political forces. This commitment reflects a firm popular belief that only democratic societies based on pluralism, respect for human rights, and the rule of law can protect and promote freedom, justice, and social progress.

Cyprus is also known for its open and efficient economic system which is based on a commitment to the concept and principles of market economy with free competition. The island enjoys a stable and high rate of economic growth (4.5 per cent annually during the period 1991–95) which compares favourably with that of EU member states. Clearly, Cyprus meets most of the economic criteria which EU countries must meet before they can join the Economic and Monetary Union (EMU). Unemployment is negligible (2.6 per cent in 1995) and foreign labour is imported to cover shortages in some sectors, like tourism and construction. In 1995, the inflation rate was 2.6 per cent, the budget deficit was less than 3 per cent of GDP, and the public debt was approximately 54 per cent of the GDP.[25] The government of Cyprus is also in the process of liberalizing interest rates and bringing relevant legislation and policies in line with EU law and practices. It should also be noted that Cyprus has already unilaterally tied its currency to the European Currency Unit (ECU) while more than half of its foreign trade, both imports and exports, is conducted with the EU.

With regard to adopting the *acquis communautaire*, including the Maastricht Treaty, Cyprus is in a position to do that without any major difficulties.[26] A problem-free accession to the EU is also guaranteed by the fact that the Eurocentric foreign policy followed by Cyprus since the collapse of the former Soviet Union, the subsequent end of the Cold War, and the weakening of the Non-Aligned Movement enjoys overwhelming domestic support.[27] An extremely high percentage of the population has a strong sense of belonging to Europe and a belief that the future of a united, secure, and prosperous Cyprus lies in its accession to the EU. This view is shared by all political parties.

WHAT CYPRUS CAN CONTRIBUTE TO THE EU

Accession to the EU involves a two-way relationship. Cyprus has a lot to gain from it, but it can also make a contribution in the creation of a united Europe that will enjoy prosperity and security. The geographic location of the island is of considerable symbolic as well as substantive significance, as it constitutes Europe's last outpost in the eastern Mediterranean. Because of its strategic position, Cyprus can also contribute in the creation of a European security system that will safeguard the defence and security interests of the EU in the region. The significance of Cyprus as a strategic outpost will be more obvious with the development of a common foreign and security policy as provided by the Maastricht Treaty.[28]

It should also be pointed out that Cyprus has excellent relations with all the countries of the Middle East. In this regard, it can become an economic, political, and cultural link between the EU and that important geopolitical region. As a member of the EU, Cyprus could serve as a bridge and an advocate for peaceful co-operation among the peoples of Europe, the Mediterranean basin, and the Middle East.

Along the same lines, it can be added that Cyprus has already been chosen by many multinational firms as a location for their regional headquarters. Several thousand offshore companies also have established offices on the island to promote their business activities in the region. For many of these firms, Cyprus was an obvious choice because of its location, the availability of highly educated managerial and technical staff, the excellent transportation and communication networks, and other infrastructure including a legal system based on internationally accepted principles of jurisprudence. These assets will be used in the direct service of the common and shared interests of the EU and its member states upon Cyprus' accession.

THE EU AND THE CYPRUS QUESTION

The EU has taken a clear and firm position on the question of Cyprus and has always considered unacceptable the status quo created by the Turkish invasion of 1974 and the continued occupation of 37 per cent of the island's territory. This position was clearly stated on numerous occasions including resolutions by the European Council and the European Parliament.

The European Council at its meeting in Dublin (June 1990) issued a declaration on Cyprus, stating that the 'European Council, deeply concerned at the situation, fully reaffirms its previous declarations and its support for the unity, independence, sovereignty and territorial integrity of Cyprus in accordance with the relevant UN resolutions'.[29] In the same resolution, the European Council reiterates 'that the Cyprus problem affects EC–Turkey relations' and calls for 'the prompt elimination of the obstacles that are preventing the pursuit of effective intercommunal talks aimed at a just and viable solution to the question of Cyprus'.[30] More recently, at its meeting at Madrid (December 1995), the European Council once again reiterated 'the importance which it attaches to making substantial efforts to achieve a just and viable solution to the question of Cyprus in line with the United Nations Security Council resolutions, on the basis of a bi-zonal and bi-community federation'.[31]

The European Parliament has adopted similar resolutions calling for a peaceful settlement on Cyprus. In a resolution adopted in 1993, it 'reaffirms its conviction that the continuation of the status quo in Cyprus is unacceptable and poses wider dangers for the region'.[32] It also 'calls upon the Government of Turkey to withdraw its occupation forces from the Republic of Cyprus in accordance with the relevant UN resolutions and calls for the Turkish troops to be replaced by United Nations peacekeeping forces'.[33] In another resolution adopted in 1995, the European Parliament 'reiterates the views it has expressed in the past on the island's reunification in the form of a sovereign, independent, bizonal and bicommunal federation, in keeping with the relevant UN resolutions and, with a view to accession, in accordance with the *acquis communautaire* of the Union'.[34]

The EU has been a firm supporter of the efforts of the UN Secretary-General aimed at a just and lasting settlement of the problem in accordance with relevant UN resolutions and high-level agreements. Such a settlement will respect the sovereignty, independence, territorial integrity, and unity of a bizonal federal republic. It will also guarantee the civil, political, and cultural rights of all Cypriots without any discrimination or restriction.

The interest of the EU in promoting a settlement on the island was also manifested in the appointment by the Council of a European observer on the Cyprus problem in February 1994.[35] The senior official of the EU Commission, Serge Abou, who was appointed observer submitted three reports that confirm the lack of any progress in the search for a solution. In his last report, which was submitted in January 1995, he suggests that the EU has a role to play in Cyprus. In his words:

> the [inter-communal] talks have also shown that the issue of Cyprus' membership of the EU is now fixed in the minds of all those concerned, something which obviously gives the EU a particular responsibility, namely to flesh out the position adopted by the Corfu European Council on the accession process and to play an active part in efforts to find a solution to the Cyprus problem.[36]

In another expression of interest in the Cyprus problem, the Council of the European Union decided to appoint a representative of the presidency to monitor developments concerning the Cyprus peace process. In January 1996, the Italian diplomat Federico Di Roberto was the first one to be appointed representative of the Italian presidency (January–June 1996) in January 1996. After six months of consultations with the parties involved, he confirmed the lack of progress in the search for a political settlement, but pointed out that the efforts should continue, with the EU supporting UN initiatives. The Irish presidency of the EU (July–December 1996) continue to monitor developments on Cyprus with the appointment of an Irish representative, Kester Heaslip, who succeeded Di Roberto.

SUMMARY AND CONCLUSION

Cyprus is at the threshold of the EU and preparing to become a full member. But the Cyprus problem is still unresolved despite the many efforts made by the UN to find a solution based on a united, federal, and bizonal republic. The EU, which has repeatedly expressed its concern over the lack of a settlement on the island, is now in a unique position to play a role in bringing about permanent peace and stability on the Mediterranean island and in the region.

The parties involved in Cyprus are either part of, or have special relations with, the EU and can appreciate and support a European initiative on Cyprus. Greece is a member of the EU while Turkey, with the establishment of the customs union, is as close to the EU as a non-member state can be. Great Britain, a major partner in the EU and a guarantor power of the independence and unity of Cyprus under the 1960 settlement of the colonial issue, is in a privileged position to play a constructive role within and outside the EU context. The Greek Cypriots and the Turkish Cypriots are faced with a unique challenge and an opportunity to resolve their differences, reunite their island, and become part of the European integration process that will offer them the security and stability they have been longing for.

The institutions, legal order, principles and policies of the EU – known as the *acquis communautaire* – can provide a conducive framework (and more) in the search for a long-overdue political settlement on Cyprus. In fact, settlement and accession could go hand-in-hand and reinforce and supplement each other. In sum, the prospect of Cyprus' accession to the EU provides a unique opportunity for all parties concerned to rise to the occasion and show their commitment to the principles and values that are as vital to individual countries and their peoples as they are to the EU and the European family of nations.

8 Conclusions

> The roads to human power and to human knowledge lie close together and are nearly the same; nevertheless, on account of the pernicious and inveterate habit of dwelling on abstractions, it is safer to begin and raise the sciences from those foundations which have relation to practice, and let the active part be as the seal which prints and determines the contemplative counterpart.
>
> Francis Bacon

A COMPLEX PROBLEM

A fundamental fact of life has been the basic premise of this book: the world of nations is characterized by interaction and interdependence which find expression in various forms of conflict and co-operation. Peoples build states to organize their activities, facilitate their domestic and external relations, and provide focus for their national loyalties in a diverse yet interlocked world. As a composite entity combining population, government, sovereignty, territory, and recognition by the international community, the state is the major actor and centre of political power for the conduct of both domestic and external politics. Although the increasing number and significance of national and international, governmental and non-governmental, organizations present challenges to the sovereign state, it is safe to say that the international system is still a state-centric one. The world of nations remains basically an arena within which states compete in the quest, exercise, and demonstration of power as a means for the promotion of what they perceive to be their national interests.

A serious problem faced by a number of states, which confirms the state-centric nature of the world system, is the politicization of ethnicity and the transformation of ethnic groups into political groups demanding autonomy, statehood, or incorporation into a larger ethnic nation-state. The ethnic fragmentation of the population of a state, coupled with the politicization of ethnicity, undermines the unity of the state and causes trouble and changes in the international system.

As the present study has shown, a domestic ethnic conflict can lead to the breakdown of a state and also have far-reaching consequences for other states, international organizations, and world order. The intermingling of ethnic and non-ethnic interests, and internal and external factors in an ethnic conflict is almost inevitable under the present conditions of global interaction and interdependence.

The case of Cyprus has been used to provide the empirical background for the exploration of certain aspects and consequences of the politicization of ethnicity and the internationalization of domestic ethnic conflict. Cyprus is not only 'one of the most complex problems on earth'[1] facing statesmen, but it is also a unique challenge and opportunity for scholars endeavouring to study, understand, and explain the complex world within which nations live and interact. As Inis Claude epigrammatically wrote in the 1960s:

> One could hardly construct a 'problem case' more fully illustrative of the complexity of world politics in our time than the real-life case of Cyprus, that island beset by traditional antipathies between ethnic groups, torn by the pulls and pressures exerted by neighboring states interested in the fate of its constituent nationalities, agonized by the conflict between majority rule and minority rights, poised between colonial status and genuine independence, and exposed to the political winds of both the East–West and the North–South struggles.[2]

FINDINGS

In this final chapter, the major observations and conclusions of this study are presented. The empirical evidence has shown that the roots of the domestic Cypriot conflict lie in the fragmented ethnic, historical, social, and institutional foundations of the Cypriot state that came into being in 1960. Since 1974, however, following the invasion of the island by Turkey, foreign occupation has become the main element of the Cyprus problem. Despite four centuries of coexistence and physical intermingling, the Greek Cypriots and the Turkish Cypriots remain separate and distinct ethnic groups divided along linguistic, religious, cultural, and political lines. The preservation of their ethnic identity could be attributed to the presence of strong cross-boundary ethnic ties and loyalties with Greece and Turkey, the dominance of religious institutions, the divisive administrative and educational systems, and the polarizing effect of ethnopolitics. With the establishment of the Republic of Cyprus, the ethnic and political fragmentation inherited from the past were institutionalized and incorporated into the state apparatus and the political process. Communal dualism became the foundation of political structures and practices that prevented the development of cross-cutting national bonds, overarching loyalties, and a unifying political culture supportive of the Cypriot state. The perfect coincidence of ethnic and political cleavages had a mutually reinforcing effect. Ethnicity was brought into the political arena and the fair political game was transformed into an implacable ethnopolitical struggle. The release of primordial sentiments of ethnic identification and group-belonging turned the quest and exercise of political power into zero-sum polemics dominated by ethnic fanaticism. Ethnopolitical immobilization was further reinforced by mutual mistrust, suspicion, fear, animosity, and uncertainty that neither the elites nor the masses were able to transcend. The underlying dynamics and agony of majority–minority relations bred temptations and intransigence that eliminated any hopes for bargaining in a give-and-take manner. Finally, the widening psychological gap, the enduring political impasse, and the consolidating state paralysis led to armed ethnic confrontation and undermining of the biethnic Cypriot state.

The role played by cross-boundary ethnic ties in the generation and internationalization of the domestic ethnic conflict has been a significant one. Ethnic bonds between the two Cypriot ethnic groups and their motherlands were manifested and preserved through common language, shared religious beliefs and practices, close educational and athletic affiliations, similar cultural and social patterns, common values, identical national symbols such as the flag and the national anthem, and common ethnic holidays, historical legacies, and national heroes. These bonds cultivated and maintained diverse national loyalties and conflicting ethnopolitical goals among the Cypriots, who looked to Greece and Turkey for ethnic identification, belonging, and protection. When violence broke out, ethnic ties served as the primary cause and vehicle for Greek and Turkish involvement in Cyprus. Ethnic co-operation across boundaries took the form of tight alliances in the political, diplomatic, and military fields. External intervention along ethnic lines sharpened and widened the conflict, thus shifting the focus of repeated crises from the domestic Cypriot setting to the likelihood of an all-out confrontation across the Aegean. The internationalization of the conflict through ethnic channels made Cyprus the focal point of Greek–Turkish antagonism and also brought into play other international actors who took sides on the issue or tried to contain and resolve the conflict.

It was also demonstrated that interference by the motherlands in support of their local ethnic groups was a matter of mutual and public expectation. The active involvement of Greece and Turkey in the conflict was the corollary of the definition of common ethnic-based goals and policies by the two parties on each side of the ethnic line. Cross-boundary ethnic co-operation covered the military as well as the diplomatic front. On the Greek side, there were some fluctuations of the relations between Athens and Nicosia due to domestic factors, but overall their collaboration had a sound ethnic basis, especially with regard to Turkish confrontation. The initial goal of *enosis* and the subsequent adoption of independence reflected a shared conception of the settlement of the problem. On the Turkish side, there was a similar ethnic-oriented consensus between Ankara and the Turkish Cypriots reflected in the joint pursuit of partition. Turkey also played a dominant role in protecting the Turkish Cypriots and handling their external affairs at the international level. This was largely due to the weakness of the Turkish Cypriots and their lack of international recognition.

The involvement of the two mainlands in the Cypriot conflict had a spill-over effect on their relations. It revived old ethnic enmity, antagonism, fear, and suspicion that were reflected in official government policies and mass manifestations. Ethnic hostility was primarily expressed in brinkmanship tactics and military activities on both Cyprus and the two sides of the Aegean. The bilateral relations of the two countries in other fields – political, economic, commercial, and cultural – were also ethnicized and heavily damaged. Mounting ethnic tension and controversies destroyed almost all channels of interaction and constructive communication between Athens and Ankara, and reduced relations between the two countries to mere diplomatic representation. Rising hostility not only prevented the two rivals from practising bilateral diplomacy, but it also undermined mediation efforts undertaken by outside 'honest brokers'. Finally, the ethnicization and intermingling of internal and external issues sharpened and complicated the conflict, thus paving the way for direct confrontation between the two countries.

With regard to superpower involvement in Cyprus, it was shown that both the USA and the Soviet Union approached the issue in the broader context of East–West antagonism and polarization, and expressed concern over the impact that the conflict might have on the local and regional balance of power. The strategic significance of the island and the implications that the conflict might have on the domestic and foreign policies of the parties involved have been the major reasons behind American and Soviet involvement in the dispute. The USA intervened to resolve repeated crises through quiet diplomacy, contain the conflict, and prevent a Greek–Turkish war. The ultimate objective of US mediation efforts and peace plans was a permanent settlement of the problem that would eliminate the causes of ethnic friction, establish Western control over Cyprus, and safeguard NATO security interests in the region. The Soviet Union saw the conflict as an opportunity to expand its influence in Cyprus and the region, and benefit from the disruption of NATO's south-eastern flank. Moscow sought to counteract American policies and goals by siding with actors holding anti-Western positions and undermining attempts at a pro-Western solution of the problem. Although both superpowers had to make occasional adjustments to their attitudes, their fundamental goals and policies remained consistent, and reflected global rivalry and bipolarity. The ethnic aspects of the Cypriot conflict were overshadowed in Washington and Moscow by strategic and ideological goals prescribed by antagonistic Cold War doctrines.

Regarding the impact of superpower intervention in Cyprus, a distinction should be drawn between the management of sharp crises involving armed clashes and the search for a lasting settlement of the problem at large. During periods of crisis, US and Soviet intervention had a moderating and containing effect on the crisis. This effect, however, was not due to collaboration between the two superpowers. It was, rather, either the result of mediation efforts by the USA, which was especially concerned over the risk of an escalation of the crisis, or it was the result of a balancing effect of US–Soviet confrontation. With regard to attempts at a permanent settlement of the problem, superpower involvement proved ineffective. The transformation of the ethnic conflict into a Cold War dispute connoting East–West rivalry and polarization prevented the two superpowers from making a constructive contribution towards a settlement of the problem. Attempts at a lasting settlement made by the USA were aimed at promotion of Western interests and, therefore, they were undermined by the Soviet Union.

The rivalry between Greece and Turkey over Cyprus had a disintegrating effect on NATO. The two Aegean allies, driven by constraints and considerations emanating from their ethnic ties with the contesting Cypriot ethnic groups, took actions contradicting their alliance bonds and commitments. Supersedure of ethnic over alliance commitments was manifested in diplomatic as well as military confrontations that at times virtually paralysed the south-eastern flank of NATO. Other negative ramifications of ethnic friction included the rise of disturbing controversies among other NATO members about the handling of the conflict. The USA and Britain tried to get NATO involved and use it as an instrument for the advancement of a pro-Western settlement of the conflict, but they failed for the following reasons: first, the members of the Western alliance at large failed to reach an agreement on how to handle the issue. Besides the USA and Britain (that is, the two leading NATO members having vital security interests in the island and the region), no other allies showed any enthusiasm in becoming involved in a conflict that they considered to be a British post-colonial problem; secondly, the conflict was politicized in the broader context of East–West antagonism, and the Soviet Union adamantly resisted intervention by the Western alliance in a small strategic non-aligned island-state; thirdly, the Greek side, fearing a favourable treatment of Turkey, rejected NATO offers for peacekeeping and peacemaking; fourthly, the UN option was open, tempting, and promising for the Greek Cypriots, who were looking for ways to neutralize Turkish and Western pressure. Because of these reasons, the Anglo-American initiatives failed, and NATO hardly played any role in containing the conflict.

The conflict over Cyprus repeatedly threatened international peace and security. The intensity and intermingling of domestic and external ethnopolitics, coupled with the presence of cross-boundary ethnic ties and controversies, sharpened and widened the domestic conflict. The threat of an all-out Greek–Turkish confrontation and the likelihood of superpower military involvement became real and imminent as the opposing ethnic factions, driven by ethnic fanaticism, proved incapable of negotiating in a give-and-take manner, and resorted to the use of force for the settlement (rather perplexing) of the conflict. The assumption of the primary peacekeeping and peacemaking roles by the UN was the corollary of a general assessment within and outside the UN that the conflict on Cyprus presented a threat to international peace and security under the UN Charter.

It was also demonstrated that the UN became a channel for the internationalization of the conflict. Since the world organization is a political institution reflecting the prevailing will of its members, it is susceptible to political exploitation. The Greek Cypriots used it to politicize the ethnic conflict at the global level and take advantage of favourable international political forces. In doing so, they used the UN as a platform for political debate, a ground for diplomatic manoeuvring, a channel for communication and publicization, a means for the mobilization of governments and world public opinion, and an instrument for collective legitimization and support.

In recent years, Cyprus has also been on the agenda of the EU but so far (summer 1996) there has been no substantive involvement in the efforts to resolve the problem. This, however, might happen in the future as Cyprus is preparing to join the European integration process and the need for a settlement on the island is becoming more urgent. The challenge and the opportunity is knocking at the door of all those involved and concerned. The EU, which has been a staunch supporter of the unity and independence of Cyprus, and is now becoming a major actor in the post-Cold War world order, is presented with a unique chance to contribute in the search for a solution. Cyprus' accession may very well turn out to be a useful tool for solving the problems that have been plaguing the island since independence.

TYING IT ALL TOGETHER

The conclusions drawn from the case of Cyprus about the interaction between ethnic conflict and the international political environment reaffirm that the world of nations is a global community caught amidst forces of independence and interdependence. Ethnic groups, states, and international organizations are struggling for power and order in a global arena that seems to be condemned to tension and disorder. On the one hand, peoples are striving to create and maintain independent states encompassing national individuality, shared values, and common interests, while on the other hand, patterns of interdependence inherent in the international system dictate interaction that results in conflict and co-operation, and the creation of international organizations. The internal dynamics of states and the global dynamics of the world system are thus interwoven to produce the complexities of domestic and international politics that are puzzling statesmen, scholars, and laymen.

The sources of domestic and international political complexities are countless. This book has focused on one of them: the ethnic heterogeneity of the world, a complex phenomenon in itself. The findings of this study cannot lead to generalizations about the political dimension of ethnicity or the ethnic dimension of politics, but they do confirm that ethnicity is an important factor that deserves special attention from those endeavouring to understand and explain the complexity, tension, and disorder within and among states. The rise of ethno-nationalism to a major political force in the twentieth century is perhaps the greatest challenge the nation-state has ever faced. Its political implications affect not only individual multiethnic states, but they also have an impact on inter-state relations and the overall performance and stability of the international system. As the present study has shown, ethnicity can be easily politicized and turned into a lever of action that can greatly influence the behaviour and relations of states and international organizations. In this regard, the ethnic factor can be seen as an important variable for the understanding of international relations.

Epilogue

Throughout the various stages of the Cyprus problem, many efforts have been made to find a solution but all of them have failed. The two communities are still separated by a widening economic gap, barbed wire, trenches, and minefields which neither side nor third parties can cross. Most of the peace efforts were carried out by the UN or in the name of the UN.

Although all UN efforts have failed, blaming the UN for failure in Cyprus would be an over-simplification. The UN is nothing else than a microcosm and a reflection of the real world which has many problems and few solutions, or no solutions at all in some cases. As an institutional arrangement through which countries interact, the UN can be efficient only if all parties involved have the political will and commitment to overcome difficulties and make genuine efforts to look for solutions. In the case of Cyprus, this has not been the case.

In a recent report to the Security Council addressing issues related to confidence-building between the two communities, the Secretary-General pointed out that no solution can be found and the status quo is unlikely 'to change on an agreed basis as long as there is, both on the island and in the region, a lack of political will for such change'.[1] Then he went on to point the finger in the direction where he thinks more has to be done in order to bridge the gap and reach a settlement. He referred to 'an already familiar scenario: the absence of agreement due essentially to the lack of political will on the Turkish Cypriot side'.[2] It is no secret, of course, that the policies and positions of the Turkish Cypriot leadership are shaped in Ankara.

But although all UN efforts have failed and no settlement has been reached so far, the continuing *de facto* division of the island, which was brought about by force, has not gained legitimacy and nobody considers it a solution. Therefore, there is still hope for a negotiated settlement on the basis of a unified bizonal federal republic on the basis of the high-level agreements of 1977 and 1979. These agreements were a significant turning point because, for the first time, the two communities agreed to seek a settlement on the basis of a bizonal bicommunal federal republic. The first agreement was reached between Makarios and Denktash on 12 February 1977 and consisted of the following four points:[3]

1 We are seeking an independent, Non-Aligned bicommunal Federal Republic.

2 The territory under the administration of each community should be discussed in the light of economic viability or productivity and land ownership.

3 Questions of principle, like freedom of movement, freedom of settlement, the right of property and other specific matters, are open for discussion, taking into consideration the fundamental basis of a bicommunal federal system and certain practical difficulties which may arise for the Turkish Cypriot community.

4 The powers and functions of the central federal government will be such as to safeguard the unity of the country, having regard to the bicommunal character of the State.

The second high-level agreement was reached between President Spyros Kyprianou and the Turkish Cypriot leader Rauf Denktash on 19 May 1979 and basically reconfirmed the 1977 Makarios–Denktash agreement. The high-level agreements provided the basic guidelines in the search for a settlement on Cyprus during the presidencies of Kyprianou (1977–88), George Vassiliou (1988–93), and Glafcos Clerides (1993–). To this day (summer 1996), the high-level agreements are generally considered an acceptable framework and a basis for the search for a peaceful political settlement on Cyprus.

Under the circumstances, a settlement based on a bizonal and bicommunal form of federation seems to be reasonable, feasible, and viable – assuming of course that all citizens will enjoy equal rights and opportunities all over the island. Given the realities of Cyprus – geography, economy, size, distribution of natural resources, demography, and the political failures of the past – a federal solution seems to be a pragmatic way out of the stalemate.

A solution to the Cyprus problem, however, cannot be an abstract construction. The settlement should meet the basic needs of the whole population and the requirements of a just, viable, functional, and lasting solution. Such a solution, by definition, will have no room for foreign armies or occupation forces. It will also be more appealing if it meets the requirements of the *acquis communautaire*, and its implementation precedes or coincides with Cyprus' accession to the EU. But this scenario, by itself, cannot be a magic formula unless it has substantive and substantial support from all parties involved and concerned. The Cypriots themselves should realize that a remedy to their problems can be sought through pacific means, evolutionary peaceful change, political and administrative adjustments, renovation of political thinking, and the cultivation of conciliatory attitudes. Certainly, the whole population will be better off if the island ceases to be a place of arms and confrontation, and the present status quo is replaced by a meaningful political order that will bring the two communities together under conditions of working and peaceful coexistence.

The forthcoming accession of Cyprus to the EU can be an excellent opportunity for all parties involved to work out their differences and benefit from the constructive support that third parties can offer.

APPENDIX 1   Treaty of Establishment

Signed at Nicosia, 16 August 1960; came into force on the date of signature in accordance with article xii.

The United Kingdom of Great Britain and Northern Ireland, the Kingdom of Greece and the Republic of Turkey of the one part and the Republic of Cyprus of the other part;

Desiring to make provisions to give effect to the Declaration made by the Government of the United Kingdom on the 17th of February, 1959, during the Conference at London, in accordance with the subsequent Declarations made at the Conference by the Foreign Ministers of Greece and Turkey, by the Representative of the Greek Cypriot Community and by the Representative of the Turkish Cypriot Community;

Taking note of the terms of the Treaty of Guarantee signed to-day by the Parties to this Treaty;

Have agreed as follows:

Article I

The territory of the Republic of Cyprus shall comprise the Island of Cyprus, together with the islands lying off its coast, with the exception of the two areas defined in Annex A to this Treaty, which areas shall remain under the sovereignty of the United Kingdom. These areas are in this Treaty referred to as the Akrotiri Sovereign Base Area and the Dhekelia Sovereign Base Area.

Article II

1. The Republic of Cyprus shall accord to the United Kingdom the rights set forth in Annex B to this Treaty.
2. The Republic of Cyprus shall co-operate fully with the United Kingdom to ensure the security and effective operation of the military bases situated in the Akrotiri Sovereign Base Area and the Dhekelia Sovereign Base Area, and the full enjoyment by the United Kingdom of the rights conferred by this Treaty.

Article III

The Republic of Cyprus, Greece, Turkey and the United Kingdom undertake to consult and co-operate in the common defence of Cyprus.

Article IV

The arrangements concerning the status of the forces in the Island of Cyprus shall be those contained in Annex C to this Treaty.

Article V

The Republic of Cyprus shall secure to everyone within its jurisdiction human rights and fundamental freedoms comparable to those set out in Section I of the European Convention for the Protection of Human Rights and Fundamental Freedoms signed at Rome on the 4th of November, 1950, and the Protocol to that Convention signed at Paris on the 20th of March 1952.

Article VI

The Arrangements concerning the nationality of persons affected by the establishment of the Republic of Cyprus shall be those obtained in Annex D to this Treaty.

Article VII

The Republic of Cyprus and the United Kingdom accept and undertake to carry out the necessary financial and administrative arrangements to settle questions arising out of the termination of British administration in the territory of the Republic of Cyprus. These arrangements are set forth in Annex E to this Treaty.

Article VIII

1. All international obligations and responsibilities of the Government of the United Kingdom shall henceforth, in so far as they may be held to have application to the Republic of Cyprus, be assumed by the Government of Cyprus.
2. The international rights and benefits heretofore enjoyed by the Government of the United Kingdom in virtue of their application to the territory of the Republic of Cyprus shall henceforth be enjoyed by the Government of the Republic of Cyprus.

Article IX

The Parties of this Treaty accept and undertake to carry out the arrangements concerning trade, commerce and other matters set forth in Annex F to this Treaty.

Article X

Any question or difficulty as to the interpretation of the provisions of this Treaty shall be settled as follows:
1. Any question or difficulty that may arise over the operation of the military requirements of the United Kingdom, or concerning the provisions of this Treaty in so far as they affect the status, rights and obligations of United Kingdom forces associated with them under the terms of this Treaty, or of Greek, Turkish and Cypriot forces, shall ordinarily be settled by negotiation between the Tripartite Headquarters of the Republic of Cyprus, Greece and Turkey and the authorities of the armed forces of the United Kingdom.
2. Any question or difficulty as to the interpretation of the provisions of this Treaty on which agreement cannot be reached by negotiation between the military authorities in the cases described above, or, in other cases, by negotiation between the Parties concerned through diplomatic channel, shall be referred for final decision to a tribunal appointed for the purpose, which shall be composed of four representatives, one each to be nominated by the Government of the United Kingdom, the Government of Greece, the Government of Turkey and the Government of the Republic of Cyprus, together with an independent chairman nominated by the President of the International Court of Justice. If the President is a citizen of the United Kingdom and Colonies or of the Republic of Cyprus or of Greece or of Turkey, the Vice-President shall be requested to act; and, if he also is such a citizen, the next senior Judge of the Court.

Article XI

The Annexes to this Treaty shall have force and effect as integral parts of this Treaty.

Article XII

This Treaty shall enter into force on signature by all Parties to it.

APPENDIX 2 Treaty of Guarantee

Signed at Nicosia, 16 August 1960; came into force on the date of signature, in accordance with article v.

The Republic of Cyprus on the one part, and Greece, Turkey and the United Kingdom of Great Britain and Northern Ireland of the other part,
1. Considering that the recognition and maintenance of the independence, territorial integrity and security of the Republic of Cyprus, as established and regulated by the Basic Articles of the Constitution, are in their common interest,
2. Desiring to co-operate to ensure respect for the state of affairs created by the Constitution,
Have agreed as follows:

Article I

The Republic of Cyprus undertakes to ensure the maintenance of its independence, territorial integrity and security, as well as respect for its Constitution.

It undertakes not to participate, in whole or in part, in any political or economic union with any state whatsoever. It accordingly declares prohibited any activity likely to promote, directly or indirectly, either union with any other State or partition of the Island.

Article II

Greece, Turkey and the United Kingdom, taking note of the undertakings of the Republic of Cyprus set out in Article I of the present Treaty, recognize and guarantee the independence, territorial integrity and security of the Republic of Cyprus, and also the state of affairs established by the Basic Articles of its Constitution.

Greece, Turkey and the United Kingdom likewise undertake to prohibit, so far as concerns them, any activity aimed at promoting, directly or indirectly, either union of Cyprus with any other State or partition of the Island.

Article III

The Republic of Cyprus, Greece and Turkey undertake to respect the integrity of the areas retained under United Kingdom sovereignty at the time of the establishment of the Republic of Cyprus, and guarantee the use and enjoyment by the United Kingdom of the rights to be secured to it by the Republic of Cyprus in accordance with the Treaty concerning the Establishment of the Republic of Cyprus signed at Nicosia on today's date.

Article IV

In the event of a breach of the provisions of the present Treaty, Greece, Turkey and the United Kingdom undertake to consult together with respect to the representations or measures necessary to ensure observance of those provisions.

In so far as common or concerned action may not prove possible, each of the three guaranteeing Powers reserves the right to take action with the sole aim of re-establishing the state of affairs created by the present Treaty.

Article V

The present Treaty shall enter into force on the date of signature. The original texts of the present Treaty shall be deposited at Nicosia.

The High Contracting Parties shall proceed as soon as possible to the registration of the present Treaty with the Secretariat of the United Nations, in accordance with Article 102 of the Charter of the United Nations.

APPENDIX 3 Treaty of Alliance

Signed at Nicosia, 16 August 1960; came into force on the date of signature in accordance with article vi.

The Kingdom of Greece, the Republic of Turkey and the Republic of Cyprus,
1. In their common desire to uphold peace and preserve the security of each of them,
2. Considering that their efforts for the preservation of peace and security are in conformity with the purposes and principles of the United Nations Charter,
    Have agreed as follows:

Article I

The High Contracting Parties undertake to co-operate for their common defense and to consult together on the problems raised by that defense.

Article II

The High Contracting Parties undertake to resist any attack or aggression, direct or indirect, directed against the independence or the territorial integrity of the Republic of Cyprus.

Article III

For the purpose of this alliance, and in order to achieve the object mentioned above, a Tripartite Headquarters shall be established on the territory of the Republic of Cyprus.

Article IV

Greece and Turkey shall participate in the Tripartite Headquarters so established with the military contingents laid down in Additional Protocol No. I annexed to the present Treaty.
    The said contingents shall provide for the training of the army of the Republic of Cyprus.

Article V

The Command of the Tripartite Headquarters shall be assumed in rotation, for a period of one year each, by a Greek, Turkish and Cypriot General Officer, who shall be appointed respectively by the Governments of Greece and Turkey and by the President and the Vice-President of the Republic of Cyprus.

Article VI

The present Treaty shall enter into force on the date of signature.

The High Contracting Parties shall proceed as soon as possible with the registration of the present Treaty with the Secretariat of the United Nations, in accordance with Article 102 of the United Nations Charter.

ADDITIONAL PROTOCOL No. I

1. The Greek and Turkish contingents which are to participate in the Tripartite Headquarters shall comprise respectively 950 Greek officers, non-commissioned officers and men, and 650 Turkish officers, non-commissioned officers and men.
2. The President and Vice-President of the Republic of Cyprus, acting in agreement, may request the Greek and Turkish Governments to increase or reduce the Greek and Turkish contingents.
3. It is agreed that the sites of the cantonments for the Greek and Turkish contingents participating in the Tripartite Headquarters, their juridical status, facilities and exemptions in respect of customs and taxes, as well as other immunities and privileges and any other military and technical questions concerning the Headquarters mentioned above shall be determined by a Special Convention which shall come into force not later than the Treaty of Alliance.
4. It is likewise agreed that the Tripartite Headquarters shall be set up not later than three months after the completion of the tasks of the Mixed Commission for the Cyprus Constitution and shall consist, in the initial period, of a limited number of officers charged with the training of the armed forces of the Republic of Cyprus. The Greek and Turkish contingents mentioned above will arrive in Cyprus on the date of signature of the Treaty of Alliance.

ADDITIONAL PROTOCOL No. II

1. A Committee shall be set up consisting of the Ministers for Foreign Affairs of the Republic of Cyprus, Greece and Turkey. It shall constitute the supreme political body of the Tripartite Alliance and may take cognizance of any question concerning the Alliance which the Governments of the three Allied countries shall agree to submit.

2. The Committee of Ministers shall meet in ordinary session once a year. In a matter of urgency the Committee of Ministers can be convened in special session by its Chairman at the request of one of the members of the Alliance. Decisions of the Committee of Ministers shall be unanimous.

3. The Committee of the Ministers shall be presided over in rotation, and for a period of one year, by each of the three Foreign Ministers. It will hold its ordinary sessions, unless it is decided otherwise, in the capital of the Chairman's country. The Chairman shall, during the year in which he holds office, preside over sessions of the Committee of Ministers, both ordinary and special.

The Committee may set up subsidiary bodies whenever it shall judge it to be necessary for the fulfillment of its task.

4. The Tripartite Headquarters established by the Treaty of Alliance shall be responsible to the Committee of Ministers in the performance of its functions. It shall submit to it, during the Committee's ordinary session, an annual report comprising a detailed account of the Headquarter's activities.

APPENDIX 4 President Makarios' Thirteen-Point Proposal to Amend the Constitution

Submitted to Vice-President Kutchuk, 30 November 1963.
Suggested Measures to Facilitate the Smooth Functioning of the State and Remove Certain Causes of Inter-Communal Friction.

The Constitution of the Republic of Cyprus, in its present form, creates many difficulties in the smooth government of the State and impedes the development and progress of the country. It contains many sui generis provisions conflicting with internationally accepted democratic principles and creates sources of friction between Greek and Turkish Cypriots.

At the Conference at Lancaster House in February, 1959, which I was invited to attend as leader of the Greek Cypriots, I raised a number of objections and expressed strong misgivings regarding certain provisions of the Agreement arrived at Zurich between the Greek and Turkish Governments and adopted by the British Government. I tried very hard to bring about the change of at least some provisions of that Agreement. I failed, however, in that effort and I was faced with the dilemma either of signing the Agreement as it stood or of rejecting it with all the grave consequences which would have ensued. In the circumstances I had no alternative but to sign the Agreement. This was the course dictated to me by necessity.

The three years' experience since the coming into operation of the Constitution, which was based on the Zurich and London Agreements, has made clear the necessity for revision of at least some of those provisions which impede the smooth functioning and development of the State.

I believe that the intention of those who drew up the Agreement at Zurich was to create an independent State, in which the interests of the Turkish Cypriot Community were safeguarded, but it could not have been their intention that the smooth functioning and development of the country should be prejudiced or thwarted, as has in fact been the case.

One of the consequences of the difficulties created by certain constitutional provisions is to prevent the Greeks and the Turks of Cyprus from co-operating in a spirit of understanding and friendship, to undermine the relations between them and cause them to draw further apart instead of closer together, to the detriment of the well-being of the people of Cyprus as a whole.

This situation causes me, as President of the State, great concern. It is necessary to resolve certain of the difficulties by the removal of some at least of the obstacles to the smooth functioning and development of the State.

146

With this end in view I have outlined below the immediate measures which I propose to be taken.

1. The right of veto of the President and the Vice-President of the Republic to be abandoned.

2. The Vice-President of the Republic to deputize for the President of the Republic in case of his temporary absence or incapacity to perform his duties.

3. The Greek President of the House of Representatives and the Turkish Vice-President to be elected by the House as a whole and not as at present the President by the Greek Members of the House and the Vice-President by the Turkish Members of the House.

4. The Vice-President of the House of Representatives to deputize for the President of the House in case of his temporary absence or incapacity to perform his duties.

5. The Constitutional provisions regarding separate majorities for enactment of certain laws by the House of Representatives to be abolished.

6. Unified Municipalities to be established.

7. The administration of Justice to be unified.

8. The division of the Security Forces into Police and Gendarmerie to be abolished.

9. The numerical strength of the Security Forces and the Defense Forces to be determined by law.

10. The proportion of the participation of Greek and Turkish Cypriots in the composition of the Public Service and the Forces of the Republic to be modified in proportion to the ratio of the population of Greek and Turkish Cypriots.

11. The number of the Members of the Public Service Commission to be reduced from ten to five.

12. All decisions of the Public Service Commission to be taken by simple majority.

13. The Greek Communal Chamber to be abolished.

APPENDIX 5 UN Security Council Resolution on the Creation of the United Nations Peacekeeping Force in Cyprus (UNFICYP)

Resolution no. 186, adopted 4 March 1964.

The Security Council,

Noting that the present situation with regard to Cyprus is likely to threaten international peace and security and may further deteriorate unless additional measures are taken to maintain peace and seek out a durable solution,

Considering the positions taken by the parties in relation to the Treaties signed at Nicosia on 16 August 1960,

Having in mind the relevant provisions of the Charter of the United Nations and its Article 2, paragraph 4, which reads: 'All members shall refrain in their international relations from the threat or use of force against the territorial integrity or political independence of any State, or in any other manner inconsistent with the Purposes of the United Nations',

1. Calls upon all Member States, in conformity with their obligations under the Charter of the United Nations, to refrain from any action or threat of action likely to worsen the situation in the sovereign Republic of Cyprus, or to endanger international peace;

2. Asks the Government of Cyprus, which has the responsibility for the maintenance and restoration of law and order, to take all additional measures necessary to stop violence and bloodshed in Cyprus;

3. Calls upon the communities in Cyprus and their leaders to act with the utmost restraint;

4. Recommends the creation, with the consent of the Government of Cyprus, of a United Nations peace-keeping force in Cyprus. The composition and size of the Force shall be established by the Secretary-General, in consultation with the Governments of Cyprus, Greece, Turkey, and the United Kingdom of Great Britain and Northern Ireland. The commander of the Force shall be appointed by the Secretary-General and report to him. The Secretary-General, who shall keep the Governments providing the Force fully informed, shall report periodically to the Security Council on its operation.

5. Recommends that the function of the Force should be, in the interest of preserving international peace and security, to use its best efforts to prevent a recurrence of fighting and, as necessary, to contribute to the maintenance and restoration of law and order and a return to normal conditions;

6. Recommends that the stationing of the Force shall be for a period of three months, all costs pertaining to it being met, in a manner to be agreed upon by them, by the Governments providing the contingents and by the Government of Cyprus. The Secretary-General may also accept voluntary contributions for that purpose;

7. Recommends further that the Secretary-General designate, in agreement with the Government of Cyprus and the Governments of Greece, Turkey and the United Kingdom, a mediator, who shall use his best endeavours with the representatives of the communities and also with the aforesaid four Governments, for the purpose of promoting a peaceful solution and an agreed settlement of the problem confronting Cyprus, in accordance with the Charter of the United Nations, having in mind the well-being of the people of Cyprus as a whole and the preservation of international peace and security. The mediator shall report periodically to the Secretary-General on his efforts.

8. Requests the Secretary-General to provide, from funds of the United Nations, as appropriate, for the remuneration and expenses of the mediator and his staff.

APPENDIX 6 Security Council Resolution Deploring the Unilateral Turkish Cypriot Declaration of Independence in Northern Cyprus

Resolution no. 541, adopted 18 November 1983.tpb 10pt

The Security Council,

Having heard the statement of the Foreign Minister of the Government of the Republic of Cyprus,

Concerned at the declaration by the Turkish Cypriot authorities issued on 15 November 1983 which purports to create an independent state in northern Cyprus,

Considering that this declaration is incompatible with the Treaty concerning the establishment of the Republic of Cyprus and the 1960 Treaty of Guarantee,

Considering therefore that the attempt to create a 'Turkish Republic in Northern Cyprus' is invalid, and will contribute to a worsening of the situation in Cyprus,

Reaffirming its resolutions 365 (1974) and 367 (1975),

Aware of the need for a solution of the Cyprus problem based on the mission of good offices undertaken by the Secretary-General,

Affirming its continuing support for the United Nations Peace-Keeping Force in Cyprus,

Taking note of the Secretary-General's statement of 17 November 1983,

1. Deplores the declaration of the Turkish Cypriot authorities of the purported secession of part of the Republic of Cyprus,

2. Considers the declaration referred to above as legally invalid and calls for its withdrawal,

3. Calls for the urgent and effective implementation of its resolutions 365 (1974) and 367 (1975),

4. Requests the Secretary-General to pursue his mission of good offices in order to achieve the earliest possible progress towards a just and lasting settlement in Cyprus,

5. Calls upon the parties to co-operate fully with the Secretary-General in his mission of good offices,

6. Calls upon all states to respect the sovereignty, independence, territorial integrity and non-alignment of the Republic of Cyprus,

7. Calls upon all states not to recognize any Cypriot state other than the Republic of Cyprus,

8. Calls upon all states and the two communities in Cyprus to refrain from any action which might exacerbate the situation,

9. Requests the Secretary-General to keep the Security Council fully informed.

APPENDIX 7   UN General Assembly Resolution on the Sovereignty and Independence of Cyprus

Resolution no. 2077 (XX), adopted 18 December 1965.

The General Assembly,

Having considered the question of Cyprus,

Recalling the Security Council Resolutions (S/5575 of 4 March 1964, S/5603 of 13 March 1964, S/5778 of 20 June 1964, S/5868 of 5 August 1964, S/5987 of 25 September 1964, S/6121 of 18 December 1964, S/6247 of 19 March 1965, and S/6569 of 10 August 1965) and Consensus (11 August 1964) adopted with regard to Cyprus,

Recalling the declaration adopted by the Conference of Heads of State or Government of Non-Aligned Countries held in Cairo on 10 October 1964 regarding the question of Cyprus (A/5763),

Noting the report of the United Nations Mediator on Cyprus submitted to the Secretary-General on March 26 1965 (A/6017),

Noting further that the Government of Cyprus is committed through its declaration of intent and memorandum (A/6039) to:

(a) The full application of human rights to all citizens of Cyprus, irrespective of race or religion,

(b) The ensuring of minority rights, and

(c) The safeguarding of the above rights as contained in the above declaration memorandum,

1. Takes cognizance of the fact that the Republic of Cyprus, as an equal member of the United Nations, is, in accordance with the Charter, entitled to and should enjoy full sovereignty and complete independence without any foreign intervention or interference;

2. Calls upon all states, in conformity with their obligations under the Charter, and in particular article 2, paragraphs 1 and 4, to respect the sovereignty, unity, independence and territorial integrity of the Republic of Cyprus and to refrain from any intervention directed against it;

3. Recommends to the Security Council the continuation of the United Nations mediation work in conformity with the resolution of 4 March 1964 (S/5575).

APPENDIX 8 UN General Assembly Resolution on the Withdrawal of Foreign Armed Forces from Cyprus

Resolution no. 3212 (XXIX), adopted 1 November 1974 by 117 votes in favour, none against and no abstentions.

The General Assembly,

Having considered the question of Cyprus,

Gravely concerned about the continuation of the Cyprus crisis, which constitutes a threat to international peace and security,

Mindful of the need to solve this crisis without delay by peaceful means, in accordance with the purposes and principles of the United Nations,

Having heard the statements in the debate and taking note of the Report of the Special Political Committee on the Question of Cyprus,

1. Calls upon all states to respect the sovereignty, independence, territorial integrity and non-alignment of the Republic of Cyprus and to refrain from all acts and interventions directed against it;

2. Urges the speedy withdrawal of all foreign armed forces and foreign military presence and personnel from the Republic of Cyprus and the cessation of all foreign interference in its affairs;

3. Considers that the constitutional system of the Republic of Cyprus concerns the Greek–Cypriot and Turkish–Cypriot communities;

4. Comments the contacts and negotiations taking place on an equal footing, with the good offices of the Secretary-General between the representatives of the two communities, and calls for the continuation with a view to reaching freely a mutually acceptable political settlement based on their fundamental and legitimate rights;

5. Considers that all the refugees should return to their homes in safety and calls upon the parties concerned to undertake urgent measures to that end;

6. Expresses the hope that, if necessary, further efforts including negotiations can take place, within the framework of the United Nations, for the purpose of implementing the provisions of the present resolution, thus ensuring to the Republic of Cyprus its fundamental right to independence, sovereignty and territorial integrity;

7. Requests the Secretary-General to continue to provide United Nations humanitarian assistance to all parts of the population of Cyprus and calls upon all states to contribute to that effort;

8. Calls upon all parties to continue to cooperate fully with the United Nations Peace-Keeping Force in Cyprus, which may be strengthened if necessary;

9. Requests the Secretary-General to continue to lend his good offices to the parties concerned;

10. Further requests the Secretary-General to bring the present resolution to the attention of the Security Council.

APPENDIX 9 Letter from Chairman Khrushchev to President Johnson

7 February 1964

Dear Mr President,

I deem it necessary to address you on behalf of the Soviet Government concerning the fact that recently the situation around Cyprus has become greatly inflamed, giving rise to the danger of serious international complications in the Mediterranean area. The reason for the tension which has arisen are well known: disagreements, long ago heated up from abroad, between the two communities on Cyprus – the Greek, comprising the majority of the population, and the Turkish – are being exploited as a pretext for unconcealed intervention in the international affairs of the Republic of Cyprus – a sovereign, independent state, a member of the United Nations.

Several powers, flouting the principles of the UN Charter and generally accepted norms of international law, are now trying to foist on the people and Government of Cyprus a solution which these powers want of problems which concern only the Cypriots; indeed they even represent the matter as if it were possible to bring Cyprus a solution of these internal problems only on foreign bayonets. In doing this, some variants of 'solutions' are being discussed – for example dispatch to Cyprus of NATO troops or troops of particular NATO countries – although in essence all these variants have one aim – actual occupation by NATO armed forces of the Republic of Cyprus which adheres to a policy of nonalignment with military blocs. In other words, the matter involves crude encroachment on the sovereignty, independence, and freedom of the Republic of Cyprus, an attempt to place this small neutral state under the military control of NATO.

For all who are interested in preservation of peace, in insuring for any states – large or small, strong or weak – opportunity to build their national life in accordance with their own interests and aspirations, the question arises: if the sovereignty of states is not to be empty words written in the UN Charter, if the right to freedom and independence is really the sacred right of all peoples, of all states, then why do they want to exclude the Republic of Cyprus from the number of those who are allowed to enjoy the blessings of sovereignty and to build the national life without external interference? Are not they thinking that sovereignty is a right of only the strong and that genuine independence is a privilege of only those who possess powerful armed forces? Are they not considering at the same time that small states like the Republic of Cyprus, having neither nuclear armament nor large armed forces, are states of some other kind, with sovereignty and rights which one need not take into account?

Such views, if the governments of the great powers and especially of the permanent members of the Security Council are guided by them, could present a serious danger for general peace and become the source of international implications fraught with grave consequences for the peoples.

Sometimes in justifying plans to send NATO troops to Cyprus they express the point of view that the Cypriots are allegedly not capable of resolving their own internal problems, cannot agree how the Greek and Turkish communities can continue to live together within the framework of a single state. But who should know better whether the Cypriots can independently, without any interference from without, overcome their internal difficulties, than the Cypriots themselves, who headed by their Government and President Makarios courageously and firmly uphold the sovereignty of their Republic, defend their notional independence, their rights? Do they really wish to make someone believe that it is easier to cope with the internal problems of Cyprus in the capitals of other states? And it is not a secret that in NATO circles they are even considering the question whether to send to Cyprus as part of so-called 'NATO forces' soldiers and officers of the West German *Bundeswehr*, although in these areas the memories of steel helmets of soldiers and officers of the *Wehrmacht*, which brought destruction and death also to the Mediterranean region in the years of World War II, are still not eradicated.

We are convinced that the Cypriots are fully capable of taking care of their internal affairs, as was declared more than once by the Government of the Republic of Cyprus, and for finding solutions to the problems before them, which will to the greatest extent correspond to their national interests. But we are ready to admit that for other states perhaps there is a different approach to this question and they may evaluate the state of affairs to the effect that it is necessary to help the Cypriot people in overcoming its internal difficulties. However, even if this were so, then in that case it would be all the more a question of giving the Cypriots good advice, if they asked for it, and not in any way of interfering in their internal affairs.

And if one speaks about an examination of the Cyprus question in an international forum, then does not there exist agreement between all states, embodied in the UN Charter, as to where, in which international organs similar questions should be examined and how this should be done without a breach of states sovereignty? Meanwhile everything is being done now just in order not to allow discussion of the Cyprus question in the Security Council, examination by which was proposed at the request of the Government of Cyprus. And this is being done notwithstanding the fact that the Security Council is precisely that organ which the UN Charter charges with guaranteeing international peace and security.

What is not being done now, in order to prevent further examination of the Cyprus question in the Security Council? They persuade the Government of Cyprus, they bring pressure to bear on it, they threaten it, near the shores of Cyprus they carry out military demonstrations, they wave the flag of a naval blockade and thereby try in every way not to allow a new appeal of the Government of Cyprus to the Security Council.

In all this is clear that they prefer to examine the Cyprus question in closed conferences, where substituting arbitrariness for the UN Charter they count on shattering the opposition of a small state – the Republic of Cyprus – by means of external pressure.

Taking into account all circumstances, which have mounted up in connection with plans to organize a military intervention against the Republic of Cyprus, I would like to declare that the Soviet Government condemns such plans, as well as in general the use of methods of such type in the practice of international relations. The Soviet Government calls upon all interested states, and first and foremost the permanent members of the Security Council, who bear the main responsibility for maintenance of international peace and security, including the US and Great Britain, to show restraint, to take realistic and comprehensive account of all consequences, which military intrusion on Cyprus might entail, and to respect the sovereignty and independence of the Republic of Cyprus.

In making this appeal which is dictated by concern for the preservation and consolidation of peace and for guaranteeing the rights of peoples, I proceed from the fact that the Soviet Union, although it does not border directly on the Republic of Cyprus, cannot remain indifferent to that situation which is developing in the area of the eastern Mediterranean – an area not so distant from the southern borders of the USSR, especially if one considers how the notion of distances has changed in our time.

It seems to me that abstention from any plans which might aggravate the situation in the area of the eastern Mediterranean and infringe upon the legal rights of the people of Cyprus to freedom and independence, would correspond not only with the interests of the Cypriots but also with our general interests. The leaders of the great powers more than once have declared that they are striving for a reduction of international tension, whether it concerns Central Europe, the Mediterranean, or any other area. If this is so then it seems to me that all their weight, all the international authority and influence of leading figures of the Soviet Union, the United States of America, Great Britain, France, and also Cyprus' neighboring states, Turkey and Greece, must be used immediately so as not to permit further inflammation of the situation around Cyprus, to extinguish passions inflamed from without, which already has so adversely affected this situation, and thereby facilitate the consolidation of peace in this important area.

I should like, Mr President, to express the hope that your Government will correctly understand the motives which guide the Soviet Government, raising anew its voice in defense of the just cause of the Republic of Cyprus, and will take the due account of the considerations set forth in this appeal.

Respectfully,
Nikita Khrushchev

APPENDIX 10 Letter from President Johnson to Premier Inonu

5 June 1964

Dear Mr Prime Minister,

I am gravely concerned by the information which I have had through Ambassador Hare from you and your Foreign Minister that the Turkish Government is contemplating a decision to intervene by military force to occupy a portion of Cyprus. I wish to emphasize, in the full friendship and frankness, that I do not consider that such a course of action by Turkey, fraught with such far-reaching consequences, is consistent with the commitment of your Government to consult fully in advance with us. Ambassador Hare has indicated that you have postponed your decision for a few hours in order to obtain my views. I put it to you personally whether you really believe that it is appropriate for your Government, in effect, to present a unilateral decision of such consequence to an ally who has demonstrated such staunch support over the years as has the United States for Turkey. I must, therefore, first urge you to accept the responsibility for complete consultation with the United States before any such action is taken. It is my impression that you believe that such intervention by Turkey is permissible under the provision of the Treaty of Guarantee of 1960. I must call your attention, however, to our understanding that the proposed intervention by Turkey would be for the purpose of effecting a form of partition of the Island, a solution which is specifically excluded by the Treaty of Guarantee. Further, that Treaty requires consultation among the Guarantor Powers. It is the view of the United States that the possibilities of such consultation have by no means been exhausted in this situation and that, therefore, the reservation of the right to take unilateral action is not yet applicable.

I must call to your attention, also, Mr. Prime Minister, the obligations of NATO. There can be no question in your mind that a Turkish intervention in Cyprus would lead to a military engagement between Turkish and Greek forces. Secretary of State Rusk declared at the recent meeting of the Ministerial Council of NATO in The Hague that war between Turkey and Greece must be considered as 'literally unthinkable'. Adhesion to NATO, in its very essence, means that NATO countries will not wage war on each other. Germany and France have buried centuries of animosity and hostility in becoming NATO allies; nothing less can be expected from Greece and Turkey. Furthermore, a military intervention in Cyprus by Turkey could lead to a direct involvement by the Soviet Union. I hope you will understand that your NATO allies have not had a chance to consider whether they have an obligation to protect Turkey against the Soviet Union if Turkey takes a step which results in Soviet intervention without the full consent and understanding of its NATO allies.

Further, Mr. Prime Minister, I am concerned about the obligations of Turkey as a member of the United Nations. The United Nations has provided forces on the Island to keep the peace. Their task has been difficult but, during the past several weeks, they have been progressively successful in reducing the incidents of violence on the Island. The United Nations Mediator has not yet completed his work. I have no doubt that the general membership of the United Nations would react in the strongest terms to unilateral action by Turkey which would defy the efforts of the United Nations and destroy any prospect that the United Nations could assist in obtaining a reasonable and peaceful settlement of this difficult problem.

I wish also, Mr. Prime Minister, to call your attention to the bilateral agreement between the United States and Turkey in the field of military assistance. Under Article IV of the Agreement with Turkey of July 1947, your Government is required to obtain United States consent for the use of military assistance for purposes other than those for which such assistance was furnished. Your Government has on several occasions acknowledged to the United States that you fully understand this condition. I must tell you in all candor that the United States cannot agree to the use of any United States supplied military equipment for a Turkish intervention in Cyprus under the present circumstances.

Moving to the practical results of the contemplated Turkish move, I feel obligated to call to your attention in the most friendly fashion the fact that such a Turkish move could lead to the slaughter of tens of thousands of Turkish Cypriots on the Island of Cyprus. Such an action on your part would unleash the furies and there is no way by which military action on your part could be sufficiently effective to prevent wholesale destruction of many of those whom you are trying to protect. The presence of the United Nations forces could not prevent such a catastrophe.

You may consider that what I said is much too severe and that we are disgraceful of Turkish interests in the Cyprus situation. I should like to assure you that this is not the case. We have exerted ourselves both publicly and privately to assure the safety of the Turkish Cypriots and to insist that a final solution of the Cyprus problem should rest upon the consent of the parties most directly concerned. It is possible that you feel in Ankara that the United States has not been sufficiently active in your behalf. But surely you know that our policy has caused the liveliest resentments in Athens (where demonstrations have been aimed against us) and has led to a basic alienation between the United States and Archbishop Makarios. As I said to your Foreign Minister in our conversation just a few weeks ago, we value very highly our relations with Turkey. We have considered you as a great ally with fundamental common interests. Your security and prosperity have been a deep concern of the American people and we have expressed that concern in the most practical terms. You and we have fought together to resist the ambitions of the Communist world revolution. This solidarity has meant a great deal to us and I would hope that it means a great deal to your Government and your people. We have no intention of lending any support to any solution of Cyprus which endangers the Turkish Cypriot community. We have not been able to find a final solution because this is, admittedly, one of the most complex problems on earth. But I wish to assure you that we have been deeply concerned about the interests of Turkey and the Turkish Cypriots and will remain so.

Finally, Mr. Prime Minister, I must tell you that you have posed the gravest issues of war and peace. These are issues which go far beyond the bilateral relations between Turkey and the United States. They not only will certainly involve war between Turkey and Greece but could involve wider hostilities because of the unpredictable consequences which a unilateral intervention in Cyprus could produce. You have your responsibilities as Chief of the Government of Turkey; I also have mine as President of the United States. I must, therefore, inform you in the deepest friendship that unless I can have your assurance that you will not take such action without further and fullest consultation I cannot accept your injunction to Ambassador Hare of secrecy and must immediately ask for emergency meetings of the NATO Council and the United Nations Security Council.

I wish it were possible for us to have a personal discussion of this situation. Unfortunately, because of the special circumstances of our present Constitutional position, I am not able to leave the United States. I do feel that you and I carry a very heavy responsibility for the general peace and for the possibilities of a sane and peaceful resolution of the Cyprus problem. I ask you, therefore, to delay any decisions which you and your colleagues might have in mind until you and I have had the fullest and frankest consultation.

Sincerely,
Lyndon B. Johnson

APPENDIX 11 Opinion of the EC Commission on the Application of Cyprus for Membership

Issued 30 June 1993; endorsed by the Council of Ministers 4 October 1993. (Excerpts. Numbers indicate paragraphs in the original text.)

8. When presenting its application for accession, the government of the Republic of Cyprus, recognized by the European Community and its Member States as the only legitimate government representing the Cypriot people, addressed the Community on behalf of the whole of the island. The application was strongly challenged by the *de facto* authorities of the northern part of the island. While acknowledging that it would be in the interests of the Turkish Cypriot community to form part of the European Community, these authorities rejected the right of the government of the Republic of Cyprus to speak for the whole of Cyprus in such an approach. They based their position on the Guarantee Treaty and the wording of the 1960 Constitution, which grants the president and vice-president (a Turkish Cypriot) a veto over any foreign policy decision, particularly any decision on joining an international organization or alliance that does not count both Greece and Turkey among its members. They consider, accordingly, that in the prevailing circumstances the Community should not take any action on the application.

The Community, however, following the logic of its established position, which is consistent with that of the United Nations where the legitimacy of the government of the Republic of Cyprus and non-recognition of the 'Turkish Republic of Northern Cyprus' are concerned, felt that the application was admissible and initiated the procedures laid down by the Treaties in order to examine it.

44. Cyprus' geographical position, the deep-lying bonds which, for two thousand years, have located the island at the very fount of European culture and civilization, the intensity of the European influence apparent in the values shared by the people of Cyprus and in the conduct of the cultural, political, economic and social life of its citizens, the wealth of its contacts of every kind with the Community, all these confer on Cyprus, beyond all doubt, its European identity and character and confirm its vocation to belong to the Community.

45. A political settlement of the Cyprus question would serve only to reinforce this vocation and strengthen the ties which link Cyprus to Europe. At the same time a settlement would open the way to the full restoration of human rights and fundamental freedoms throughout the island and encourage the development of pluralist democracy.

46. The Commission is convinced that the results of Cyprus's accession to the Community would be increased security and prosperity and that it would help bring the two communities on the island closer together. If there were to be a political settlement, the prospect of the progressive re-establishment on fundamental liberties would help overcome the inevitable practical difficulties which would arise during the transition period in regard to the adoption of the relevant Community legislation. In regard to economic aspects, this opinion has shown that, in view of the progress toward a customs union achieved thus far, the adoption of the *acquis communautaire* by Cyprus will pose no insurmountable problems. The Commission is not underestimating the problems that the economic transition poses. However, the economy of the southern part of the island has demonstrated an ability to adapt and seems ready to face the challenge of integration provided that the work already started on reforms and on opening up to the outside world is maintained, notably in the context of the customs union. This opinion has also shown that there will be a greater chance of narrowing the development gap between north and south in event of Cyprus's integration with the Community.

The government of the Republic of Cyprus shares this conviction. Even though they object to the conditions under which the application for membership was made, the leaders of the Turkish Cypriot community are fully conscious of the economic and social benefits that integration with Europe would bring their community.

47. This opinion has also shown that Cyprus's integration with the Community implies a peaceful, balanced and lasting settlement of the Cyprus question – a settlement which will make it possible for the two communities to be reconciled, for confidence to be re-established and for their respective leaders to work together. While safeguarding the essential balance between the two communities and the right of each to preserve its fundamental interests, the institutional provisions contained in such a settlement should create the appropriate conditions for Cyprus to participate normally in the decision-making process of the European Community and in the correct application of Community law throughout the island.

48. In view of all the above and in the expectation of significant progress in the talks currently being pursued under the auspices of the Secretary-General of the United Nations, the Commission feels that a positive signal should be sent to the authorities and the people of Cyprus confirming that the Community considers Cyprus eligible for membership and that as soon as the prospect of a settlement is surer, the Community is ready to start the process with Cyprus that should eventually lead to its accession.

49. The United Nations Secretary-General is aware that he can count on the Community's support in his continued endeavours to produce a political settlement of the Cyprus question.

Even before such a settlement is forthcoming, the Commission undertakes to use all the instruments available under the Association Agreement to contribute, in close cooperation with the Cypriot government, to the economic, social and political transition of Cyprus towards integration with the Community.

If the Council agrees, and in the hope of facilitating the conduct of the future accession negotiations, the Commission is willing to begin immediately talks with the government of Cyprus. These talks would serve to familiarize the Cypriot authorities with all the elements that constitute the *acquis communautaire*, partly in order to allow them to prepare their negotiating position under the best possible conditions and partly to permit an assessment of the need for any technical co-operation and assistance that their country might require to adopt and implement Community legislation and the policies and instruments that will be needed for its integration and to prepare the way, in due course, for the north of the island to catch up economically.

The Commission also undertakes to examine the issue of Cyprus's future institutions and their compatibility with the requirements of active participation in the day-to-day running of the Community in the event of accession.

50. The Community must ensure, moreover, that the general assessment to be carried out in the context of the 1996 intergovernmental conference resolved in greater efficiency in the operation of the institutions of an enlarged Community – and one that could well be enlarged further – while at the same time providing Cyprus, and any other new Member State of a similar size with a guarantee that it will receive appropriate treatment in the decision-making process and in the discharging of its responsibilities.

51. Lastly, the Commission must envisage the possibility of the failure of the intercommunal talks to produce a political settlement of the Cyprus question in the foreseeable future, in spite of the endeavors of the United Nations Secretary-General. Should this eventuality arise, the Commission feels that the situation should be reassessed in view of the positions adopted by each party in the talks and that the question of Cyprus's accession to the Community should be reconsidered in January 1995.

APPENDIX 12
Conclusions of the European Council at Corfu Regarding Cyprus

Adopted at the meeting of 24-25 June 1994 held in Corfu.
(Excerpts from the section on applicant countries.)

The European Council welcomes the significant progress made regarding the application by Cyprus and Malta for accession to the European Union and considers that an essential stage in the preparation process could be regarded as completed.

The European Council asks the Council and the Commission to do their utmost to ensure that the negotiations with Malta and Cyprus with a view to the conclusion of the forth financial protocols, intended in particular to support the efforts of Malta and Cyprus towards integration into the European Union, are brought to a rapid conclusion.

The European Council notes that in theses conditions the next phase of enlargement of the Union will involve Cyprus and Malta.

The European Council, recalling relevant decisions of the Council of 4 October 1993, 18 April 1994 and 13 June 1994, reaffirms that any solution of the Cyprus problem must respect the sovereignty, independence, territorial integrity and unity of the country, in accordance with the relevant United Nations resolutions and high-level agreements.

APPENDIX 13   European Parliament Resolution on Cyprus' Application for Membership of the European Union

Adopted 12 June 1995.
The European Parliament,

- having regard to the application for membership of the European Union submitted by Cyprus on 4 July 1990,
- having regard to the Commission Opinion of 30 June 1993,
- having regard to the Council's Conclusion of 4 October 1993,
- having regard to its resolution on the situation in Cyprus and on the enlargement of the Union,

whereas at the European Council meetings in Corfu and Essen (June and December 1994) it was agreed that Cyprus and Malta should be included in the next phase of enlargement of the Union,

- having regard to the resolutions of the UN Security Council on the situation in Cyprus and the report by the Secretary General of the United Nations on his mission of good offices,
- having regard to the Conclusions of the Council on Cyprus of 6 March 1995,
- having regard to the Conclusions of the European Council held in Cannes on 26-27 June 1995,
- having regard to Rule 148 of its Rules of Procedure,
- having regard to the report of the Committee on Foreign Affairs, Security and Defence Policy (A4-0156/95),

A. whereas Cyprus's vocation to be part of Europe and its eligibility for membership of the Union are confirmed in the Opinion of the Commission and the Conclusions of the Council on the membership application,
B. whereas this eligibility was reconfirmed by the Council in March 1995 upon re-examination of the membership application by Cyprus,
C. whereas the European Council in Cannes decided that negotiations for the accession of Cyprus would begin six months after the end of the 1996 Intergovernmental Conference,

D. whereas Cyprus has cultural and historical, as well as economic and political, links with the Member States of the European Union and, therefore, its membership is of importance to all Member States,

E. whereas negotiations on the Cyprus question are still continuing under UN auspices, with a view to reaching a fair and lasting peace agreement,

F. wishing to see a more decisive involvement by the European Union in efforts to secure a just and lasting settlement of the Cyprus problem,

1. Endorses the Commission opinion and the Council's Conclusions on the membership application and confirms Cyprus's vocation and its eligibility for membership of the Union;

2. Reiterates the views it has expressed in the past on the island's reunification in the form of a sovereign, independent, bi-zonal and bi-communal federation, in keeping with the relevant UN resolutions and, with a view to accession, in accordance with the *acquis communautaire* of the Union;

3. Points out that the Union considers the island to be a single entity, with a legitimate and internationally recognized government, and that the status quo is unacceptable, as was reaffirmed in the UN Security Council Resolution 939/94 (paragraphs 1 and 2);

4. Notes the UN Secretary-General's report of 22 November 1993 and supports his call to the two sides on the island, as well as Turkey and Greece, to 'work more effectively for a negotiated settlement, in return for the great efforts of the international community' (paragraph 102 of the report);

5. Notes the UN Secretary General's report of 30 May 1994 which speaks of a deadlock in the inter-community talks, over both the substance of the Cyprus problem and the confidence-building measures, owing to the absence of political will on the part of the Turkish Cypriot side (paragraph 53);

6. Notes the report by the Union observer to the inter-community talks and deplores the state of deadlock reached in the negotiations;

7. Deplores the recent resolutions by the Turkish Cypriot 'parliament';

8. Believes nevertheless that the UN Secretary-General should continue his efforts to find a peace settlement and calls on the international community to take all possible steps to reduce the tension between the two parties;

9. Welcomes the substantive discussions which have taken place between the Union and the Cyprus authorities which should enable Cyprus to prepare for the accession negotiations in the best possible circumstances;

10. Considers that the accession of Cyprus is an autonomous process and that Cyprus should not be a hostage of relations between the Union and Turkey, as the Commission and the Council have confirmed in various statements;

11. Calls for resources of the Fourth Financial Protocol to be employed to support efforts by the Cypriot Government to achieve harmonization with the *acquis communautaire*;

12. Believes that not only the opening of negotiations on accession but also accession itself can help speed up a peaceful settlement in Cyprus and considers that membership should benefit both communities;

13. Points to the positive role which Cyprus will play by enhancing the Union's contribution to peace and security in Europe, particularly in the eastern Mediterranean;

14. Repeats that enlargement must be accompanied by changes;

15. Refers to the Conclusion of the EU Council of Ministers fixing opening of the accession negotiations with Cyprus and Malta six months after the end of the Intergovernmental Conference of 1996; calls, accordingly, on the Council and the Member States to commit themselves to that effect with a view to the prompt accession of Cyprus to the EU;

16. Welcomes the structured dialogue between Cyprus and the European Union, as agreed at the Associated Council of 12 June 1995, and calls for the details of this dialogue to be modelled on the structured dialogue between the EU and the countries of central and eastern Europe;

17. Calls on the Commission to pursue the dialogue with the Turkish Cypriot community so as to ensure that the democratic forces in the northern part of the island are kept abreast of progress in the ongoing process of accession;

18. Calls on the Commission to act in concert with the Government of Cyprus, in order to make the Turkish community in the northern part of Cyprus aware of the benefits of accession and calls also for a joint action to be undertaken by the Union to accelerate the peace process in Cyprus;

19. Calls on the institutions of the European Union to examine the possibility of a joint action with a view to solving the Cyprus problem, taking into account the international rule of law and the relevant UN resolutions;

20. Instructs its President to forward this resolution to the Council, the Commission, the Governments of the Member States and the Government of Cyprus.

Notes

1 CONCEPTUAL CONSIDERATIONS AND ANALYTICAL CONTEXTS

1 R. O. Keohane and J. S. Nye, *Power and Interdependence*, 2nd edn. (Glenview, IL: Scott, Foresman, 1989), p. 8.
2 L. R. Brown, *World Without Borders: The Interdependence of Nations* (New York: Foreign Policy Association, 1972).
3 J. L. Ray, *Global Politics*, 5th edn. (Boston: Houghton Mifflin, 1992).
4 C. W. Kegley, Jr. and E. R. Wittkopf, *The Global Agenda*, 2nd edn. (New York: Random House, 1988).
5 F. S. Pearson and M. J. Rochester, *International Relations: The Global Condition in the Late Twentieth Century* (New York: McGraw-Hill, 1992).
6 The three quotes in this sentence come from the titles of international relations textbooks indicating that the 'global approach' has also entered the classroom.
7 A. L. Bennett, *International Organizations: Principles and Issues*, 5th edn. (Englewood Cliffs, NJ: Prentice Hall, 1991), p. 21.
8 J. N. Rosenau, 'Introduction', in his edited work *Linkage Politics* (New York: Free Press, 1969), p. 2.
9 S. Hoffman, *Primacy or World Order: American Foreign Policy since the Cold War* (New York: McGraw-Hill, 1978), p. 111.
10 Examples of works which use the global system as a framework of reference and analysis are Keohane and Nye, *Power and Interdependence*; A. M. Scott, *The Dynamics of Interdependence* (Chapel Hill: University of North Carolina Press, 1982); Hoffman, *Primacy or World Order*; A. Inkeles, 'The Emerging Social Structure of the World', *World Politics*, 27 (1975), 467–95; P. J. Katzenstein, 'International Interdependence: Some Long-Term Trends and Recent Changes', *International Organization*, 29 (1975), 1021–34; I. Wallerstein, *The Modern World System* (New York: Academic Press, 1974); Brown, *World Without Borders*; C. A. McLeland, *Theory and the International System* (New York: Macmillan, 1966); R. N. Rosecrance, *Action and Reaction in World Politics* (Boston: Little, Brown, 1963); M. A. Kaplan, *System and Process in International Politics* (New York: Wiley, 1962).
11 J. Rothschild, *Ethnopolitics: A Conceptual Framework* (New York: Columbia University Press, 1981), p. 3.
12 Following are some of the scholars who have paid special attention to ethnic groups and their politics: J. Rex and B. Drury (eds.), *Ethnic Mobilisation in a Multi-Cultural Europe* (Aldershot: Avebury, 1995); T. R. Gurr and B. Harff, *Ethnic Conflict in World Politics* (Boulder, CO: Westview Press, 1994); R. Jenkins, 'Rethinking Ethnicity: Identity, Categorization and Power', *Ethnic and Racial Studies*, 17 (1994) 197–223; G. Gottlieb, *Nation Against State: A New Approach to Ethnic Conflicts, the Decline of*

Sovereignty, and the Dilemmas of Collective Security (New York: Council on Foreign Relations, 1993); T. R. Gurr, *Minorities at Risk: A Global View of Ethnopolitical Conflicts* (Washington, D.C.: US Institute of Peace, 1993); M. I. Midlarsky (ed.), *The Internationalization of Communal Strife* (London: Routledge, 1992); P. R. Brass, *Ethnicity and Nationalism: Theory and Comparison* (New Delhi: Sage, 1991); K. M. de Silva and J. R. May (eds.), *Internationalization of Ethnic Conflict* (New York: St. Martin's Press, 1991); A. Heraclides, *The Self-Determination of Minorities in International Politics* (London: Frank Cass, 1991); D. L. Horowitz, *Ethnic Groups in Conflict* (Berkeley: University of California Press, 1985); F. L. Shiels (ed.), *Ethnic Separatism and World Politics* (Lanham, MD: University Press of America, 1984); J. Kreijci and V. Velimski, *Ethnic and Political Nations in Europe* (New York: St. Martin's Press, 1981); A. Suhrke and L. Noble (eds.), *Ethnic Conflict in International Relations* (New York: Praeger, 1977); A. Said and L. R Simmons (eds.), *Ethnicity in an International Context* (New Brunswick, NJ: Transaction Books, 1976).

13 A. Said and L. R. Simmons, 'The Ethnic Factor in World Politics', in their edited volume *Ethnicity in an International Context*, p. 19.

14 Gurr and Harff, *Ethnic Conflict in World Politics*, p. xiii.

15 S. Huntington, 'The Clash of Civilizations', *Foreign Affairs*, 72, 3 (1993), p. 22.

16 Gurr and Harff, *Ethnic Conflict in World Politics*, p. 2.

17 Ibid., p. 139.

18 Shiels, *Ethnic Separatism and World Politics*, p. 1.

19 Gurr and Harff, *Ethnic Conflict in World Politics*, p. 10.

20 Q. Wright, 'The Nature of Conflict', *The Western Political Quarterly*, 4 (June 1951), p. 194.

21 L. A. Coser, *The Functions of Social Conflict* (New York: Free Press, 1956), p. 3.

22 R. M. Burkey, *Ethnic and Racial Groups: The Dynamics of Dominance* (Manlo Park, CA: Benjamin-Cummings, 1978), p. 1.

23 R. A. Shermerhorn, *Comparative Ethnic Relations: A Framework for Theory and Research* (New York: Random House, 1970), p. 12.

24 Gurr and Harff, *Ethnic Conflict in World Politics*, p. 15.

25 G. P. Murdock, *Ethnographic Atlas* (Pittsburgh: University of Pittsburgh Press, 1967).

26 W. Connor, 'Nation-Building or Nation-Destroying?' *World Politics*, 24 (1972), 319–55.

27 Gurr and Harff, *Ethnic Conflict in World Politics*, p. 10.

28 Ibid.

29 J. M. Rosenau, 'Pre-theories and Theories of Foreign Policy', in R. B. Farrell (ed.), *Approaches to Comparative and International Politics* (Evanston, IL: Northwestern University Press, 1966), pp. 27–92.

30 W. F. Hanrieder, 'International Organizations and International Systems', *The Journal of Conflict Resolution*, 10 (1966), p. 297.

31 See *Worldwide Peacekeeping Operations* (Washington, D.C.: Central Intelligence Agency, 1993) and *The Blue Helmets: A Review of United Nations Peace-keeping*, 2nd edn. (United Nations, 1990).

32 H. Morgenthau, *Politics Among Nations: The Struggle for Power and Peace*, 4th edn. (New York: Knopf, 1967), p. 25.
33 Ibid., p. 5.
34 J. W. Burton, *International Relations: A General Theory* (Cambridge: Cambridge University Press, 1965), p. 46.
35 Some classic works on diplomacy are R. P. Barston, *Modern Diplomacy* (London: Longman, 1988); B. Sen, *A Diplomat's Handbook of International Law and Practice*, 3rd edn. (Dordrecht: Martinus Nijhoff, 1988); H. Nicolson, *Diplomacy*, 3rd edn. (London: Oxford University Press, 1963).
36 Barston, *Modern Diplomacy*, p. 1.

2 BACKGROUND OF THE DOMESTIC ETHNIC CONFLICT

1 The strategic significance of Cyprus lies primarily in its position relative to the land and sea routes connecting Europe and the Mediterranean with the Middle East. This was convincingly shown during the Second World War and the 1956 Suez crisis when the island (then a British colony) was used to support military operations in the region. In the first case, Cyprus was used as an air base, refuelling station, and naval support centre for military operations in south-eastern Europe, North Africa, and the Middle East. During the Suez crisis, Britain and France used Cyprus as a starting point for launching their attacks on the Suez canal.
2 Article 1 of the Cyprus Convention between Britain and Turkey stated:

> If Batoum, Ardahan, Kars, or any of them shall be retained by Russia, and if any attempt shall be made at any future time by Russia to take possession of any further territories of His Imperial Majesty the Sultan in Asia, as fixed by the Definitive Treaty of Peace, England engages to join His Imperial Majesty the Sultan in defending them by force of arms.
>
> In return, His Imperial Majesty the Sultan promises to England to introduce necessary Reforms, to be agreed upon later between the two Powers, into the government, and for the protection of the Christian and other subjects of the Porte in these territories.
>
> And in order to enable England to make necessary provision for executing her engagement, His Imperial Majesty the Sultan further consents to assign the Island of Cyprus to be occupied and administered by England.
>
> For the complete text of the treaty, see G. Hill, *A History of Cyprus*, 4 vols. (Cambridge: Cambridge University Press, 1940–52), vol. IV, pp. 300–4.

3 Article 20 of the treaty of Lausanne stated: 'Turkey hereby recognizes the annexation of Cyprus proclaimed by the British Government on the 5th of November, 1914.' For the complete text of the treaty, see F. L. Israel (ed.), *Major Peace Treaties of Modern History 1648–1967* (New York: McGraw-Hill, 1967), pp. 2301–67.
4 According to the 1960 census, the population of Cyprus was 572,707, distributed as follows: Greek Cypriots 447,901 (78.20%); Turkish Cypriots

103,822 (18.13%); others (mainly Maronites, Armenians, and Latins) 20,984 (3.66%).

5 For detailed statistics and analyses of the demography of Cyprus see L. W. St John-Jones, *The Population of Cyprus* (London: Maurice Temple Smith, 1983); G. Karouzis, *Proposals for a Solution to the Cyprus Problem* (Nicosia: Government Printing Office, 1976); A. Melamid, 'The Geographical Distribution of Communities in Cyprus', *The Geographical Review*, 46 (July 1956), 355–74.

6 In the seventeenth century, the sultan of the Ottoman Empire granted the title of ethnarch (ethnic political leader) to the archbishop of Cyprus. Thus, the religious leader became also *ex officio* political leader of the Greek Cypriot community. That practice remained unchanged until Cyprus became independent in 1960. That explains, to some degree, why it was easy for Archbishop Makarios to be elected first president of Cyprus.

7 For detailed discussions on the position and role of the Church of Cyprus under the Ottomans and the British, see the following works: F. R. Walsh and M. T. Walsh, 'Church and State in Cyprus', *The Texas Quarterly*, 3 (Autumn 1960), 268–73; Hill, *History of Cyprus*, vol. IV, pp. 305–400, 509–606; and J. Hackett, *A History of the Orthodox Church of Cyprus* (New York: Burt Franklin, 1901).

8 The word *millet* is of Arabic origin. It appears in the Koran with the meaning of religion. In the Ottoman Empire it came to mean religious group. For discussions on the concept of *millet* and the principles and nature of Ottoman administration see A. E. Vacalopoulos, *The Greek Nation, 1453–1669: The Cultural and Economic Background of Modern Greek Society*, translated from Greek with an introduction by Ian and Phania Moles (New Brunswick, NJ: Rudgers University Press, 1976), pp. 125–6; B. Lewis, *The Emergence of Modern Turkey*, 2nd edn. (London: Oxford University Press, 1968), pp. 333–7; Z. N. Zeine, *The Emergence of Arab Nationalism – With a Study of Arab-Turkish Relations in the Near East*, 2nd edn. (Beirut: Khayats, 1966), pp. 19–33; and H. J. Miller, *The Loom of History* (New York: Harper, 1958), pp. 325–6. For remarks on the application of the *millet* system in Cyprus see H. D. Purcell, *Cyprus* (New York: Praeger, 1968), pp. 169–75; and H. Luke, *Cyprus: A Portrait and an Appreciation* (London: Harrap, 1957), pp. 179–80.

9 Kitromilides and Couloumbis write about the preservation of the *millet* system under British rule: 'Political representation in the Legislative Council reflected the traditional system of social organization based on religious communities (*millets*), which was retained by the British and which formed the fundamental principle of their handling of the politics of Cyprus. In the context of this policy, the *millet* system was gradually politicized and provided the organizational foundation for the national differentiation of the Cypriots.' See P. M. Kitromilides and T. A. Couloumbis, 'Ethnic Conflict in a Strategic Area: The Case of Cyprus', in A. Said and L. R. Simmons (eds.), *Ethnicity in an International Context* (New Brunswick, NJ: Transaction Books, 1976), p. 169.

10 The idea of *enosis* dates back to the creation of the modern Greek state in 1830. It became a political issue when the British took control of Cyprus in 1878. Under Ottoman rule its propagation was not allowed. The Greek

Cypriots saw the change from Ottoman of British rule as a first step towards the achievement of *enosis*. For accounts of the emergence of the idea of *enosis* and the evolution of the *enosis* movement see A. M. Walker, 'Enosis in Cyprus: Dhali, a Case Study', *The Middle East Journal*, 38 (Summer 1984): 474–94; M. Attalides, *Cyprus: Nationalism and International Politics* (New York: St. Martin's Press, 1979), pp. 22–35; D. Alastos, *Cyprus in History: A Survey of Five Thousand Years*, 2nd edn. (London: Zeno, 1976), pp. 330–59; Royal Institute for International Affairs, *Cyprus: Background to Enosis* (London: Chatham House, 1958); and Hill, *History of Cyprus*, vol. IV, pp. 488–568.

11 The following two measures illustrate the segregationist character of the British policy: first, the Greek and Turkish members of the legislative council were elected separately by the two communities. And secondly, during the Greek Cypriot revolt against British colonial rule (1955–59), a special police force consisting primarily of Turkish Cypriots was set up by the colonial administration to fight the Greek Cypriot guerrillas.

12 Purcell, *Cyprus*, p. 245.

13 Britain dispatched to Cyprus a force of over 30 000 to fight the guerrillas and maintain order. During the period 1955–59, approximately 600 people were killed and 1400 injured in the hostilities. Detailed figures were given by the *Daily Telegraph* (20 February 1959).

14 For detailed accounts of domestic and international developments during the period 1955–59, see N. Crashaw, *The Cyprus Revolt: An Account of the Struggle for Union with Greece* (London: Allen and Unwin, 1978); C. Foley and W. I. Scobie, *The Struggle for Cyprus* (Stanford: Hoover Institution Press, 1975); P. Treymayne, *Below the Tide* (Boston: Houghton Mifflin, 1959); and R. P. Fairfield, 'Cyprus: Revolution and Resolution', *The Middle East Journal*, 13 (Summer 1959): 235–48.

15 For a standard work on the Greek appeals to the UN and other developments in international diplomacy see S. G. Xydis, *Cyprus: Conflict and Conciliation, 1954–58* (Columbus: Ohio State University Press, 1967).

16 UN doc. A/2703, letter dated 16 August 1954, from the Greek prime minister to the Secretary-General requesting the inclusion of the Cyprus issue in the agenda of the General Assembly.

17 On 26 February 1957, the General Assembly adopted Resolution 1013 (XI) which expressed the earnest desire for 'a peaceful, democratic and just solution' that would be 'in accordance with the purposes and principles of the Charter of the United Nations'. On 5 December 1958, the General Assembly adopted Resolution 1287 (XIII) which, in essence, was a repetition of Resolution 1013 (XI).

18 For analyses of the Zürich and London settlement in the context of internal and external politics of Britain, Greece, and Turkey see Royal Institute for International Affairs, *Cyprus: The Dispute and the Settlement* (London: Chatham House, 1959); and E. Baker, 'The Settlement in Cyprus', *Political Quarterly*, 30 (September 1959): 244–53.

19 For extensive analyses and interpretations of the legal and political aspects and consequences of the 1960 founding treaties see R. S. J. Macdonald, 'International Law and the Conflict in Cyprus', *The Canadian Yearbook of International Law*, 29 (1981): 3–49; T. Ehrlich, *Cyprus, 1958–1967: Inter-*

national Crises and the Role of Law (New York: Oxford University Press, 1974).

20 Treaty of Guarantee, art. 1.

21 Ibid., art. 4.

22 The constitution can be found in A. P. Blaustein and G. H. Flauz (eds.), *Constitutions of the Countries of the World* (Dobbs Ferry: Oceana, 1972). For extensive analyses of the Cyprus constitution see the following works: Z. M. Nedjadigil, *The Cyprus Conflict: A Lawyer's View* (Nicosia: Tezel, 1982); C. G. Tornaritis, *Cyprus and Its Constitutional and Other Legal Problems*, 2nd edn. (Nicosia: n.p., 1982); S. Kyriakides, *Cyprus: Constitutionalism and Crisis Government* (Philadelphia: University of Pennsylvania Press, 1968); T. W. Adams, 'The First Republic of Cyprus: A Review of an Unworkable Constitution', *The Western Political Quarterly*, 19 (September 1966): 475–90; and S. A. de Smith, *The New Commonwealth and Its Constitutions* (London: Stevens, 1964).

23 Article 2 of the constitution identified the two communities as follows: '(1) the Greek Community comprises all citizens of the Republic who are of Greek origin and whose mother tongue is Greek or who share the Greek cultural traditions or who are members of the Greek-Orthodox Church; (2) the Turkish Community comprises all citizens of the Republic who are of Turkish origin and whose mother tongue is Turkish or who share the Turkish cultural traditions or who are Moslems.'

24 Constitution, art. 1.

25 Ibid., art. 4.

26 These figures were later changed to fifty-four Greek Cypriots and twenty-four Turkish Cypriots.

27 Constitution, art. 78.

28 Ibid., art. 173.

29 Ibid., art. 182.

30 G. D. Camp, 'Greek-Turkish Conflict over Cyprus', *Political Science Quarterly*, 95 (Spring 1980), p. 49.

31 T. W. Adams and A. J. Cottrell, *Cyprus Between East and West* (Baltimore: Johns Hopkins University Press, 1968), p. 7.

32 Both sides prepared contingency plans for military and diplomatic action in the event of a flare-up and a breakdown of communal relations. The Greek Cypriot plan was revealed for the first time in 1967 when it was published in the Greek Cypriot newspaper *Patris* (21 April 1967). The Turkish Cypriot plan was published in the *Cyprus Bulletin* (2 March 1964). Government officials from both sides were involved in the secret preparations. President Makarios, commenting on the existence of irregular groups, said: 'There are such people on both sides. The Greeks were afraid of Turkish attack, and the Turks feared we would attack.' Quoted in *Keesing's Contemporary Archives* (1964) p. 20113. For an extensive report on the underground organizations and their activities see the *Guardian*, 30 December 1963.

33 Memorandum submitted by President Makarios to Vice-President Kutchuk on 30 November 1963, under the heading 'Suggested Measures to Facilitate the Smooth Functioning of the State and Remove Certain Causes of Intercommunal Friction.'

34 Ibid.
35 UN Charter, preamble.

3 THE IMPACT OF CROSS-BOUNDARY ETHNIC TIES

 1 G. Hill, *A History of Cyprus*, 4 vols (Cambridge: Cambridge University Press, 1940–52), vol. IV, p. 496.
 2 There is a question as to whether it was Bishop Kyprianos of Citium or Archbishop Sophronios who included these words in his welcome address. For more clarifications, refer to Hill, *History of Cyprus*, vol. IV, pp. 297–8 and D. Alastos, *Cyprus in History: A Survey of Five Thousand Years*, 2nd edn. (London: Zeno Publishers, 1976), p. 308.
 3 Hill cites several sources to state that 'the general feeling among Greeks and Turks appeared to be one of welcome for the new dispensation and hope for the future'. See Hill, *History of Cyprus*, vol. IV, p. 297.
 4 Hill mentions several incidents where the Turkish Cypriots expressed their opposition to agitation for *enosis*. See especially Chapter 8, 'Enosis', in *History of Cyprus*, vol. IV.
 5 H. D. Purcell, *Cyprus* (New York: Praeger, 1968), p. 229.
 6 In 1950, in a plebiscite organized by the Orthodox Church 95.6 per cent of the Greek Cypriots had voted for *enosis*.
 7 UN doc. A/2703, letter dated 16 August 1954, from the Greek prime minister to the UN Secretary-General requesting the inclusion of the Cyprus issue in the agenda of the General Assembly.
 8 The riots were organized and co-ordinated by the 'Cyprus is Turkish Association', a government-supported society with approximately 100 000 members. The position of this association was that in case of a British withdrawal, Cyprus should be handed back to Turkey. For more details on the goals and activities of the 'Cyprus is Turkish Association', see *The Manchester Guardian*, 30 July 1955, and *The Times*, 26 January 1957.
 9 For detailed reports on the causes and consequences of the violent anti-Greek riots, see *The New York Times*, 15 and 17 April 1957, and 7 September 1958; and *The Times* (London), 12 April, 20 June and 13 July 1957; and 8 December 1958.
10 In 1923, at the signing of the Treaty of Lausanne, which regulates minority issues between Greece and Turkey, there were approximately 150 000 Greeks living in Istanbul. This number has been reduced to approximately 2 500 as a result of ill-treatment, especially during periods of tension in Greek–Turkish relations. For more information, see M. K. Leighton, 'The Antagonists: Greece and Turkey', *Conflict Studies*, No. 109, July 1979.
11 For an authoritative account and interpretation of the domestic Turkish reactions to the Cyprus dispute in the 1950s, see F. Tachau, 'The Face of Turkish Nationalism as Reflected in the Cyprus Dispute', *The Middle East Journal*, 13 (Summer 1959): 262–72.
12 UN doc. A/C.1/SR.977, 25 November 1958, statement by the Turkish representative at the General Assembly.

13 On 26 February 1957, the General Assembly adopted Resolution 1013 (XI) which expressed the earnest desire for 'a peaceful, democratic and just solution' that would be 'in accordance with the purposes and principles of the Charter of the United Nations'. On 5 December 1958, the General Assembly adopted Resolution 1287 (XIII) which, in essence, was a repetition of Resolution 1013 (XI).

14 Article 2 of the Treaty of Guarantee provides that Greece, Turkey, and the United Kingdom 'recognize and guarantee the independence, territorial integrity and security of the Republic of Cyprus, and also the state of affairs established by the Basic Articles of its Constitution'. Article 4 provides that 'In the event of a breach of the provisions of the present Treaty, Greece, Turkey and the United Kingdom undertake to consult together with respect to the representations or measures necessary to ensure observance of those provisions. In so far as common or concerned action may not prove possible, each of the three guaranteeing Powers reserves the right to take action with the sole aim of re-establishing the state of affairs created by the present Treaty.'

15 The impact of the Cyprus colonial problem on Greek–Turkish relations in the 1950s is the focus of the following articles: R. P. Fairfield, 'Cyprus: Revolution and Resolution', *The Middle East Journal*, 13 (Summer 1959): 235–48; and P. Pipinellis, 'The Greco-Turkish Feud Revived', *Foreign Affairs*, 37 (January 1959): 306–16.

16 A good background on the social, cultural, and religious patterns and practices of the two communities is provided in E. K. Keefe et al., *Area Handbook for Cyprus* (Washington, D.C.: Government Printing Office, 1971), especially chapters 5 and 6, 'Social System' and 'Religion', pp. 89–122.

17 In 1967, the number of Cypriot students abroad was approximately 4700, distributed as follows: Greek Cypriots: Greece 2500, Britain 1000, other countries 100. Turkish Cypriots: Turkey 1200, and an insignificant number in other countries. Source: Purcell, *Cyprus*, pp. 67–9.

18 Ethnic origin, language, cultural traditions, and religion are the criteria used by the constitution of Cyprus to classify the Cypriots into Greeks and Turks. Article 2 provides: 'For the purposes of this Constitution (1) the Greek Community comprises all citizens of the Republic who are of Greek origin and whose mother tongue is Greek or who share the Greek cultural traditions or who are members of the Greek-Orthodox Church; (2) the Turkish Community comprises all citizens of the Republic who are of Turkish origin and whose mother tonge is Turkish or who share the Turkish cultural traditions or who are Moslems.'

19 Quoted in *Keesing's* (1963), p. 19257.

20 F. Kutchuk, 'Reply to the President's Memorandum'.

21 For some revealing first-hand information on the secret dispatch of Greek troops to Cyprus, see A. Papandreou, *Democracy at Gunpoint: The Greek Front* (New York: Doubleday, 1970), p. 132.

22 UN doc. S/PV. 1143, 9–11 August 1964, para. 42, statement by the Greek representative at the Security Council.

23 Ibid., para. 143, statement by the American representative at the Security Council.

24 Article 1 of the Treaty of Guarantee provides that Cyprus 'undertakes not to participate, in whole or in part, in any political or economic union with any State whatsoever. It accordingly declares prohibited any activity likely to promote, directly or indirectly, either union with any other State or partition of the Island.'

25 For a controversial work on AKEL and its role in Cypriot politics see T. W. Adams, *AKEL: The Communist Party of Cyprus* (Stanford: Hoover Institution, 1971).

26 The Communist Party of Greece was outlawed in 1947 during the civil war. It was legalized again in 1974 after the fall of the military regime and the restoration of democracy.

27 Any study of the Cyprus issue must take into account the variable 'Makarios'. The charismatic Orthodox archbishop dominated Cypriot politics from 1950 to 1977. For extensive accounts of his character, life, policies, and legacies, see S. Mayes, *Makarios: A Biography* (New York: St. Martin's Press, 1981); and P. N. Vanezis, *Makarios: Pragmatism and Idealism* (London: Abelard-Shuman, 1974).

28 See, for example, the widely publicized, domestically and internationally, joint communiqué issued after the Makarios–Papandreou talks in Athens on 13 April 1964. Refer to *Keesing's* (1964), pp. 20121–2; *Facts on File* (1964), p. 113; and the Greek and Greek Cypriot press of 14 April 1964.

29 Refer to *Keesing's* (1964), pp. 20113–25 and *Facts on File* (1964), pp. 33–4.

30 Quoted in Papandreou, *Democracy at Gunpoint*, pp. 131–2.

31 Quoted in *Facts on File* (1964), p. 210.

32 The friction over minority issues caused Greece to appeal to the Security Council. For detailed accounts about facts and arguments presented by both sides, see UN docs. S/5665 and S/5702, letters dated 2 April and 12 May 1964 from the representative of Greece to the Secretary-General; and doc. S/5957, letter dated 10 September 1964, from the representative of Turkey to the Secretary-General.

33 For reports and analyses of the measures taken by Turkey against the Greek minority see 'Turkey: Lashing Out', and 'Greece: Playing it Cool', The *Economist* (18 April 1964), pp. 252–3.

34 UN doc. S/5677, letter dated 2 May 1964, from the representative of Turkey to the Secretary-General.

35 The Treaty of Lausanne of 1923 provided for the balanced protection of minorities in Greece and Turkey. For the text of the treaty, see F. L. Israel (ed.), *Major Treaties of Modern History, 1648–1967* (New York: McGraw-Hill, 1967).

36 UN doc. S/5665.

37 From the opening statement by Duncan Sandys at the London conference on 15 January 1964. Quoted in *Keesing's* (1964), p. 20115.

38 UN doc. S/PV. 1095 (18 February 1964), para. 55, statement by the British representative at the Security Council.

39 George Ball played a key role in the management of the repeated crises during 1963–64. In his revealing memoirs, he gives a detailed account of the many obstacles he faced as a troubleshooter and mediator in the troubled zone. See G. Ball, *The Past Has Another Pattern: Memoirs* (New York: Norton, 1982), especially chapter 23, 'Cyprus', pp. 337–59.

40 Quoted in E. Weintel and C. Bartlett, *Facing the Brink: An Intimate Study of Crisis Diplomacy* (New York: Scribner's Sons, 1967), p. 20.

41 A major source of tension and hostility between the Greek military regime and Makarios was the latter's open criticism of dictatorial rule and doctrine, 'particularly in Greece, the country where democracy was born and cradled'. For a remarkable document on the strained Athens–Nicosia relations see Makarios' open letter to the Greek junta dated 2 July 1974. It is published in *Keesing's* (1974), pp. 2661–2; and the *Sunday Times* (London), 21 July 1974.

42 For a detailed account on Sisco's mission, see L. Stern, 'Bitter Lessons: How We Failed in Cyprus', *Foreign Policy*, 19 (Summer 1975): 34–78.

43 H. Kissinger, *Years of Upheaval* (Boston: Little, Brown, 1982), p. 1191.

44 This attitude was reflected in a nationally broadcasted speech of President Phaidon Ghizikis on the day of the Turkish invasion. He said: 'Greeks be calm and show faith in the right of the Greek race and our brilliant traditions.' Quoted in the *New York Times*, 21 July 1974.

45 For detailed accounts on developments in Greece during the summer of 1974, see C. M. Woodhouse, *Karamanlis: The Restorer of Greek Democracy* (Oxford: Clarendon, 1982).

46 For Callaghan's statement on the breakdown of the Geneva conference, see *Keesing's* (1974), pp. 26709–10.

47 Resolution of the Turkish Cypriot 'assembly' approving the 'declaration of independence', 15 November 1983.

48 Quoted in the *New York Times*, 16 November 1983.

49 Ibid.

50 Security Council Resolution 541 (1983), which was adopted on 18 November 1983, stated: 'The Security Council... Deplores the declaration of The Turkish Cypriot authorities of the purported secession of part of the Republic of Cyprus; Considers the declaration referred above as legally invalid and calls for its withdrawal;... Calls upon all states to respect the sovereignty, independence, territorial integrity and non-alignment of the Republic of Cyprus; Calls upon all states not to recognize any Cypriot state other than the Republic of Cyprus.'

51 In January 1984, the Cyprus government submitted a framework for a comprehensive settlement of the problem on the basis of a federal bizonal state with the Turkish Cypriots controlling 25 per cent of the island. For the full text of the proposal see the *Cyprus Bulletin*, 15 May 1984.

4 ETHNOPOLITICS AND SUPERPOWER POLITICS

1 For more details on the strategic importance of Cyprus see J. C. Campbell, *Defence of the Middle East* (New York: Harper and Brothers, 1960), pp. 197–9; Sir J. Harding, 'The Cyprus Problem in Relation to the Middle East', *International Affairs*, 34 (July 1958): 291–6; and G. Hill, *A History of Cyprus*, 4 vols. (Cambridge: Cambridge University Press, 1940–52), vol. IV, chapter 26, 'Strategic Considerations'.

2 The following works provide detailed analyses of the domestic and international aspects of the Cyprus problem in the 1950s: N. Crawshaw, *The*

Cyprus Revolt: An Account of the Struggle for Union with Greece (London: Allen & Unwin, 1978); and S. G. Xydis, *Cyprus: Conflict and Reconciliation, 1954–58* (Columbus: Ohio State University Press).

3 For extensive studies on the many aspects of Soviet–American rivalry in the Middle East and the Mediterranean during the Cold War, see G. Lenczowski, *The Middle East in World Affairs*, 4th edn. (Ithaca: Cornell University Press, 1980); Y. Evron, *The Middle East: Nations, Superpowers, and Wars* (New York: Praeger, 1973); and J. C. Hurewitz (ed.), *Soviet–American Rivalry in the Middle East* (New York: Praeger, 1969).

4 For an elaborate account on the sources of American interest in Cyprus refer to T. W. Adams, 'The American Concern in Cyprus', *The Annals of the American Academy of Political and Social Sciences*, 401 (May 1972), 95–105.

5 Treaty of Alliance, article 4.

6 The British telecommunication and radar installations on the Troodos mountain (6400 feet above sea level), and the Royal Air Force base at Akrotiri are the most vital British military posts in the region. The Akrotiri sovereign base is one of the largest RAF stations in the world outside the United Kingdom.

7 Sir John Harding, field marshal and last British governor of Cyprus, wrote characteristically about the strategic importance of Cyprus with regard to NATO and 'the regional struggle against international communism which at the moment has focused itself on the Middle East . . . The use of Cyprus as a command post, as an operational air-base, and for certain other military purposes is indispensable to our ability to support – militarily – the right flank of NATO and the Baghdad Pact.' See Harding, 'The Cyprus Problem', p. 292.

8 The following works provide a good background on Soviet concerns and objectives in the Middle East: *Soviet Objectives in the Middle East*, Report of a Study Group of the Institute for the Study of Conflict (London: ISC, 1974); G. Lenczowski, *Soviet Advances in the Middle East* (Washington, D.C.: American Enterprise Institute, 1971); and J. Wynfred, *Soviet Penetration into the Middle East* (New York: National Strategy Information Center, 1971).

9 The following works focus on Soviet concerns, objectives, and policy on Cyprus: K. Mackenzie, 'Cyprus: The Ideological Crucible', *Conflict Studies*, no. 26 (September 1972); and T. W. Adams and A. J. Cottrell, *Cyprus Between East and West* (Baltimore: Johns Hopkins University Press, 1968).

10 For an insightful and informative article on the motives, goals, and difficulties of British intervention see A. Verrier, 'Cyprus: Britain's Security Role', *The World Today*, 20 (March 1964): 131–7.

11 Superpower intervention in Greece and Turkey in the 1940s is the focus of the following works: B. R. Kuniholm, *The Origins of the Cold War in the Near East: Great Power Conflict and Diplomacy in Iran, Turkey, and Greece* (Princeton: Princeton University Press, 1980); C. M. Woodhouse, *The Struggle for Greece, 1941–49* (London: Hart-Davis, MacGibbon, 1976); and S. Xydis, *Greece and the Great Powers, 1944–47: Prelude to the Truman Doctrine* (Thessaloniki: Institute for Balkan Studies, 1963).

12 See Johnson's message to President Makarios and Vice-President Kutchuk, dated 25 December 1964. This message, along with a letter from Johnson to President Gursel of Turkey are published in *The Department of State Bulletin*, vol. 50, no. 1282 (20 January 1964), p. 90. Secretary of State Dean Rusk and spokesman Robert McClosky, expressing US concern over the eruption of fighting in December 1963, emphasized that 'the US had a major interest in the Eastern Mediterranean and will do whatever it can' to restore peace. Refer to *The Department of State Bulletin*, vol. 50, no. 1287 (24 February 1964), pp. 283–4.

13 G. Ball, *The Past Has Another Pattern: Memoirs* (New York: Norton, 1982), p. 340. Ball provides a detailed and authoritative account of US intervention in Cyprus in 1964.

14 Ibid., p. 342.

15 The text of Ball's proposal and Makarios' statement of rejection are published in *Keesing's* (1964), pp. 20116–17.

16 Ball, *The Past Has Another Pattern*, p. 345.

17 Refer to the *New York Times*, 1 January 1964, 'Soviet Pledges Support'. It writes: 'The Soviet Ambassador in Nicosia Pavel Yermosin delivered a note to President Makarios indicating the full support of the Kremlin for the Greek Cypriots and the independence, sovereignty, and territorial integrity of Cyprus. The Soviet Union condemns any attempt at foreign intervention in the internal affairs of Cyprus under whatever pretext that might be realized.' For similar statements see also *Pravda*, 1 January and 8 February 1964.

18 Refer to Adams and Cottrell, *Cyprus Between East and West*, p. 35.

19 From Khrushchev's letter to Johnson, dated 7 February 1964. The letter is published in *The State Department Bulletin*, vol. 50, no. 1291 (23 March 1964), pp. 447–8.

20 Ibid. Extensive commentaries expressing similar views appeared in *Pravda* and *Isvestiya* throughout 1964. See, for example, Khrushchev's statement in *Isvestiya*, 9 July 1964. He wrote that 'the imperialists, inciting national conflicts between the Greek and Turkish communities are seeking to fasten on Cyprus a new occupation'. He also warned Turkey for its 'adventurous design' on Cyprus and threatened reprisals.

21 UN doc. S/PV. 1096, 19 February 1964, para. 18. Similar accusations appeared also in the Soviet press. *Pravda*'s UN correspondent, for example, reported that the goal of the Western powers at the Security Council 'was to confirm their plans for occupation and partition of the island'. See *Pravda*, 5 March 1964.

22 *The State Department Bulletin*, vol. 51, no. 1307 (13 July 1964), p. 49.

23 Ball, *The Past Has Another Pattern*, p. 355.

24 For a revealing account of the Washington talks, see A. Papandreou, *Democracy at Gunpoint: The Greek Front* (New York: Doubleday, 1970), pp. 133–7. He writes that at one point the American Secretary of Defense, Robert McNamara, threatened the Greek premier that in case of a Greek–Turkish confrontation the powerful Turkish air force 'would literally burn up the Greek countryside'. Papandreou responded: 'Allow me to remind you, however, that Turkey neighbors on a country that has a much more powerful air force. It is more than likely that this

air force would be drawn into the conflict were the Turks to attack.' Ibid., p. 135.

25 The Acheson plan was made public by President Makarios. It was submitted in two versions both of which are published in H. I. Salih, *Cyprus: The Impact of Diverse Nationalism on a State* (Alabama: University of Alabama Press, 1978), pp. 47–50.

26 From the joint communiqué issued after the Papandreou–Makarios talks in Athens on 30 July 1964. Quoted in *Keesing's* (1964), p. 20269.

27 From a statement by Makarios. Quoted in *Keesing's* (1964), p. 20269.

28 For an interesting analysis of Makarios' sources of power, see K. Markides, *The Rise and Fall of the Cyprus Republic* (New Haven: Yale University Press, 1987), chapter 2, 'Makarios' Power and Authority'.

29 Dean Acheson's speech 'Cyprus: The Anatomy of the Problem', delivered before the Chicago Bar Association, 24 March 1965. In that speech, Acheson gave an account of the Cyprus problem and the Geneva conference.

30 Adlai Stevenson in a discussion with Ball on the handling of the Cyprus problem. Quoted in Ball, *The Past Has Another Pattern*, p. 341.

31 Quoted in L. Stern, *The Wrong Horse: The Politics of Intervention and the Failure of American Diplomacy* (New York: Time Books, 1977), p. 84.

32 Quoted in *Keesing's* (1964), p. 20266.

33 UN doc. S/PV. 1153, 17 September 1964, para. 80.

34 Ibid., para. 93.

35 Ibid., para. 76.

36 During 1964–65, Cyprus received from the Soviet Union $70 million in arms, half of which was a gift. Refer to Adams and Cottrell, *Cyprus Between East and West*, p. 44.

37 Joint communiqué issued in Moscow after the conclusion of the agreement. Quoted in *Keesing's* (1964), p. 20371.

38 Quoted in *Keesing's* (1964), p. 20266.3

39 Quoted in UN doc. S/PV. 1153, 17 September 1964, paras. 85 and 91.

40 It is worth mentioning that despite the collapse of the Soviet Union, AKEL continues to be a powerful political party. At the parliamentary elections which were held on 26 May 1996, it received 33 per cent of the votes.

41 A detailed calendar of Cypriot–Communist bloc activities in 1968 which was compiled by the American embassy in Nicosia includes 111 entries. The calendar is published in T. W. Adams, *AKEL: The Communist Party of Cyprus* (Stanford: Hoover Institution Press, 1971), pp. 223–36.

42 The following editorial from AKEL's daily *Haravghi*, 17 September 1969, is quite illustrative of the role and impact of Soviet connections with AKEL and the Cypriot government: 'The Soviet Union supports Cyprus' independence, sovereignty, and territorial integrity. The Soviet Union has always consistently and steadily supported this position, which is in keeping with the officially proclaimed government line. As the Cypriot people well know, this support has had vigorous expression not only in the political sector, with the well-known Soviet statements on Cyprus during every crucial phase of our problem, and in the diplomatic field, with the important speeches of Soviet delegates at the United Nations and other

international organizations – this support has also been manifested in the most practical, and we would say saving manner, in the form of military and financial aid the Soviet Union granted Cyprus in the most difficult moments of its modern history.'

43 Quoted in C. Vance, *Hard Choices: Critical Years in American Foreign Policy: Memoirs* (New York: Simon and Schuster, 1983), p. 144.

44 During his nine-day peace mission, Vance travelled four times to Greece, three times to Turkey, and twice to Cyprus. For a report on his role during the November crisis, see The *Economist*, 9 December 1967, pp. 1031–2. Unfortunately, Vance in his memoirs devotes only a short paragraph to the 1967 crisis.

45 *Economist*, 15 December 1967, p. 1031.

46 The rationale behind US support for the Greek military regime (1967–74) was reflected in the following statement from a testimony of Deputy Secretary of Defense David Packard: 'I am not supporting the attitude of the (Greek) government but I am simply saying that our military considerations are overriding. Furthermore, I think we have a better chance to influence the (Greek) government to change if we continue to work with them than if we turn our back to them.' Testimony before the House of Representatives Committee on Foreign Affairs, 27 April 1971. For more background on US policy towards the Greek military government see 'Greece, Spain, and the Southern NATO Strategy', Hearings before the Committee on Foreign Affairs, US House of Representatives, 92 Cong., 1st Sess., September 1971; and 'Political and Strategic Implications of Homeporting in Greece', Joint Hearings before the Subcommittee on the Near East of the Committee of Foreign Affairs, US House of Representatives, 92nd Cong., 2nd Sess., April 1972.

47 Stern, *The Wrong Horse*, p. 86.

48 From an official Soviet statement published in *Pravda*, 23 November 1967.

49 UN doc. S/PV. 1383, 24/25 November 1967, para. 78, statement by the Soviet representative at the Security Council.

50 Ibid., para. 81.

51 Ball, *The Past Has Another Pattern*, p. 357.

52 For an informative report on Grivas' role in 1964, see 'Grivas into Action', *Economist*, 4 July 1964, pp. 27–8.

53 For an authoritative account on the 1967 crisis see L. P. Battle and D. P. Williams, *Cyprus: A Decade of Crises* (Washington, D.C.: Middle East Institute, 1976). Battle was Assistant Secretary of State for Near Eastern Affairs and directed the 'crisis center' at the State Department during the 1967 crisis.

54 White House press release dated 5 December 1967, published in *The State Department Bulletin*, vol. 57, no. 1487, 25 December 1967, p. 859.

55 Quoted in *Facts on File*, 20 July 1974, p. 571.

56 For an insightful commentary on the consequences of the coup see 'The Coup that Backfired', *The Nation*, 3 August 1974, p. 66.

57 Quoted in *Facts on File* (1974), p. 571.

58 UN doc. S/PV. 1793, 15 August 1974, para. 10.

59 For extensive works on Soviet–Turkish and American–Turkish relations, see A. Z. Rubinstein, *Soviet Policy toward Turkey, Iran, and Afghanistan: The*

Dynamics of Influence (New York: Praeger, 1982); and G. S. Harris, *Troubled Alliance: Turkish–American Problems in Historical Perspective, 1945–71* (Washington, D.C.: American Enterprise Institute, 1972).

60 Quoted in Stern, 'Bitter Lessons', p. 57.

61 Ibid., p. 60.

62 Refer to State Department press release no. 309, 22 July 1974.

63 For more details on the US role, policy, and concerns in the 1974 crisis, see the following two revealing interviews: James Schlesinger, Secretary of Defense, with 'CBS: Face the Nation'. It is published in *Face the Nation, 1974* (Metuchen: Scarecrown, 1975); and Henry Tasca, American Ambassador to Athens, with *Newsweek*, 2 September 1974, p. 34.

64 Kissinger, *Years of Upheaval*, p. 1191.

65 Quoted in Stern, *The Wrong Horse*, p. 117.

66 The following studies examine in detail the role of the Greek lobby in the Turkish embargo affair: C. Hackett, 'Ethnic Politics in Congress: The Turkish Embargo Experience', in A. Said (ed.), *Ethnicity and US Foreign Policy* (New York: Praeger, 1981), pp. 33–62; and S. M. Hicks and T. A. Couloumbis 'The "Greek Lobby": Illusion or Reality', in Said, *Ethnicity and US Foreign Policy*, pp. 63–96.

67 As Hicks and Couloumbis conclude, 'the Greek–American lobby and considerations of voter repercussions were only one of many factors in a senator's or a congressman's decision to vote in favor of an arms embargo on Turkey'. Ibid., p. 90. Hackett reaches a similar conclusion, but stresses that the embargo reflected primarily a 'breakdown of executive-legislative cooperation on foreign affairs'. He explains that the policy pursued by the Nixon/Ford–Kissinger Administration on Cyprus was the 'most glaring failure', and that the Congress was expressing its disapproval of this policy by imposing the embargo to which the administration was strongly opposed. See Hackett, 'Ethnic Politics in Congress', pp. 48–9. For an insightful and informative article on the president versus the Congress theme see J. G. Tower, 'Congress versus the President: The Formulation and Implementation of Foreign Policy', *Foreign Affairs*, 60 (Winter 1981/82): 229–46.

68 For more details on the negative impact that the embargo had on US military interests in the region, see US Senate, Committee on Foreign Relations, 'Turkey, Greece, and NATO: The Strained Alliance' (Washington, DC: Government Printing Office, 1980); and the testimony of Secretary of Defense Harold Brown in 'The Military Aspects of Banning Arms Aid to Turkey', US Senate, Committee on Armed Forces, Hearings, 95th Cong., 2nd Sess., 28 June 1978.

69 *Pravda*, 28 February 1975.

70 Rubinstein, *Soviet Policy Toward Turkey, Iran, and Afghanistan*, p. 28.

71 Quoted in the *Guardian*, 30 September 1975.

5 ETHNIC RIVALS VS NATO ALLIES

1 For extensive works on the concept of alliance and its role in international politics, see O. R. Holsti, P. T. Hopman, and J. D. Sullivan, *Unity and*

Disintegration in International Alliances: Comparative Studies (New York: Wiley, 1973); F. A. Beer (ed.), *Alliances: Latent War Communities in the Contemporary World* (New York: Holt, Rinehart, and Winston, 1970); J. R. Friedman, C. Bladen, and S. Rosen, *Alliance in International Politics* (Boston: Allyn and Bacon, 1970); R. Neustadt, *Alliance Politics* (New York: Columbia University Press, 1970); G. Liska, *Nations in Alliance*, 2nd edn. (Baltimore: Johns Hopkins University Press, 1968); and E. H. Fedder, 'The Concept of Alliance', *International Studies Quarterly*, 12 (March 1968): 65–85.

2 R. E. Osgood, *Alliances and American Foreign Policy* (Baltimore: Johns Hopkins University Press, 1968), p. 19.

3 The following are some of the many works focusing on the origin, formation, and scope of NATO: L. S. Kaplan, *The United States and NATO: The Formative Years* (Lexington: The University Press of Kentucky, 1984); T. P. Ireland, *Creating the Atlantic Alliance: The Origins of the North Atlantic Treaty Organization* (Westport: Greenwood, 1981); E. H. Fedder, *NATO: The Dynamics of Alliance in the Postwar World* (New York: Dodd, Mead, 1973); *NATO: Facts about the North Atlantic Treaty Organization* (Brussels: NATO Information Service, 1969); E. V. der Beugel, *From Marshall Plan to Atlantic Partnership* (New York: Elsevier, 1966); and E. Furniss (ed.), *The Western Alliance: Its Status and Prospects* (Columbus: Ohio State University Press, 1965).

4 The North Atlantic Treaty, article 5.

5 Following are some of the works focusing on the internal difficulties of NATO: R. W. Tucker and L.Wringley (eds.), *The Atlantic Alliance and Its Critics* (New York: Praeger, 1983); H. A. Kissinger, *The Troubled Partnership: A Reappraisal of the Atlantic Alliance* (Garden City: Doubleday, 1966); T. W. Stanley, *NATO in Transition: The Future of the Atlantic Alliance* (New York: Praeger, 1965); A. J. Cottrell and J. E. Dougherty, *The Politics of the Atlantic Alliance* (New York: Praeger, 1964); and R. E. Osgood, *NATO: The Entangling Alliance* (Chicago: University of Chicago Press, 1962).

6 The following articles deal with Greek–Turkish friction over Cyprus in the 1950s and its implications for NATO: S. G. Xydis, 'Toward "Toil and Moil" in Cyprus', *Middle East Journal* (Winter 1966): 1–19; and P. Pipinellis, 'The Greco–Turkish Feud Revived', *Foreign Affairs*, 37 (January 1959): 306–16.

7 For more details on the role played by NATO in connection with the settlement of the Cypriot colonial problem see T. W. Adams and Alvin J. Cottrell, 'The Cyprus Conflict', *Orbis*, 8 (Spring 1964): 66–83; and Royal Institute for International Affairs, *Cyprus: The Dispute and the Settlement* (London: Chatham House Memoranda, 1959).

8 A. J. Cottrell and J. E. Dougherty, *The Politics of the Atlantic Alliance* (New York: Praeger, 1964), p. 214.

9 Quoted in R. P. Stebbins, *The United States in World Affairs, 1959* (New York: Harper, 1960), p. 191.

10 The following works deal with the impact that the Cypriot conflict has had on Greek–Turkish relations in the light of NATO concerns: P. T. Hart, *Two NATO Allies at the Threshhold of War, Cyprus: A Firsthand Account of Crisis*

Management, 1965–1968 (Durham: Duke University Press, 1990); A. Borowiec, *The Mediterranean Feud* (New York: Praeger, 1983); M. M. Ball, 'Turkey's New National Security Concept: What It Means for NATO', *Orbis*, 23 (Fall 1979): 609–31; J. C. Campbell, 'The Mediterranean Crisis', *Foreign Affairs*, 53 (July 1975): 605–24; and P. Windsor, 'NATO and the Cyprus Crisis', The Institute of Strategic Studies, Adelphi paper no. 14, 1964.

11 For an informative report on the secret dispatch of Greek and Turkish troops to Cyprus see 'Soldiers of the Night', in the *Economist*, 18 July 1964, pp. 253–4.

12 A. Papandreou, *Democracy at Gunpoint: The Greek Front* (New York: Doubleday, 1970), p. 132.

13 See UN doc. S/PV 1153, 17 September 1964.

14 For an interesting analysis of NATO's reaction to the outbreak of intercommunal violence see Windsor, 'NATO and the Cyprus Crisis'.

15 For an authoritative source of information about the origin of the NATO plan see G. Ball, *The Past Has Another Pattern: Memoirs* (New York: Norton, 1982), pp. 340–3.

16 Ball, *The Past Has Another Pattern*, p. 338.

17 For the complete text of the NATO proposal see *Keesing's* (1964), p. 20116.

18 Statement by Secretary of State for Commonwealth Relations Duncan Sandys in the House of Commons, 689 H.C. Deb. (5th ser., 1964), p. 841.

19 For purposes of comparison, one could mention that UNFICYP, which was created in March 1964, and had to cope with more severe crises, never exceeded 6500.

20 Glafcos Clerides, president of the House of Representatives, in an interview with the BBC, reported in *The Washington Post*, 31 January 1964.

21 From Makarios' statement of rejection of the NATO proposal. For the complete text of the statement, see *Keesing's* (1964), p. 20116.

22 For an insightful report on the Soviet reaction to the NATO plan see 'Khrushchev warns NATO on Intervention in Cyprus', in the *New York Times*, 8 February 1964.

23 Letter from Khrushchev to the heads of government of Britain, the USA, France, Greece, and Turkey, dated 7 February 1964. The letter was published in *The Department of State Bulletin*, vol. 50, no. 1291 (23 March 1964), 447–8.

24 Ibid.

25 Ball, *The Past Has Another Pattern*, p. 353.

26 From Johnson's letter to Inonu, dated 5 June 1964.

27 From Inonu's letter to Johnson, dated 15 June 1964. The entire letter is published in *The Middle East Journal*, 20 (Summer 1966): 388–93.

28 Ibid.

29 From Johnson's welcome address to Inonu in Washington. White House press release, 22 June 1964.

30 See 'Turkey Ready to Quit Alliance', in the *New York Times*, 17 April 1964.

31 From a conversation between George Papandreou and George Ball, quoted in Papandreou, *Democracy at Gunpoint*, p. 133.

32 Ibid., p. 136.

33 Ibid., p. 135.

34 The expressed position of German neutrality could be seen as a reaction to the severe Soviet reaction against the possibility of dispatching West German troops to Cyprus. In his letter of 7 February 1964, to President Johnson, Chairman Khrushchev made specific reference to that possibility and strongly rejected sending 'to Cyprus as part of the so-called "NATO-forces" soldiers and officers of the West German *Bundeswehr*, although in these areas the memories of steel helmets of soldiers and officers of the *Wehrmacht*, which brought destruction and death also to the Mediterranean region in the years of World War II, are still not eradicated'.

35 From a statement by the French Minister of Information M. Perrefitte, quoted in *Keesing's* (1964), p. 20116. With regard to the French pro-Greek position on Cyprus, Windsor writes: 'And behind Greece, ready to profit from the dissensions of Western polycentrism stood France, unwilling to see the Cyprus crisis taken up by NATO, but willing to back Greece in its dispute with the other member of the Alliance, Turkey.' Windsor, 'NATO and the Cyprus Crisis', p. 4.

36 Adams and Cottrell, 'The Cyprus Conflict', p. 23.

37 J. Stegenga, *The United Nations Force in Cyprus* (Columbus: Ohio State University Press, 1968), p. 45.

38 Windsor, 'NATO and the Cyprus Crisis', p. 5.

39 Refer to C. M. Woodhouse, *Karamanlis: The Restorer of Greek Democracy* (Oxford: Clarendon, 1982), pp. 217–19.

40 Quoted in L. Stern, *The Wrong Horse: The Politics of Intervention and the Failure of American Diplomacy* (New York: Time Books, 1977), p. 119.

41 From Kissinger's press conference, on 22 July 1974. Refer to State Department press release no. 309, 22 July 1974.

42 See Woodhouse, *Karamanlis*, p. 216.

43 For an insightful analysis of the causes and consequences of the Greek withdrawal from NATO, see P. Lambropoulos, 'Cyprus, NATO, and the Greek Future', *The Nation*, 28 September 1974, pp. 267–9.

44 The statement, which was widely publicized in the Greek and international press, is given in *Keesing's* (1974), p. 26710.

45 The Turkish invasion of Cyprus was code-named 'Attila operation' after the king of the Huns known as the 'scourge of God'.

46 The impact of the 1974 Cyprus crisis and its aftermath on the regional balance of power is discussed in the following works: K. Mackenzie, 'Greece and Turkey: Disarray in NATO's Southern Flank', *Conflict Studies*, no. 154, 1984; R. J. Rander, 'Cyprus and the Great Power Balance', in *Encyclopaedia Britannica: 1975 Book of the Year*, pp. 216–17; and M. K. Leighton, 'The Antagonists: Greece and Turkey', *Conflict Studies*, no. 109, 1979.

6 THE ROLE OF THE UNITED NATIONS

1 For some standard works on the origin, creation, and scope of the UN, see *Everyone's United Nations* (1986), a UN publication; I. L. Claude,

Jr., *Swords into Plowshares*, 4th edn. (New York: Random House, 1971); L. M. Goodrich, E. Hambro, and A. P. Simmons, *United Nations Charter: Commentary and Documents* (New York: Columbia University Press, 1969); and L. M. Goodrich, *The United Nations* (London: Stevens, 1960).

2 C. C. O'Brien, *Conflicting Concepts of the UN* (Leeds: Leeds University Press, 1964), p. 2.

3 The following works provide extensive analyses of the many aspects of the politicization of the UN: D. A. Kay (ed.), *The Changing United Nations: Options for the United States, Proceedings of the Academy of Political Science*, vol. 32, no. 4, 1977; J. G. Stoessinger, *The United Nations and the Superpowers*, 2nd edn. (New York: Random House, 1970); I. L. Claude, Jr., *The Changing United Nations* (New York: Random House, 1967); H. G. Nicholas, *The United Nations as a Political Institution*, 4th edn. (New York: Oxford University Press, 1971).

4 For a standard work on the five Greek recourses to the General Assembly, see S. G. Xydis, *Cyprus: Conflict and Conciliation, 1954–1958* (Columbus: Ohio State University Press, 1967).

5 UN doc. S/5488, letter dated 26 December 1963, from the representative of Cyprus to the president of the Security Council.

6 Ibid.

7 For a coverage of the London conference see *Keesing's* (1964), pp. 20115–17. Also, the British delegate gave an extensive account and an assessment of the London conference before the Security Council; see UN doc. S/PV. 1095, 18 February 1964, paras. 33–96.

8 H. D. Purcell, *Cyprus* (New York: Praeger, 1968), pp. 333–4. Article 33 of the UN Charter provides: 'The parties to any dispute, the continuance of which is likely to endanger the maintenance of international peace and security, shall, first of all, seek a solution by negotiation, enquiry, mediation, conciliation, arbitration, judicial settlement, resort to regional agencies or arrangements, or other peaceful means of their choice.'

9 See the provisions of the UN Charter, Article 33.

10 See *Keesing's* (1964), p. 20115. Refer also to the Greek Cypriot press of 4 January 1964.

11 UN doc. S/5545, letter dated 15 February 1964, from the representative of Cyprus to the president of the Security Council.

12 For a regular coverage of UN involvement in Cyprus since 1964, including reviews of discussions and resolutions of the Security Council and the General Assembly, see the *UN Monthly Chronicle* (after 1976 named *UN Chronicle*).

13 On 1 January 1964, Makarios communicated his intention to abrogate the Treaty of Guarantee. On 4 April 1964, he repeated that intention. Refer to R. Stephens, *Cyprus: A Place of Arms: Power Politics and Ethnic Conflict in the Eastern Meditteranean* (London: Pall Mall, 1966), pp. 185–6; *Keesing's* (1964) pp. 20115 and 20121; and the *New York Times*, 2 January 1964.

14 For detailed accounts on the economic, military, and political situation in Cyprus after the eruption of ethnic violence, see UN doc. S/6102, 12

December 1964, and UN doc. S/5950, 10 September 1964. Both documents include reports of the Secretary-General to the Security Council on the situation in Cyprus.

15 Later those figures changed and today the parliament is supposed to have fifty-six Greek Cypriots and twenty-four Turkish Cypriots.

16 The *Economist*, 8 February 1964, p. 478, suggests that there might have been some Soviet incitement for the Cypriot appeal to the UN. It writes: 'This eagerness (of the Greek Cypriots) to take cover under the so-called UN "umbrella" may not be unconnected with the Russians' keen display of interest in the Cyprus problem and with the new vistas opened up by the voting strength of so many new Afro-Asian states in the UN which, unlike Cyprus, came into existence through self-determination.'

17 *Economist*, 7 March 1964, p. 865. A week later, in the issue of 14 March 1964, p. 979, the *Economist* wrote about the role of the British peacekeeping troops: 'That their sympathies lie with the Turks is undeniable; it has become inherent in the situation, even though the Turks themselves are now complaining that the British are not protecting them effectively.'

18 Makarios rejected the Anglo-American proposal for a NATO peacekeeping force because it was not under the auspices of the Security Council. As he explained, 'it is necessary that any force stationed in Cyprus should be under the Security Council, which is the only international organ created for and entrusted with the preservation of peace'. From Makarios' note to the British and American governments, 4 February 1964. The note is quoted in *Keesing's* (1964), p. 20116.

19 UN doc. S/5491, telegram from the vice-president of the Republic of Cyprus to the Secretary-General. Kutchuk's complaint was based on article 48(f) of the constitution which provided that the vice-president had 'the right of final veto on decisions of the council of ministers concerning foreign affairs'.

20 Besides the Turkish side, no other party raised questions about the legality of the Greek Cypriot appeal. It is, however, interesting to note that the Soviet Union was the leading supporter of the constitutionality and legitimacy of the Makarios government and its appeal to the UN.

21 G. Ball, *The Past Has Another Pattern: Memoirs* (New York: Norton, 1982), pp. 344–5.

22 Ibid., p. 340.

23 Ibid., p. 345.

24 *Time* magazine, 21 February 1964, p. 34.

25 Refer to the *Christian Science Monitor*, 18 February 1964.

26 UN doc. S/5543, letter dated 15 February 1964, from the representative of Britain to the president of the Security Council.

27 J. Stegenga, *The United Nations Force in Cyprus* (Columbus: Ohio State University Press, 1968), p. 48.

28 The discussion took place during ten consecutive meetings of the Security Council from 18 February to 4 March 1964 (meetings 1093–1102). For an insightful analysis of the discussion and the viewpoints advanced by the various parties, see Stegenga, *The United Nations Force in Cyprus*, pp. 46–72.

29 UN doc. S/PV. 1095, 18 February 1964, para. 214.
30 UN doc. S/PV. 1098, 27 February 1964, para. 109.
31 UN doc. S/PV. 1096, 19 February 1964, para. 74.
32 For an extensive analysis of the legal and political aspects of the Treaty of Guarantee in the light of the UN Charter, see R. St J. Macdonald, 'International Law and the Conflict in Cyprus', *The Canadian Yearbook of International Law*, 29 (1981): 3–49.
33 UN doc. S/PV. 1098, 27 February 1964, para. 109.
34 UN doc. S/PV. 1096, 19 February 1964, para. 33.
35 Ibid., para. 50.
36 Security Council resolution 183/1964, adopted 4 March 1964.
37 *Cyprus Mail*, 5 March 1964.
38 Stegenga, *The United Nations Force in Cyprus*, pp. 57–8.
39 *Economist*, 15 February 1964, p. 580.
40 E. Weintel and C. Bartlett, *Facing the Brink: An Intimate Study of Crisis Diplomacy* (New York: Scribner's Sons, 1967), p. 20.
41 *The State Department Bulletin*, vol. 50, no. 1289 (9 March 1964), p. 375.
42 UN doc. S/PV. 1096, 18 February 1964, para. 77.
43 UN doc. S/PV. 1098, 27 February 1964, para. 79.
44 *Economist*, 14 March 1964, p. 979.
45 D. W. Wainhouse, *International Peacekeeping at the Crossroads: National Support, Experience and Prospects* (Baltimore: Johns Hopkins University Press, 1973), p. 348.
46 *New York Times*, 18 February 1964.
47 This is the title of an insightful commentary displaying the grave dangers involved in the tactics of brinkmanship followed by the ethnic rivals on and around Cyprus. See the *Economist*, 19 September 1964, pp. 1114–15.
48 K. Waltheim, *Building the Future Order: The Search for Peace in an Interdependent World* (New York: Free Press, 1980), p. 43.
49 Stegenga, *The United Nations Force in Cyprus*, p. 59.
50 For extensive accounts on the many aspects of the UN peace keeping operation in Cyprus, see V. Coufoudakis, 'United Nations Peacekeeping and the Cyprus Question', *The Western Political Science Quarterly*, 29 (1976): 457–73; Stegenga, *The United Nations Force in Cyprus*; J. M. Boyd, 'Cyprus: Episode in Peacekeeping', *International Organization*, 20 (Winter 1966): 1–17; and R. Higgins, 'Basic Facts on the UN Force in Cyprus', *The World Today*, 20 (August 1964): 347–50.
51 For an insightful commentary on Makarios' undermining of the Geneva conference and the Acheson plan see 'Archiepiscopal Sabotage', *Economist*, 29 August 1964, p. 799.
52 UN doc. S/6253, 6 March 1965, 'Report of the United Nations Mediator on Cyprus to the Secretary-General'.
53 Ibid., para. 163.
54 Ibid., para. 168.
55 For an account of the Turkish views on Plaza's role and report see Z. M. Nedjatigil, *The Cyprus Conflict: A Lawyer's View* (Nicosia: Tezel, 1982), pp. 25–7.

56 UN doc. A/5752/ADD.1, explanatory memorandum accompanying the Cypriot requests for the inclusion of the 'Question of Cyprus' in the agenda of the General Assembly in 1964 and 1965.

57 Ibid.

58 General Assembly Resolution 1514 (XV) of 14 December 1960. The resolution provided that alien domination was contrary to the UN Charter and that all peoples had a right to self-determination.

59 The UN involvement in the Congo crisis is the focus of the following works: E. W. Lefever, *The Crisis in the Congo: A UN Force in Action* (Washington, D.C.: The Brookings Institution, 1965); S. Hoffmann, 'In Search of a Thread: The UN in the Congo Labyrinth', *International Organization* (Spring 1962): 331–61; and K. Gordon, *UN in the Congo* (New York: Carnegie Endowment for International Peace, 1962).

60 *Economist*, 14 March 1964, p. 979.

61 *The Times* (London), 17 February 1964. For more comments on the analogy between Cyprus and the Congo, see *The Christian Science Monitor*, 8 and 18 February 1964.

62 General Assembly, 20th plenary session, 1358 meeting, 12 October 1965, para. 47.

63 General Assembly Resolution 2077 (XX), 18 December 1965.

64 J. G. Stoessinger, *The United Nations and the Superpowers: United States–Soviet Interaction at the United Nations*, 2nd edn. (New York: Random House, 1970), p. 82.

65 A. Boyd, *Fifteen Men on a Powder Keg: A History of the UN Security Council* (London: Methuen, 1971), p. 293.

66 General Assembly Resolution 3212 (XXIX), 1 November 1974.

67 F. C. Ikle, *How Nations Negotiate* (New York: Harper and Row, 1964), p. 21.

68 Claude, *The Changing United Nations*, p. 74.

69 Ibid., p. 73.

70 *The Christian Science Monitor*, 18 June 1984.

71 Quoted in *The Christian Science Monitor*, 21 June 1984.

7 THE EUROPEAN UNION AND THE CYPRUS PROBLEM

1 This chapters draws on an article by the author which appeared in the spring 1996 issue of the *Mediterranean Quarterly* under the title 'Cyprus at the Threshold of the European Union' (Vol. 7, No. 2: 112–22).

2 Treaty of the European Union (also known as the Maastricht Treaty), art. A. The treaty was signed on 7 February 1992 at Maastricht (The Netherlands) and went into force on 1 November 1993.

3 For extensive accounts on the evolution of Cyprus–EU relations, see Y. Kranidiotis et al. (eds.), *Cyprus–EU: Evolution and Prospects of Cyprus' Relations with the European Community* (Nicosia: Popular Bank EU Division, 1994), in Greek; P. Ifestos and C. Tsardanidis, *The Cyprus–EC Association Agreement* (Athens: Papazisis, 1991), in Greek; Y. Kranidiotis, 'Relations between Cyprus and the European Community', *Modern Greek*

Studies Yearbook, 8 (1992), published by the University of Minnesota, Modern Greek Studies Programme; C. Tsardanidis, 'The European Community and the Cyprus Problem since 1974', *Journal of Political and Military Sociology*, Vol. 16, no. 2 (1988): 155–71; C. Tsardanidis, 'The EC–Cyprus Association Agreement: 1973–1983. A Decade of Troubled Relationship', *Journal of Common Market Studies*, 21 (1984): 371–6.

4 The protocol was signed on 19 October 1987, and went into effect on 1 January 1988.

5 It should be noted that the association agreement was signed between Cyprus and the European Economic Community (EEC) while the application for membership was for the European Communities (EC), that is the European Coal and Steel Community (ECSC), the European Economic Community (EEC), and the European Atomic Energy Committee (EAEC).

6 For a comprehensive presentation and analysis of facts and issues related to the economy of Cyprus, see D. Christodoulou, *Inside the Cyprus Miracle: The Labours of an Embattled Mini-Economy* (Minneapolis: *Modern Greek Studies Yearbook*, Supplement 2, University of Minnesota, Modern Greek Studies Programme, 1992).

7 *Commission Opinion on the Application by the Republic of Cyprus for Membership*, para. 8; hereafter cited as *Opinion*.

8 *Opinion*, para. 8.

9 *Opinion*, para. 48.

10 *Opinion*, para. 10.

11 *Opinion*, para. 47.

12 *Conclusions* of the Council of General Affairs, 4 October 1993.

13 For the purposes of the substantive talks, twenty working groups and dozens of sub-groups were formed on the Cypriot side. These groups were composed of public servants and delegates of semi-government agencies and the private sector. The talks covered almost all chapters of the *acquis communautaire* under the following headings: 1. External trade policy and relations; 2. Free movement of goods, customs union; 3. Free movement of services, right of establishment; 4. Free movement of capital; 5. Free movement of persons, employment and social policy, education; 6. Common agricultural policy, fisheries; 7. Industrial policy, energy; 8. Common transport policy; 9. Economic and monetary union; 10. Common foreign and security policy; 11. Co-operation in home and justice affairs; 12. Environment; 13. Competition policy, consumer protection; 14. Regional policy, structural funds, cohesion fund; 15. Company law; 16. Statistics; 17. Taxation; 18. Telecommunications; 19. Enterprise policy, distributive trade, tourism, co-operatives; 20. Research and technology policy.

14 *Conclusions of the Presidency*, Corfu European Council, 24–25 June 1994.

15 *Conclusions of the Presidency*, Cannes European Council, 26–27 June 1995.

16 *Conclusions of the Presidency*, Madrid European Council, 15–16 December 1995.

17 The establishment of the Turkey–EU customs union was the culmination of a long process which started with an association agreement that was signed on 12 September 1963 and went into effect on 1 January 1964.

18 Resolution adopted by the Cyprus–EU Association Council, 8 June 1995.
19 Protocol, art. 1.
20 Protocol, art. 5, para. 2.
21 Resolution on Cyprus' Application for Membership of the European Union, adopted by the European Parliament on 12 July 1995.
22 The criteria for accession to the EU were spelled out in a report of the Commission entitled *Europe and the Challenge of Enlargement*, which was presented to, and endorsed by the Lisbon European Council (June 1992). The report provides that:

> Membership implies the acceptance of the rights and obligations, actual and potential, of the community system and its institutional framework, the Community's *acquis* as it is known. That means:
>
> - the contents, principles and political objectives of the Treaties, including the Maastricht Treaty;
> - legislation adopted in implementation of the Treaties, and the jurisprudence of the Court;
> - the declarations and resolutions adopted in the Community framework;
> - the international agreements, and the agreements between Member States connected with the Community's activities.

23 *Opinion*, para. 47.
24 *Opinion*, para. 44.
25 Facts, figures, and information on the economy refer to the free part of the Republic of Cyprus under administration by the government of Cyprus and not occupied by Turkey. Source: Antonis Malaos, 'How Ready is the Cyprus Economy for Accession to the EU?' *Phileleftheros* (newspaper, Nicosia) 20, 21, 22 May 1996 (in Greek). Malaos is the Director General of the Ministry of Finance of the Republic of Cyprus.
26 This is confirmed by the *Opinion*, para. 46, which states that 'the adoption of the *acquis communautaire* by Cyprus will pose no insurmountable problems'.
27 The *Opinion*, para. 22, makes it clear that 'Cyprus must also give up its membership of the Non-Aligned Movement of which it was a founder-member and in which it continues to participate actively'. Cyprus will have no problem abandoning the Non-Aligned Movement before or upon accession to the EU.
28 One of the main objectives of the EU (known as the second pillar) is 'to assert its identity on the international scene, in particular through the implementation of a common foreign and security policy including the eventual framing of a common defence policy, which might lead to a common defence'. Treaty on the European Union, art. B.
29 Declaration on Cyprus adopted by the European Council at its meeting in Dublin, 26 June 1990.
30 Ibid.
31 *Conclusions of the Presidency*, Madrid European Council, 15–16 December 1995.

32 Resolution on Cyprus adopted by the European Parliament on 21 January 1993.
33 Ibid.
34 Resolution on Cyprus' Application for Membership of the European Union, adopted by the European Parliament on 12 July 1995. The resolution also points out that the EU 'considers the island to be a single entity, with a legitimate and internationally recognized government and that the status quo is unacceptable'.
35. The terms of reference of the European observer were as follows: 'prior to the review scheduled for January 1995 of the question of Cyprus' accession to the European Union, to report periodically to the Council on the implications of political developments in Cyprus for the Union's *acquis communautaire*, including the progress of the UN Secretary-General's good offices mission for Cyprus'.
36 *European Observer's Report on Cyprus*, para. 11, issued 23 January 1995.

8 CONCLUSIONS

1 Letter from President Johnson to Premier Inonu, dated 5 June 1964.
2 I. Claude, 'Foreword', in J. Stegenga, *The United Nations Force in Cyprus* (Columbus: Ohio State University Press, 1968), p. 3.

EPILOGUE

1 Report of the Secretary-General on his Mission of Good Offices in Cyprus, UN doc. S/1994/629, para. 52, 30 May 1994.
2 Ibid., para. 53.
3 UN doc. S/12323, para. 5, 30 April 1977.
4 UN doc. S/13369, 31 May 1979. The Kyprianou–Denktash agreement provided also that priority would be given to the resettlement of Varosha and that the demilitarization of the Republic of Cyprus would be discussed. Varosha is part of the city of Famagusta. Until 1974 it was inhabited by Greek Cypriots. Today it is an uninhabited ghost town, fenced off by the Turkish occupation army.

Select Bibliography

ACHESON, D. 'Cyprus: The Anatomy of the Problem', Chicago Bar Record, 46 (8) (1965), 349–56.

ADAMS, T. W. *Cyprus: A Possible Prototype for Terminating the Colonial Status of a Strategically Located Territory.* Unpublished Ph.D. dissertation, University of Oklahoma, 1962.

ADAMS, T. W. *US Army Area Handbook for Cyprus.* Washington, D.C.: Government Printing Office, 1964.

ADAMS, T. W. 'The First Republic of Cyprus: A Review of an Unworkable Constitution', *The Western Political Quarterly*, 19 (1966), 475–90.

ADAMS, T. W. *AKEL: The Communist Party of Cyprus.* Stanford: Hoover Institution Press, 1971.

ADAMS, T. W. 'The American Concern in Cyprus', *The Annals of the American Academy of Political and Social Sciences*, 401 (1972), 95–105.

ADAMS, T. W. and COTTRELL, A. J. 'The Cyprus Conflict', *Orbis*, 8 (1964), 66–83.

ADAMS, T. W. and COTTRELL, A. J. *Cyprus Between East and West.* Baltimore: Johns Hopkins University Press, 1968.

ALASTOS, D. *Cyprus Guerrilla: Grivas, Makarios and the British.* London: Heinemann, 1960.

ALASTOS, D. *Cyprus in History: A Survey of Five Thousand Years*, 2nd edn. London: Zeno Publishers, 1976.

ALEXANDRIS, A. 'Imbros and Tenedos: A Study of Turkish Attitudes toward the Ethnic Island Communities since 1923', *Journal of the Hellenic Diaspora*, 7 (1980), 5–31.

ATHENIAN (pseudonym for Roufos, R.) *Inside the Colonel's Greece.* New York: Norton, 1972.

ATTALIDES, M. (ed.) *Cyprus Reviewed.* Nicosia: Jus Cypri Association, 1977.

ATTALIDES, M. *Cyprus: Nationalism and International Politics.* New York: St. Martin's Press, 1979.

AUSLAND, J. C. and RICHARDSON, H. F. 'Crisis Management: Berlin, Cyprus, Laos', *Foreign Affairs*, 44 (1976), 161–94.

AVEROFF-TOSSIZZA, E. *Lost Opportunities: The Cyprus Question, 1950–1963.* New York: New Rochelle, 1986.

BAHCHELI, T. *Greek–Turkish Relations Since 1955.* Boulder, CO: Westview Press, 1989.

BAKER, E. 'The Settlement in Cyprus', *Political Quarterly*, 30 (1959), 244–53.

BALL, G. *The Past Has Another Pattern: Memoirs.* New York: Norton, 1982.

BALL, M. M., 'Turkey's New National Security Concept: What It Means for NATO', *Orbis*, 23 (1979), 609–31.

BARSTON, R. P. 'Cyprus: The Unresolved Problem, 1963–1970', *India Quarterly*, 27 (1971), 114–21.

BARSTON, R. P. (ed.) *The Other Powers: Studies in the Foreign Policies of Small States.* London: Allen and Unwin, 1973.

BARSTON, R. P. *Modern Diplomacy.* London: Longman, 1988.
BARTH, F. (ed.) *Ethnic Groups and Boundaries: The Social Organization of Cultural Difference.* Boston: Little, Brown 1969.
BEER, F. A. *Integration and Disintegration in NATO.* Columbus: Ohio State University Press, 1969.
BELL, W. and FREEMAN, W. (eds.) *Ethnicity and Nation Building.* Beverly Hills: Sage, 1974.
BENNETT, A. L. *International Organizations: Principles and Issues,* 5th edn. Englewood Cliffs, NJ: Prentice Hall, 1991.
BITSIOS, D. *Cyprus: The Vulnerable Republic.* Thessaloniki: Institute for Balkan Studies, 1975.
BLAY, S. K. L. 'Self-Determination in Cyprus: The New Dimensions of an Old Conflict', *Australian Yearbook of International Law,* 10 (1987), 67–100.
BOLL, M. 'Turkey's new National Security Concept: What It Means for NATO', *Orbis,* 23 (1979), 609–31.
BOLUKBASI, S. *The Superpowers and the Third World: Turkish American Relations and Cyprus.* Lanham, MD: University Press of America, 1988.
BOROWIEC, A. *The Mediterranean Feud.* New York: Praeger, 1983.
BOYD, J. M. 'Cyprus: Episode in Peacekeeping', *International Organization,* 20 (1) (1966), 1–17.
BRASS, P. R., (ed.) *Ethnic Groups and the State.* Totowa, NJ: Barnes and Noble, 1985.
BRASS, P. R. *Ethnicity and Nationalism: Theory and Comparison.* New Delhi: Sage Publications, 1991.
BROWN, L. R. *World Without Borders: The Interdependence of Nations.* New York: Foreign Policy Association, 1972.
BRUCE, L. H. 'Cyprus: A Last Chance', *Foreign Policy,* 58 (1985), 115–33.
BUNGE, F. M. *Cyprus: A Country Study.* Washington, D.C.: The American University, 1980.
BURKEY, R. M. *Ethnic and Racial Groups: The Dynamics of Dominance.* Manlo Park, CA: Benjumin-Cummings, 1978.
BURTON, J. W. *International Relations: A General Theory.* Cambridge: Cambridge University Press, 1965.
BURTON, J. W. *Systems, States, Diplomacy and Rules.* Cambridge: Cambridge University Press, 1968.
BURTON, J. W. 'Resolution of Conflict', *International Studies Quarterly,* 16 (1972), 5–22.
BYFORD, J. W. *Grivas and the Story of EOKA.* London: Hale, 1959.
CAMP, G. D. 'Greek–Turkish Conflict over Cyprus', *Political Science Quarterly,* 95 (1980), 43–70.
CAMPBELL, J. C. *Defense of the Middle East.* New York: Harper and Brothers, 1960.
CAMPBELL, J. C. 'The Mediterranean Crisis', *Foreign Affairs,* 53 (1975), 605–24.
CAMPBELL, J. C. 'The United States and the Cyprus Question, 1974–75', in V. Coufoudakis V (ed.) *Essays on the Cyprus Conflict.* New York: Pella, 1976.

CATSIAPIS, J. 'France and the Cyprus Issue', *Hellenic Studies*, 4 (1) (1996), 15–42; in French with an extensive summary in English.

CHRISTODOULOU, D. *Inside the Cyprus Miracle: The Labours of an Embattled Mini-Economy*. Minneapolis: Modern Greek Studies Yearbook Supplement 2, 1992.

CLERIDES, G. *Cyprus: My Deposition*, 4 vols. Nicosia: Alithia Publishing, 1989–92.

CLERIDES, G. 'Reflections on the Cyprus Problem', *Modern Greek Studies Yearbook*, 10/11 (1994/95), 1–6.

CLOGG, R. A. 'Greece and the Cyprus Crisis', *The World Today*, 30 (1974), 364–8.

CLOGG, R. A. *A Short History of Modern Greece*. Cambridge: Cambridge University Press, 1979.

CLOGG, R. A. and YANNOPOULOS, G. (eds.) *Greece under Military Rule*. New York: Basic Books, 1972.

CONNOR, W. 'Nation Building or Nation Destroying?' *World Politics*, 24 (1972), 319–55.

CONSTANTINIDES, S. 'Greek Foreign Policy: Theoretical Orientations and Praxis', *Hellenic Studies*, 4 (1) (Spring 1996), 43–61.

CONSTANTINOU, D. 'Difficult Days in Cyprus', *World Marxist Review*, 17 (1974), 123–6.

CONSTANTINOU, S. T. 'The Changing Spatial Aspects of the Population of Cyprus', *Modern Greek Studies Association*, 10/11 (1994/95), 205–31.

CONSTAS, D. (ed.) *The Greek–Turkish Conflict in the 1990s: Domestic and External Influences*. London: Macmillan Press 1991.

CONSTAS, D. and STAVROU, T. (eds.) *Greece Prepares for the Twenty-First Century*. Washington, D.C: Woodrow Wilson Center Press, 1995.

COSER, L. A. *The Functions of Social Conflict*. New York: Free Press, 1956.

COTTRELL, A. J. and Dougherty, J. E. *The Politics of the Atlantic Alliance*. New York: Praeger, 1964.

COUFOUDAKIS, V. 'United States Foreign Policy and the Cyprus Question: A Case Study in Cold War Diplomacy', in T. A. Couloumbis, and S. M. Hicks (eds.) *US Foreign Policy Toward Greece and Cyprus: The Clash of Principle and Pragmatism*. Washington, D.C.: The Center for Mediterranean Studies, 1975.

COUFOUDAKIS, V. 'United Nations Peacekeeping and the Cyprus Question', *The Western Political Quarterly*, 29 (1976), 457–73.

COUFOUDAKIS, V. (ed.) *Essays on the Cyprus Conflict*. New York: Pella, 1976.

COUFOUDAKIS, V. 'The Greek American Lobby and Its Influence on Greek Foreign Policy, 1974–1979', *Mediterranean Quarterly*, 2 (4) (1991), 70–82.

COUFOUDAKIS, V. 'Greek Foreign Policy in the Post-Cold War Era: Issues and Challenges', *Mediterranean Quarterly*, 7 (3) (1996), 26–41

COULOUMBIS, T. A. *Greek Political Reaction to American and NATO Influences*. New Haven: Yale University Press, 1966.

COULOUMBIS, T. A. 'The Greek Junta Phenomenon', *Polity*, 6 (1974), 345–74.

COULOUMBIS, T. A. 'Five "Theories" Regarding Kissinger's Policy toward the Cyprus Crisis', *Internationals Studies Notes*, 6 (1975), 12–17.

COULOUMBIS, T. A. *The United States, Greece, and Turkey: The Troubled Triangle.* New York: Praeger, 1983.

COULOUMBIS, T. A. and HICKS, S. M., (eds.) *US Foreign Policy toward Greece and Cyprus: The Clash of Principle and Pragmatism.* Washington, D.C.: The Center for Mediterranean Studies, 1975.

COULOUMBIS, T. A. and IATRIDES, J. O. (eds.) *Greek–American Relations: A Critical Review.* New York: Pella, 1980.

CRASHAW, N. 'Cyprus After Kophinou', *The World Today,* 24 (1968) 428–35.

CRASHAW, N. 'Subversion in Cyprus', *The World Today,* 27 (1971), 25–32.

CRASHAW, N. *The Cyprus Revolt: An Account of the Struggle for Union with Greece.* London: Allen and Unwin, 1978.

CRASHAW, N. 'Cyprus After Makarios: Prospects for a Settlement', *The World Today,* 34 (1978), 31–8.

CRAWFORD, J. *The Creation of States in International Law.* Oxford: Clarendon Press, 1979.

CYPRUS RESEARCH CENTER. *Yearbook,* 1992 and 1993, separate volumes, Nicosia.

DENKTASH, R. *The Cyprus Triangle.* Winchester: Allen and Unwin, 1982.

DURRELL, L. *Bitter Lemons.* London: Faber and Faber, 1957.

EDEN, A. *Full Circle.* Boston: Houghton, Mifflin, 1960.

EHRLICH, T. 'Cyprus, the "Warlike Isle": Origins and Elements of the Current Crisis', *Stanford Law Review,* 18 (1966), 1021–98.

EHRLICH, T. *Cyprus, 1958–1967: International Crises and the Role of Law.* New York: Oxford University Press, 1974.

EMILIOU, N. 'The Prohibition of the Use of Force in International Law and the Cyprus Problem', *Modern Greek Studies Yearbook,* 10/11 (1994/95) 171–204.

EVRIVIADES, M. L. 'The Problem of Cyprus', *Current History,* 70 (1976), 18–21, 38–42.

EVRIVIADES, M. L. 'The US and Cyprus: The Politics of Manipulation in the 1985 UN Cyprus High Level Meeting', Occasional Research Paper no. 3. Athens: Institute of International Relations, 1992.

EVRIVIADES, M. and BOURANTONIS, D. 'Peacekeeping and Peacemaking: Some Lessons from Cyprus', *International Peacekeeping,* 1 (1994), 395–412.

EVRON, Y. *The Middle East: Nations, Superpowers, and Wars.* New York: Praeger, 1973.

FAIRFIELD, R. P. 'Cyprus: Revolution and Resolution', *The Middle East Journal,* 13 (1959), 235–48.

FOLEY, C. *Legacy of Strife: Cyprus from Rebellion to Civil War,* 2nd edn. Baltimore: Penguin Books, 1964.

FOLEY, C. and SCOBIE, W. I. *The Struggle for Cyprus.* Stanford: Hoover Institution Press, 1975.

FRANKEL, J. 'Britain's Behavior in the Cyprus Crisis, 1974', *Jerusalem Journal of International Relations,* 3 (1978), 229–44.

FREY, F. *The Turkish Political Elite.* Cambridge: Massachussets Institute of Technology Press, 1965.

GALLEN, J. 'Turkey as a Self-Inflicted Wound: The Narrowing Options for US Defense Policy', *Armed Forces Journal International* (1980), 62–73.

GEORGE, A. L. *Presidential Decisionmaking in Foreign Policy: The Effective Use of Information and Advice.* Boulder: Westview, 1980.

GOBBI, H. J. *Rethinking Cyprus.* Tel Aviv: Aurora, 1993.

GORDON, K. J. 'The UN in Cyprus', *International Journal*, 19 (1964), 326–47.

GOTTLIEB, G. *Nation Against State: A New Approach to Ethnic Conflicts, the Decline of Sovereignty, and the Dilemmas of Collective Security.* New York: Council on Foreign Relations, 1993.

GRIVAS, G. *The Memoirs of General Grivas*, ed. C. Foley. New York: Praeger, 1965.

GROOM, A. J. R. 'Cyprus: Back in the Doldrums', *The Round Table*, 300 (1986), 362–83.

GROOM, A. J. R. 'Cyprus: Separate but Together?' *Journal of Modern Hellenism*, 4 (1987), 129–43.

GURKAN, I. *NATO, Turkey, and the Southern Flank: A Mideastern Perspective.* New York: National Strategy Information Center, 1980.

GURR, T. R. *Minorities at Risk: A Global View of Ethnopolitical Conflicts.* Washington, D.C.: US Institute of Peace, 1993.

GURR, T. R. and HARFF, B. *Ethnic Conflict in World Politics.* Boulder, CO: Westview Press, 1994.

HAASS, R. 'Cyprus Moving Beyond Solution', *The Washington Quarterly*, 10 (2) (1987), 183–90.

HACKETT, C. 'Ethnic Politics in Congress: The Turkish Embargo Experience', in A. Said (ed.) *Ethnicity and US Foreign Policy.* New York: Praeger, 1981.

HACKETT, J. *A History of the Orthodox Church of Cyprus.* New York: Burt Franklin, 1901.

HALE, W. M. and NORTON, J. R., 'Turkey and the Cyprus Crisis', *The World Today*, 30 (1974), 364–8.

HANRIEDER, W. F. 'International Organizations and International Systems', *The Journal of Conflict Resolution*, 10 (1966).

HARBOTTLE, M. *The Impartial Soldier.* London: Oxford University Press, 1970.

HARDING, J. (Sir), 'The Cyprus Problem in Relation to the Middle East', *International Affairs*, 34 (3) (1958), 291–6.

HARRIS, G. S. *Troubled Alliance: Turkish–American Problems in Historical Perspective, 1945–1971.* Washington, D.C.: American Enterprise Institute, 1972.

HART, P. T. *Two NATO Allies at the Threshold of War, Cyprus: A Firsthand Account of Crisis Management, 1965–1968.* Durham: Duke University Press, 1990.

HERACLIDES, A. *The Self-Determination of Minorities in International Politics.* London: Frank Cass, 1991.

HIGGINS, R. 'Basic Facts on the UN Force in Cyprus', *The World Today*, 20 (1964), 347–50.

HILL, G. (Sir), *A History of Cyprus*, 4 vols. Cambridge: Cambridge University Press, 1940–52.

HITCHENS, C. *Hostage to History: Cyprus from the Ottomans to Kissinger.* New York: Noonday Press, 1989.

HOFFMAN, S. *Primacy or World Order: American Foreign Policy since the Cold War.* New York: McGraw-Hill, 1978.

HOME, G. C. *Cyprus Then and Now.* London: Dent, 1960.

HOROWITZ, D. L. *Ethnic Groups in Conflict.* Berkeley: University of California Press, 1985.

HOWARD, H. N. *Turkey, the Straits, and US Foreign Policy.* Baltimore: Johns Hopkins University Press, 1975.

HUNT, D. 'The Use of Force in the Middle East: the Case of Cyprus', *The Mediterranean Quarterly*, 2 (1) (1991), 66–70.

HUNTINGTON, S. 'The Clash of Civilizations', *Foreign Affairs*, 72 (3), (1993).

HUREWITZ, J. C. (ed.) *Soviet–American Rivalry in the Middle East.* New York: Praeger, 1969.

IATRIDES, J. O. *Balkan Triangle: Birth and Decline of an Alliance across Ideological Boundaries.* The Hague: Mouton, 1978.

IERODIAKONOU, L. *The Cyprus Question.* Stockholm: Almquist and Wiksell, 1971.

IFESTOS, P. *European Political Cooperation: Towards a Framework of Supranational Diplomacy?* Aldershot: Avebury, 1987.

INKELES, A. 'The Emerging Social Structure of the World', *World Politics*, 27 (1975), 467–95.

IOANNIDES, C. P. *In Turkey's Image: The Transformation of Occupied Cyprus into a Turkish Province.* New York: Caratzas, 1991.

IOANNIDES, C. P. (ed.) *Cyprus: Domestic Dynamics, External Constraints.* New Rochelle, NY: Caratzas, 1992.

ISRAEL, F. L. (ed.) *Major Peace Treaties of Modern History 1648–1967.* New York: McGraw-Hill, 1967.

JAMES, A. *The Politics of Peace-keeping.* London: Praeger, 1969.

JAMES, A. 'The UN Force in Cyprus', *International Affairs*, 65 (1989), 481–500.

JAMES, A. *Peacekeeping in International Politics.* New York: St. Martin's Press, 1990.

JENKINS, R. 'Rethinking Ethnicity: Identity, Categorization and Power', *Ethnic and Racial Studies*, 17 (1994), 197–23.

JOSEPH, J. S. 'The UN as an Instrument of National Policy: The Case of Cyprus', *Cyprus Review*, 1 (2), (1989) 46–64.

JOSEPH, J. S. 'The International Dimensions of the Cyprus Problem', *Cyprus Review*, 2 (2) (1990), 15–39.

JOSEPH, J. S. 'Cyprus Gains Independence', in F. N. Magill (ed.) *Great Events from History II: Human Rights*, 5 vols. (Pasadena, CA: Salem Press, 1992), pp. 1084–9.

JOSEPH, J. S. 'Greek and Turkish Inhabitants of Cyprus Clash over Political Rights', in F. N. Magill (ed.) *Great Events from History II: Human Rights*, 5 vols. (Pasadena, CA: Salem Press, 1992), pp. 1218–23.

JOSEPH, J. S. 'A United Nations Force is Deployed in Cyprus', in F. N. Magill (ed.) *Great Events from History II: Human Rights*, 5 vols. (Pasadena, CA: Salem Press, 1992), pp. 1236–40.

JOSEPH, J. S. 'The International Power Broker: A Critical View of the Foreign Policy of Archbishop Makarios', *Mediterranean Quarterly*, 3 (2) (1992), 7–33.

JOSEPH, J. S. 'Ethnic Loyalties vs. Allied Commitments: Greek–Turkish Conflict over Cyprus as a Source of Strain for NATO', *Thetis*, 2 (1995), 235–43.

JOSEPH, J. S. 'Cyprus at the Threshold of the European Union', *Mediterranean Quarterly*, 7 (2) (1996), 112–22.

JOSEPH, J. S. 'The Spill-Over Effect of Cross-Boundary Ethnic Bonds in a Conflict Situtation: The Greek–Cypriot–Turkish Triangle', *Thetis*, vol. 3 (1996), 311–22.

KALOUDIS, G. S. *The Role of the UN in Cyprus from 1964 to 1979*. New York: Peter Lang, 1991.

KAPLAN, M. A. *System and Process in International Politics*. New York: Wiley, 1962.

KATZENSTEIN, P. J. 'International Interdependence: Some Long-Term Trends and Recent Changes', *International Organization*, 29 (1975), 1021–34.

KEEFE, E. K. et al. *Area Handbook for Cyprus*. Washington, D.C.: Government Printing Office, 1971.

KEGLEY, C. W. Jr. and WITTKOPF, E. R. *The Global Agenda*, 2nd edn. New York: Random House, 1988.

KEOHANE, R. O. and Nye, J. S. *Power and Interdependence*, 2nd edn. Glenview, IL: Scott, Foresman, 1989.

KISSINGER, H. *Years of Upheaval*. Boston: Little, Brown, 1982.

KITROMILIDES, P. M. 'Greek Irredentism in Asia Minor and Cyprus', *Middle Eastern Studies*, 26 (1) (1990), 3–17.

KITROMILIDES, P. M. and COULOUMBIS, T. A. 'Ethnic Conflict in a Strategic Area: The Case of Cyprus', in A. Said and L. R. Simmons (eds.) *Ethnicity in an International Context*. New Brunswick: Transaction Books, 1976.

KITROMILIDES, P. M. and EVRIVIADES, M. *Cyprus*, rev. edn. Oxford: Clio Press, 1995.

KOSLIN, A. P. *The Megali Idea: A Study of Greek Nationalism*. Ph.D. Dissertation. Johns Hopkins University, Baltimore, 1958.

KOUMOULIDES, J. T. A. (ed.) *Cyprus in Transition 1960–1985*. London: Tigraph, 1986.

KOUSOULAS, D. G. *Modern Greece: Profile of a Nation*. New York: Scribner's Sons, 1974.

KRANIDIOTIS, Y. N. 'Relations between Cyprus and the European Community', *Modern Greek Studies Yearbook*, 8 (1992), 165–206.

KREIJCI, J. and VELIMSKY, V. *Ethnic and Political Nations in Europe*. New York: St. Martin's Press, 1981.

KUNIHOLM, B. R. *The Origins of the Cold War in the Near East: Great Power Conflict and Diplomacy in Iran, Turkey, and Greece*. Princeton: Princeton University Press, 1980.

KYPRIANOU, S. 'Cyprus: A Continuing Search for Peace', *World Affairs Journal*, 1 (1982), 19–26.

KYRIAKIDES, S. *Cyprus: Constitutionalism and Crisis Government*. Philadelphia: University of Pennsylvania Press, 1968.

LANDAU, J. M. *Radical Politics in Turkey.* Leiden: Brill, 1974.

LANDAU, J. M. 'Johnson's 1964 Letter to Inonu and the Greek Lobbying at the White House', *Turkish Yearbook of International Relations*, 14 (1974), 45–58.

LARRABEE, S. 'Balkan Security', *Adelphi Paper* no. 135. London: International Institute for Strategic Studies, 1977.

LEE, D. E. *Great Britain and the Cyprus Convention Policy of 1878.* Cambridge: Harvard University Press, 1934.

LEIGHTON, M. K. 'The Antagonsists: Greece and Turkey', *Conflict Studies*, No. 109 (July 1979), 3–22.

LENCZOWSKI, G. *Soviet Advances in the Middle East.* Washington, D.C.: American Enterprise Institute, 1971.

LENCZOWSKI, G. *The Middle East in World Affairs.* 4th edn. Ithaca: Cornell University Press, 1980.

LEWIS, B. *The Emergence of Modern Turkey*, 2nd edn. London and New York: Oxford University Press, 1968.

LEWIS, J. W. *The Strategic Balance in the Mediterranean.* Washington: D.C.: American Enterprise Institute, 1976.

LIJPHART, A. *Democracy in Plural Societies: A Comparative Exploration.* New Haven: Yale University Press, 1977.

LOIZOS, P. 'The Progress of Greek Nationalism in Cyprus, 1878–1970', in J. Davies (ed.) *Choice and Change: Essays in Honour of Lucy Mair.* London: London School of Economics, 1974.

LOIZOS, P. *The Greek Gift: Politics in a Cypriot Village.* New York: St. Martin's Press, 1975 and Oxford: Blackwell, 1975.

LUKE, H. (Sir) *Cyprus Under the Turks, 1571–1878.* London: Oxford University Press, 1921.

LUKE, H. (Sir) *Cyprus: A Portrait and an Appreciation.* London: Harrap, 1957.

LUMSDEN, M. 'The Cyprus Conflict as a Prisoner's Dilemma Game', *Journal of Conflict Resolution*, 17 (1973), 7–32.

MACDONALD, R. St J. 'International Law and the Conflict in Cyprus', *The Canadian Yearbook of International Law*, 29 (1981), 3–49.

MACKENZIE, K. 'Greece and Turkey: Disarray in NATO's Southern Flank', *Conflict Studies*, no. 154, 1984;

MACKENZIE, K. 'Cyprus: The Ideological Crucible', *Conflict Studies*, no. 26, 1972.

McDONALD, R. 'Cyprus: The UN Tries Again', *The World Today*, 40 (1984), 420–7.

McLELAND, C. A. *Theory and the International System.* New York: Macmillan, 1966.

MAIER, F. *Cyprus: From Earliest Time to Present Day.* London: Eleck Books, 1968.

MARKIDES, K. *The Rise and Fall of the Cyprus Republic.* New Haven: Yale University Press, 1977.

MARKIDES, K. and COHN, S. F. 'External Conflict/Internal Cohesion: A Reevaluation of an Old Theory', *American Sociological Review*, 47 (February 1982), 88–98.

MAYES, S. *Cyprus and Makarios.* London: Putnam, 1960.

MAYES, S. *Makarios: A Biography.* New York: St. Martin's Press, 1981.
MELAMID, A. 'The Geographical Distribution of Communities in Cyprus', *The Geographical Review*, 46 (3) (1956), 355–74.
MELAMID, A. 'Partitioning Cyprus: A Class Exercise in Applied Political Geography', *The Journal of Geography*, 59 (1960), 118–22.
MIDLARSKY, M. I. (ed.) *The Internationalization of Communal Strife.* London: Routledge, 1992.
MIKES, G. 'Letter from Cyprus', *Encounter*, 24 (1963), 87–92.
MODIANO, M. S. 'Greek Political Troubles', *The World Today*, (1965) 33–42.
MONTVILLE, J. V. (ed.) *Conflict and Peacemaking in Multiethnic Societies.* Lexington, MA: Lexington Books, 1990.
MORGENTHAU, H., *Politics Among Nations: The Struggle for Power and Peace.* 4th edn. New York: Knopf 1967.
MOSKOS, C. C. Jr. *Greek-Americans: Struggle for Success.* Englewood Cliffs: Prentice Hall, 1980.
MULLER, H. *The Loom of History.* New York: Harper, 1958.
MURDOCK, G. P. *Ethnographic Atlas.* Pittsburgh: University of Pittsburgh Press, 1967.
NAHUMI, M. 'Cyprus: The Solution and Its Dangers', *New Outlook*, 2 (1959), 3–10.
NEDJATIGIL, Z. M. *The Cyprus Conflict: A Lawyer's View.* Nicosia: Tezel, 1982.
NEDJATIGIL, Z. M. *The Cyprus Question and the Turkish Position in International Law.* Oxford: Oxford University Press, 1989.
NEUMAN, S. G. (ed.) *Small States and Segmented Societies: National Political Integration in a Global Environment.* New York: Praeger, 1976.
NICOLSON, H. *Diplomacy.* 3rd edn. London: Oxford University Press, 1963.
NIMETZ, M. 'The Cyprus Problem Revisited', *Mediterranean Quarterly*, 2 (1) (1991), 58–65.
NORDLINGER, E. A. *Conflict Regulation in Divided Societies.* Harvard University Press, 1972.
NURI, E. *Turkey: A Country Study.* Washington, D.C.: The American University, Foreign Area Studies.
OBERLING, P. *The Road to Bellapais: The Turkish Cypriot Exodus to Northern Cyprus.* New York: Columbia University Press, 1982.
PANTELI, S. *A New History of Cyprus: From the Earliest Times to the Present Day.* London: East–West Publications, 1984.
PAPAIOANNOU, E. 'For a Sovereign and United Cyprus', *World Marxist Review*, 18 (March 1975), 29–37.
PAPANDREOU, A. *Democracy at Gunpoint: The Greek Front.* New York: Doubleday, 1970.
PATRICK, R. A. *Political Geography and the Cyprus Conflict: 1963–1971.* Ontario: Department of Geography, University of Waterloo, 1976.
PEARSON, F. S. and ROCHESTER, M. J. *International Relations: The Global Condition in the Late Twentieth Century.* New York: McGraw-Hill, 1992.
PELCOVITS, N. A. and KRAMER, K. L. 'Local Conflict and UN Peacekeeping', *International Studies Quarterly*, 20 (1976), 533–52.

PERSIANIS, P. 'The Greek-Cypriot Educational Policy in Cyprus as an Expression of Conflict at the Political, Cultural, and Socio-Economic Levels', *Modern Greek Studies Yearbook*, 10/11 (1994/95), 89–116.

PIPINELLIS, P. 'The Greco-Turkish Feud Revived', *Foreign Affairs*, 37 (1959), 306–16.

POLLIS, A. 'Intergroup Conflict and British Colonial Policy: The Case of Cyprus', *Comparative Politics*, 5 (1973), 575–99.

POLLIS, A. 'International Factors and the Failure of Political Integration in Cyprus', in S. G. Newman (ed.) *Small States and Segmented Societies: National Political Integration in a Global Environment*. New York: Praeger, 1976.

POLLIS, A. 'Cyprus: Nationalism vs. Human Rights', *Universal Human Rights*, 1 (1979), 89–102.

POLYVIOU, P. G. *Cyprus: The Tragedy and the Challenge*. Washington, D.C.: The American Hellenic Institute, 1975.

POLYVIOU, P. G. *Cyprus: Conflict and Negotiation, 1960–1980*. London: Holmes and Meier, 1980.

PSOMIADES, H. J. 'The Cyprus Dispute', *Current History*, 48 (1965), 269–76, 305–6.

PURCELL, H. D. *Cyprus*. New York: Praeger, 1968.

RAMADY, M. A. 'The Role of Turkey in Greek–Turkish Cypriot Relations', in V. Coufoudakis (ed.) *Essays on the Cyprus Conflict*. New York: Pella, 1976.

RAY, J. L. *Global Politics*, 5th edn. Boston: Houghton Mifflin, 1992.

REES, D. 'Southern Europe: NATO's Crumbling Flank', *Conflict Studies*, no. 60 (1975).

REX, J. and DRURY, B. (eds.) *Ethnic Mobilisation in a Multi-Cultural Europe*. Aldershot: Avebury, 1995.

RICHARDSON, H. F., 'Crisis Management; Berlin, Cyprus, Laos', *Foreign Affairs*, 44 (1966), 291–303.

RINGER, B. R. and LAWLESS, E. R., *Race-Ethnicity and Society*. New York: Routledge, 1989.

ROSECRANCE, R. N. *Action and Reaction in World Politics*. Boston: Little, Brown, 1963.

ROSENAU, J. N. 'Pre-Theories and Theories of Foreign Policy', in R. B. Farrell (ed.) *Approaches to Comparative and International Politics*. Evanston, IL: Northwestern University Press, 1966.

ROSENAU, J. N., (ed.) *Linkage Politics*. New York: Free Press, 1969.

ROSENBAUM, N. 'Cyprus and the United Nations: An Appreciation of Parliamentary Diplomacy', *Canadian Journal of Economics and Political Science*, 33 (1967), 218–31.

ROSSI, M. 'Cyprus: Defense vs. Nationalism', *Foreign Policy Bulletin*, 35 (1956), 105–7.

ROSSI, M. 'NATO Gains by Cyprus Settlement', *Foreign Policy Bulletin*, 38 (1959), 121–2.

ROSSIDES, E. 'Cyprus and the Rule of Law', *Syracuse Journal of International Law*, 17 (1991), 22–90.

ROSTOW, D. 'Turkey's Travails', *Foreign Policy*, 58 (1979), 82–102.

ROTHSCHILD, J. *Ethnopolitics: A Conceptual Framework*. New York: Columbia University Press, 1981.

ROUSSEAS, S. *The Death of Democracy: Greece and the American Conscience*. New York: Grove Press, 1968.

ROYAL INSTITUTE FOR INTERNATIONAL AFFAIRS, *Cyprus: The Dispute and the Settlement*. London: Chatham House Memoranda, 1959.

RUBINSTEIN, A. Z. *Soviet Policy toward Turkey, Iran, and Afghanistan: The Dynamics of Influence*. New York: Praeger, 1982.

RYAN, S. 'Ethnic Conflict and the United Nations', *Ethnic and Racial Studies*, 13 (1990), 25–49.

SAID, A. (ed.) *Ethnicity and US Foreign Policy*. New York: Praeger, 1981.

SAID, A. and SIMMONS, L. R. (eds.) *Ethnicity in an International Context*. New Brunswick, NJ: Transaction Books, 1976.

SALEM, N. (ed.) *Cyprus: A Regional Conflict and Its Resolution*. London: Macmillan, 1992.

SALIH, H. I. *Cyprus: The Impact of Diverse Nationalism on a State*. Alabama: University of Alabama Press, 1978.

SCHEFFER, D. J. 'Human Rights and the New World Order', *Modern Greek Studies Yearbook*, 8 (1992), 207–19.

SCOTT, A. M. *The Dynamics of Interdependence*. Chapel Hill: University of North Carolina Press, 1982.

SEN, B. *A Diplomat's Handbook of International Law and Practice*, 3rd edn. Dordrecht: Martinus Nijhoff, 1988.

SEZER, D. B. 'Turkey's Security Policies', Adelphi Paper no. 164. London: International Institute for Strategic Studies, 1981.

SHERMERHORN, R. A. *Comparative Ethnic Relations: A Framework for Theory and Research*. New York: Random House, 1970.

SHIELS, F. L. (ed.) *Ethnic Separatism and World Politics*. Lanham, MD: University Press of America, 1984.

SILVA, K. M. de and MAY, J. R. (eds.) *Internationalization of Ethnic Conflict*. New York: St. Martin's Press, 1991.

SIRMEN, A. 'The Notion of the Small State: Cyprus, Its Security and Survival', in P. Worsley and P. Kitromilides (eds.) *Small States in the Modern World: The Conditions for Survival*. Nicosia: Zavallis, 1979.

SMITH, S. A. de. *The New Commonwealth and Its Constitutions*. London: Stevens, 1964.

SOUTER, D. 'An Island Apart: A Review of the Cyprus Problem', *Third World Quarterly*, 6 (3) (1984), 657–74.

SPYRIDAKIS, C. A. *A Brief History of Cyprus*. 3rd edn. Nicosia: Zavallis, 1964.

STAVROU, N. A. *Allied Politics and Military Interventions: The Political Role of the Greek Military*. Athens: Papazeses, 1977.

STEARNS, M. *Entangled Allies: US Policy Toward Greece, Turkey, and Cyprus*. New York: Council of Foreign Relations Press, 1992.

STEGENGA, J. *The United Nations Force in Cyprus*. Columbus: Ohio State University Press, 1968.

STEPHENS, R. *Cyprus, A Place of Arms: Power Politics and Ethnic Conflict in the Eastern Mediterranean*. London: Pall Mall, 1966.

STERN, L. 'Bitter Lessons: How We Failed in Cyprus', *Foreign Policy*, 19 (1975), 34–78.

STERN, L. *The Wrong Horse: The Politics of Intervention and the Failure of American Diplomacy*. New York: Time Books, 1977.

St JOHN-JONES, L. W. *The Population of Cyprus*. London: Maurice Temple Smith, 1983.

SUHRKE, A. and NOBLE, L. G. (eds.) *Ethnic Conflict in International Relations*. New York: Praeger, 1977.

TACHAU, F. 'The Face of Turkish Nationalism as Reflected in the Cyprus Dispute', *The Middle East Journal*, 13 (3) (1959), 262–72.

THEODORIDES, J. 'The United Nations Peacekeeping Force in Cyprus', *International and Comparative Law Quarterly*, 31 (4) (1982), 765–83.

THEOPHANOUS, A. *The Political Economy of a Federal Cyprus*. Nicosia: Intercollege Press, 1996.

THEOPHYLACTOU, D. A. *Security, Identity and Nation Building*. Aldershot: Avebury, 1995.

THEOPHYLACTOU, D. A. 'A "German Solution" for Cyprus' Reunification or United Nations "Enforcement of Peace?" ' *Mediterranean Quarterly*, 6 (3) (1995), 39–51.

THOMAS, A. J. Jr. and THOMAS, A. V. W. 'The Cyprus Crisis, 1974– 75: Political and Judicial Aspects', *Southwest Law Journal*, 29 (Summer 1976), 513–46.

TORNARITIS, C. G. *Cyprus and Its Constitutional and Other Legal Problems*. 2nd edn. Nicosia: n.p., 1982.

TSARDANIDIS, C. 'The EC–Cyprus Association Agreement: 1973–1983. A Decade of Troubled Relationship', *Journal of Common Market Studies*, 21 (1984), 371–6.

TSARDANIDIS, C. *Politics of the EEC–Cyprus Association Agreement, 1982–1987*. Nicosia: Cyprus Research Center, 1988.

TSARDANIDIS, C. 'The European Community and the Cyprus Problem since 1974', *Journal of Political and Military Sociology*, 16 (2) (1988), 155– 71.

UNITED NATIONS, *The Blue Helmets: A Review of United Nations Peacekeeping*. 2nd edn. UN publication, 1990.

VACALOPOULOS, A. E. *The Greek Nation, 1453–1669: The Cultural and Economic Background of Modern Greek Society*. New Brunswick, NJ: Rutgers University Press, 1976.

VALI, F. *Bridge Across the Bosporus: The Foreign Policy of Turkey*. Baltimore: Johns Hopkins University Press, 1971.

VALI, F. *The Turkish Straits and NATO*. Stanford: Hoover Institution Press, 1972.

VANCE, C. *Hard Choices: Critical Years in American Foreign Policy: Memoirs*. New York: Simon and Schuster, 1983.

VANEZIS, P. N. *Makarios: Faith and Power*. London: Abelard-Schuman, 1971.

VANEZIS, P. N. *Makarios: Pragmatism and Idealism*. London: Abelard-Schuman, 1974.

VANEZIS, P. N. *Cyprus: The Unfinished Agony*. London: Abelard-Schuman, 1977.

VASSILIOU, G. 'Managing Ethnic Conflicts in the New World Order: The Case of Cyprus', *Modern Greek Studies Yearbook*, 10/11 (1994/95), 7–16.

VATIKIOTIS, P. J. *Greece: A Political Essay*. Beverly Hills: Sage, 1974.

VATIKIOTIS, P. J. 'Greece and the Crisis in the Mediterranean', *Millennium*, 4 (1975), 75–81.

VEREMIS, T. *Greek Security Considerations: A Historical Perspective*. Athens: Papazeses, 1980.

VERRIER, A. 'Cyprus: Britain's Security Role', *The World Today*, 20 (1964), 131–7.

VOLKAN, V. D. *Cyprus, War and Adaptation: A Psychoanalytic History of the Two Ethnic Groups in Conflict*. Charlottesville: University Press of Virginia, 1979.

WAINHOUSE, D. W. *International Peacekeeping at the Crossroads: National Support, Experience and Prospects*. Baltimore: Johns Hopkins University Press, 1973.

WALKER, A. M. 'Enosis in Cyprus: Dhali, a Case Study', *The Middle East Journal*, 38 (1984), 474–94.

WALLERSTEIN, I. *The Modern World System*. New York: Academic Press, 1974.

WALSH, F. R. and WALSH, M. T. 'Church and State in Cyprus', *The Texas Quarterly*, 3 (1960), 268–73.

WEINTEL, E. and BARTLETT, C. *Facing the Brink: An Intimate Study of Crisis Diplomacy*. New York: Scribner's Sons, 1967.

WHITE, G. W. 'The Turkish Federated State of Cyprus: A Lawyer's View', *The World Today*, 37 (1981), 135–41.

WINDSOR, P. 'NATO and the Cyprus Crisis', Adelphi Paper no. 14. London: Institute for Strategic Studies, 1964.

WOLFE, J. H. 'Cyprus: Federation under International Safeguards', *Publius*, 18 (2) (1988), 75–89.

WOODHOUSE, C. M. *The Struggle for Greece, 1941–49*. London: Hart-Davis, MacGibbon, 1976.

WOODHOUSE, C. M. *Karamanlis: The Restorer of Greek Democracy*. Oxford: Clarendon, 1982.

WORSLEY, P. and KITROMILIDES, P. (eds.) *Small States in the Modern World: The Conditions of Survival*. Manchester: University of Manchester, 1976.

WRIGHT, Q. 'The Nature of Conflict', *The Western Political Quarterly*, 4 (1951), 193–201.

WYNFRED, J. *Soviet Penetration into the Middle East*. New York: National Strategy Information Center, 1971.

XYDIS, S. G. *Greece and the Great Powers, 1944–47: Prelude to the Truman Doctrine*. Thessaloniki: Institute for Balkan Studies, 1963.

XYDIS, S. G. 'Toward "Toil and Moil" in Cyprus', *Middle East Journal*, 20 (1966), 1–19.

XYDIS, S. G. *Cyprus: Conflict and Conciliation, 1954–58*. Columbus: Ohio State University Press, 1967.

XYDIS, S. G. *Cyprus: Reluctant Republic*. The Hague: Mouton, 1973.

YAVUZ, M. H. 'Cyprus and International Politics', *The Cyprus Review*, 4 (2) (1992), 135–43.

ZENTNER, J. 'The 1972 Turkish Opium War: Needle in the Haystack Diplomacy', *World Affairs*, 136 (1973), 36–47.

Index